"This is as raw and real as it gets. Kollmann's experience on crime scenes and in the crime lab shines through on every page. For everyone who wants to know just how human, funny, and tenacious real CSI people are!"
—**Connie Fletcher,** author of *Every Contact Leaves a Trace: Crime Scene Experts Talk About Their Work, from Discovery Through Verdict*

"Informative, witty . . . Kollmann delivers terse commentary and gory detail while puncturing common misconceptions about forensics."
—*Booklist*

"Fans of *CSI* and *Court TV*, your book has arrived. Kollmann has the enthusiasm, wit, and natural storytelling ability to make this memoir sparkle. Highly enjoyable."
—*Publishers Weekly*

"Detailed, honest, and gross . . . good practical advice."
—*Tampa Tribune*

"Fans of TV's *CSI* franchise will relish these gritty stories."
—*Sacramento Bee* (AP national)

"For the *CSI*-obsessed: Do you scratch your head over how those fabulous actors on *CSI* and its many spinoffs can work with equipment so state-of-the-art that it allows them to interrogate and arrest suspects, looking great in the process? Then this book is the necessary dose of reality check for you. With more than a decade's experience of crime scene investigation (including several in Baltimore County's police department), Dana Kollmann is well equipped to give the real scoop on the life of a CSI—from a plastic bag mistaken for a dead body to the mind-numbing paperwork to, yes, sucking on a dead man's finger. If Kollmann occasionally wields her gallows humor with a bit too much blunt force, she deserves kudos for telling the truth about *CSI* land: that TV glamor masks a far more complex profession."
—*Baltimore Sun*

Never Suck a Dead Man's Hand

Curious Adventures of a CSI

Dana Kollmann

CITADEL PRESS
Kensington Publishing Corp.
www.kensingtonbooks.com

CITADEL PRESS BOOKS are published by

Kensington Publishing Corp.
119 West 40th Street
New York, NY 10018

All Kensington titles, imprints, and distributed lines are available at special quantity discounts for bulk purchases for sales promotions, premiums, fund-raising, educational, or institutional use. Special book excerpts or customized printings can also be created to fit specific needs. For details, write or phone the office of the Kensington sales manager: Kensington Publishing Corp., 119 West 40th Street, New York, NY 10018, attn: Sales Department; phone 1-800-221-2647.

CITADEL PRESS and the Citadel logo are Reg. U.S. Pat. & TM Off.

First hardcover printing: February 2007
First trade paperback printing: February 2008

10 9 8 7 6 5 4 3 2

Printed in the United States of America

ISBN-13: 978-0-8065-4126-6
ISBN-10: 0-8065-4126-1

Electronic edition:

ISBN-13: 978-0-8065-3159-5 (e-book)
ISBN-10: 0-8065-3159-2 (e-book)

Death sneaks up on you the way a windshield
sneaks up on a bug.
—Anonymous

I dedicate this book to all the bugs I've loved before.

What you are now . . .

What I am you will be . . .

Contents . . .

Never Suck a
Dead Man's Hand

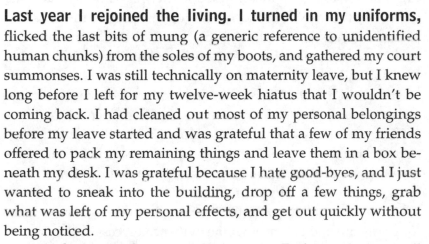

Introduction . . .

Last year I rejoined the living. I turned in my uniforms, flicked the last bits of mung (a generic reference to unidentified human chunks) from the soles of my boots, and gathered my court summonses. I was still technically on maternity leave, but I knew long before I left for my twelve-week hiatus that I wouldn't be coming back. I had cleaned out most of my personal belongings before my leave started and was grateful that a few of my friends offered to pack my remaining things and leave them in a box beneath my desk. I was grateful because I hate good-byes, and I just wanted to sneak into the building, drop off a few things, grab what was left of my personal effects, and get out quickly without being noticed.

My plan worked. It was 2:00 A.M. on a Friday, and I knew all too well that everyone would be busting their chops running from one Crime Lab call to the next. I placed the last of my uniforms on my supervisor's desk along with my pepper spray, conduct and field manuals, keys, biohazardous equipment bag, respirator, rubber boots, and identification card. I couldn't help but notice her calendar and the big letters under March 7 that read: DANA BACK ON SHIFT 1. I felt a lump growing in my throat and blinked back the tears that had begun to well up in my eyes. I couldn't believe that I was doing it. I was quitting. I was never coming back. Never, ever again.

I picked up my ID card and looked at the photograph one last time. It was discolored from being exposed to fingerprint powder every day for the past ten years of my life and deep gouges ran through my face from the card being swiped hundreds of times through the readers that secured the Lab. Even without the discoloration and gouges, it was still an awful picture of me, but I smiled thinking back to the morning it had been taken. I had been on overtime because of a stabbing in the pouring rain the night before. A woman beat the hell out of her husband with a frying pan and then stabbed him, all because he complained about the way she cooked his fish. When she was finished punishing him, she threw the frying pan off the balcony. I remembered getting rain soaked as I photographed the frying pan, a spatula, and the poor little lake trout filets that were hanging in the azaleas. I looked a wreck in the photograph, but had the excuse of being soaking wet, covered in grease, and smelling like fish. I shoved the card under my pile of uniforms.

I walked into the Lab's main area and took down the placard above my desk that had my name on it. Then I peeled my name off my mailbox. I didn't bother to look through the mail that had accumulated over the past three months. If it was important, they knew where they could find me. I grabbed what remained of my things, turned off the light, and left.

It was a straight shot to the elevator, but I decided to take the long way out and cut through the evidence processing laboratory. The room was pitch dark with only a dim ray of light from the street eleven floors below casting a faint glow on the superglue chamber. I set my things on the evidence table and walked over to the window. Everything outside looked so quiet and peaceful. It was such an irony that the most spectacular view was from the very room where evidence from the most heinous and violent of crimes passed through for processing.

I sat down on the radiator and looked around the dark lab. I wondered how many hours of my life had been spent surrounded by these four walls. I sat there in the dark for a long time—just thinking. It was difficult to believe that a decade had passed since I walked through the Crime Lab doors for the first time, green with experience but so eager to learn. I wouldn't have believed it if someone told me that I would eventually become the most senior civilian investigator in the Lab whose experience would be topped only by one detective. I didn't regret a single moment of my time spent in Crime Lab, but what I did regret was allowing the job to become such a core component of my life and letting my personal identity become so inextricably intertwined with the work that I did. I wished that I had listened to the words of the firearms examiner a few years before when he said that I would "love this place more than this place would ever love me." He was right. Although I felt like I was an integral part of the unit, I was really nothing more than a number and the Lab would continue—with or without me. That stung.

My decision to leave the Crime Lab had been a long time in coming. I struggled with the idea for well over a year, but it wasn't until my husband, Bob, and I brought our infant son home from Guatemala that I realized that I needed to reevaluate my priorities. I no longer wanted to work midnight shift, have rotating days off, or be faced with an endless stream of overtime. I wanted to spend Christmas *under* the tree, not looking at the guy who made himself into an ornament and dangled lifelessly from its branches. I didn't want the cranberry sauce on the Thanksgiving dinner table to remind me of blood clots anymore. And I didn't want the Fourth of July fireworks to take me back to the time when they misfired and landed in a crowd of spectators. I wanted a job where you'd get in trouble for saying things such as "He needs his rectum swabbed" or "Can you fish that rubber out of the toilet for me?" I wanted a normal life.

My walk on the wild side started years before. My mother didn't care what I did for a living, as long as I wore a dress to work. My father just hoped I'd find someone willing to pay me to do something, anything. My brother held a prayer vigil in an attempt to convince God to land me a job in another country. And me—I wanted to work with dead people.

So there I sat, strapped in what looked like an electric chair. A huge, rude, inhospitable mass of muscle sat behind a nearby table and studied a piece of graph paper that was spewing from an antiquated-looking polygraph machine. I wanted a job as a civilian crime scene investigator (CSI) more than I had ever wanted anything before, but the steps involved in landing one of these coveted positions seemed to never end. I had applied for this job over a year ago and although I had passed the panel interview, physical assessment, and background investigation, I still had to get through the damn polygraph and psych exam.

My interest in death was my parents' fault. My dad, a city cop turned firefighter, had become quite familiar with the crime-laden streets of Baltimore and quickly realized my brother and I would become corner hoodlums if we attended the public school in our district. In 1972, we packed up the Monte Carlo and moved to the boonies. We escaped crime all right, along with the other pleasures of urban living such as municipal pools, community playgrounds, and corner stores. My friends and I spent the long summer days engaged in contests to see who could pick the most beetles off the rose bushes. One of our favorite pastimes involved exploring the woods for witches and evidence of the sect of half-human, half-monkey people who lived on Derby Drive a million years before us. We found the bones of the monkey people along with the remains of small animals that provided proof our ancestors were meat eaters. I slept with the bones of the monkey people tucked between my mattress and box spring for nearly a year until my dad discovered them while trying to identify the source of the foul smell that constantly emanated from my room. Seems one of the bones still had a little meat on it.

By the time I entered high school, my friends had found other pastimes, but not me. One Friday afternoon my mother came home from work and discovered what she thought was dinner simmering on the stove. She opened the lid to her stainless steel crab pot and discovered six dissected cat carcasses boiling away. I tried to explain that I had volunteered to stew the cats to get rid of the soft tissue so my anatomy and physiology class could study the skeletons the following Monday, but my words fell on her furious deaf ears. She threatened to call the men with straightjackets that wrap teenage girls in cold, wet sheets and take them away to their new bedrooms with padded walls. As ordered, I carried the pot of cats to the deck so my father could see what I had done when he came home. He just stood over the cats while shaking his head and commented how the crabs would forever taste of formaldehyde. Over the weekend, the water in the pot froze and the cats wouldn't budge. My mother grounded me for what seemed like an eternity and I was the object of my classmates' ridicule after it was announced that we would be studying the skeletal system from pictures in our textbook.

As I approached high school graduation, I decided I really wanted a career working with the mummies, skeletons, and bog people that I had read about in *National Geographic* magazine. I announced my decision to major in archaeology, but my mother was less than thrilled. I was reminded that archaeology involved dirt and digging and that those "dirty looking earth-mamas" didn't wear dresses to work. The following fall I found myself inserting Foley catheters into grumpy old men. Somehow, I had been enrolled in the prestigious Union Memorial Hospital School of Nursing. The program was excellent, so excellent that I knew I absolutely hated it from day one. In the first few months, my weekly marches to impromptu sensitivity training had worn a rut in the hospital corridor. I studied nursing long enough to shave a dead guy's face and then I quit.

After nursing school, things seemed to fall in place. I wound up studying archaeology and amazed my mother by actually landing a full-time job as nothing other than an archaeological field technician (AKA Shovel bum) within a week of graduation. I returned to school a few years later and obtained a graduate degree in forensics and was hell-bent on working as a CSI, even if that meant letting a stranger wire me to a chair and ask me probing questions.

I stared blankly at the wall and waited for the polygraph examiner to ask me the next question. I had already been yelled at for moving even though I hadn't twitched a muscle and wound up sighing from the stress of the attack. Apparently, deep breathing was also a no-no because I was berated for oxygenating my blood and then made the grave error of offering an apology. It was becoming all too clear why the examiner wore her weapon on her hip and I figured applicants she didn't like left the interview with a severe case of "lead poisoning." Intimidation was a big part of the polygraph process and I just had to play the game. My thoughts were interrupted by another question. "Other than what we've talked about, have you ever stolen anything?" Her voice was dry and monotone. I didn't like her.

I was silent for a moment as I thought about the question. My heart was racing and I could hear my pulse pound in my ears. I had already confessed to the pens, adhesive notepads, and correction fluid I unintentionally "stole" from former employers. The examiner's eyes shifted between the polygraph printout and me as she waited for my answer. "No," I stated with all the confidence in the world.

The examiner glared at me for a moment and then screeched her felt-tipped pen across the graph paper as she made a series of mysterious circles and slashes. This made my heart beat faster than it already was and my hands trembled. I feared this would register as deception on her stupid little machine. I glanced at her out of the corner of my eye and caught her smirking as she subtly shook her head. She did it because she knew I was looking at her.

When my brother and I were kids, my parents told us we had to be good or Jesus would put black marks on our souls. We really didn't know what would happen if we exceeded the maximum allotted number of black marks, but that was precisely what made them so scary. Every few Sunday afternoons we were dragged into confession since it served as the spray and wash for our souls and restored our innocence. My fear of Jesus and his black marks had kept me on the straight and narrow and I had done absolutely nothing that would prevent me from getting this job—not even the incident that involved the backhoe and peach schnapps.

I had also been polygraphed by two other police departments and was waiting for the next step of their application processes. With three agencies in the game, I prayed that someone would hire me. Having lost all self-confidence and feeling about as big as an ant, I waited for what would be the final question; a question that would foreshadow the bizarre road I was about to travel as a CSI. In the most serious voice she asked, "Have you ever engaged in a sexual act with a chicken?"

WWhhaatt? Did I hear that right? I took a moment to contemplate the logistics of getting it on with a chicken. I was particularly confused about what part of the chicken would go where. I'd have to give this one more thought on the way home. I didn't even care if I passed this test anymore and decided to answer with something other than the structured yes-no response. In a tone as dry and serious as the examiner's, I answered, "A couple of jackasses maybe, but no ma'am, never a chicken."

When I walked into the Police Department Training Academy on February 13, 1995, I thought I was opening the doors to a brand-new career. What I didn't know was that these doors also invited me into a world that was much different than the one in which I had been living.

I would spend the next decade in a place where people called 911 to report aliens in their televisions and kangaroos on the beltway. A universe where women carried their cigarettes in unimaginable places and men requested ambulances because they couldn't maintain erections. A realm where pigs and dingoes replaced dogs and cats as indoor house pets and families barbecued chicken on their linoleum floors. A realm where people died holding Tombstone pizza boxes and bodies were tossed next to DEAD END and NO DUMPING road signs. Never did I think that I would have a dead man's fingers go in my mouth or have a corpse fall on me. This is the stuff you don't see on television, won't read in a novel, and is just too damn weird to make up! Allow me to share with you the true stories that I'm forbidden to tell at my dinner table. Turn off your television and let me tell you the way it *really* is.

CHAPTER 1

Cock-and-Bull . . .

Before you even ask the question, the answer is no! No, no, no, no, no! No, you can't get fingerprints off of rocks! No, I don't watch *CSI*! No, crime scene investigators don't interview suspects! No, I wasn't interested in the O. J. case! No, I wasn't a cop (and no, I didn't decide to do Crime Lab work because I couldn't get into the police academy)! No, luminol doesn't glow blue hours after it's sprayed! No, Crime Lab doesn't respond to only murders and high-profile crimes! No, I didn't wear a miniskirt and heels to work. *And No*, I don't know who the hell killed JonBenet Ramsey!

So, where did all these misnomers come from? You guessed it—Hollywood. Anyone who has recently done any channel surfing knows that television is flooded with forensic programs. These highly popular shows, like *CSI*, *Without a Trace*, *Navy NCIS*, and *Crossing Jordan* represent a recent trend in prime-time crime dramas—a trend where scripts no longer revolve around the characters, but around science. In today's cop shows, state-of-the-art laboratories replace interrogation rooms, microscopes take the place of handcuffs, and the only high-speed action you'll see is in the form of photography. Through the use of fancy gadgets, wild camera stunts, and a case clearance rate approaching 100 percent, these shows have successfully transformed the stereotype of science from something geeky into a discipline that is now hot and sexy.

There is also an array of fact-based forensic shows such as *Cold Case Files*, *New Detectives*, *Forensic Files*, *FBI Files*, *Autopsy*, *Body of Evidence*, *I Detective*, and *Dr. G.: Medical Examiner*—just to name a few. Through the profiling of real cases, these programs validate the methods, techniques, and instruments that viewers see being utilized in the fictional crime dramas and emphasize the fact that forensic possibilities are limitless given the technology we now hold in the palms of our hands.

But this inundation of television with forensic programs, including the fact-based ones, also has a downside. By portraying forensic evidence as the key witness in case after case and in show after show, attorneys are finding that many jurors have unrealistic expectations about what forensic science is, what it can do, and, more important; what it cannot do. We are learning that most jurors actually anticipate the presentation of forensic evidence at trial and await the testimony of experts in the fields of serology, latent prints, firearms, blood spatter, documents, computers, toxicology, footwear, and so on. If forensics doesn't play a prominent role in a case, or if no forensically valuable evidence was recovered from a crime scene, then interested parties increasingly develop the misguided notion that a case is weak or that the police and CSIs were negligent in their duties. The reality of the matter is that many, many, many cases are still solved on the basis of good detective work and good detective work alone. Forensic evidence is not always there, it does not always solve the crime, and it is not infallible.

Another effect of these prime-time crime lab dramas can be seen on university campuses throughout the country. Over the past few years, there has been a dramatic and well-documented increase in the number of undergraduate- and graduate-level forensic science programs as well as mounting numbers of students declaring forensics as their major. In 2005 at Buffalo State College, over 150 students were enrolled in the forensic chemistry program compared to the 40 who were reported for 1996. At West Virginia University, forensics majors jumped from 4 in 1999 to 400 in 2006, and the renowned John Jay School of Criminal Justice in

New York reports similar growth, with the number of majors increasing from 554 to 762 in recent years. An Internet search for "undergraduate forensic programs" results in nearly 1.6 million hits, so I won't continue with the statistics. Even high schools are getting a piece of the action. If you don't know how to prepare and evaluate DNA autoradiographs or determine the time of death from blowfly larvae, just ask a tenth grader.

The unfortunate part about the huge number of wannabe CSIs deluging forensic science programs is that far too many have a Hollywood mentality about a Hell's Kitchen kind of job. At the risk of sounding clichéd, I have to say that television and the real world really are two *entirely* separate entities. I have been teaching graduate- and undergraduate-level forensic science courses at a local university for about seven years and while my lectures are designed to give students a basic knowledge of the interdisciplinary facets of the discipline and introduce them to the theory, methods, and techniques of CSI, I find it is just as important to deconstruct the stereotypes of the field that pervade too many of these young and impressionable minds. I feel strongly about this because I know that the dreams of many students, or maybe I should call them starlets, will be shattered when they discover that the job of a real CSI involves duties and a wardrobe nothing like those portrayed on *CSI*. I don't recall Gil Grissom responding to any "burglary" calls where the only evidence of the crime was a stranger's turd found floating in the toilet, and when was the last time Catherine Willows came home after handling a decomp and found a dead maggot in her bra? Did Warrick Brown ever earn overtime because a junkie died after eating the living room sofa? And I must have missed the episode where Sara Sidle was directed to process a tree house for latent prints.

I find that many students think that if they study hard and graduate with a high grade point average, doors to crime labs across the nation will magically open and they will be beckoned inside, handed a fingerprint brush and a jar of powder, and put to work experimenting on the individuality of nose hairs and the possibility of determining the brand of toilet paper from residues recovered from butt cheeks. Nothing could be further from the truth.

Thanks in part to all the forensic programs, there is absolutely fierce competition for positions in the field. Many jurisdictions require CSI wannabes to be a police officer with several years of experience in patrol before they are eligible for a position in the Crime Lab. That isn't to say that forensic science students need to start jogging a mile a day and practicing their trigger pull, because other departments only allow civilian investigators into the Lab. What catches many job applicants and interns off guard is the background check. Forensics and integrity go together like maggots and a decomp, so those who have been packing funny tobacco into their Philly Blunts, or have had a felony conviction, a recent DUI or misdemeanor conviction, a negative employment history, a poor driving record, recurrent financial problems, or a dishonorable discharge from the military might as well forget it. The closest these people will get to a position in forensics is selling popcorn at the movies for the premiere of *Bone Collector II*.

If students do land a CSI position in a middle-sized city suburb, they'll quickly realize that there isn't time for any of those nose hair or butt cheek experiments because they will be constantly running from call to call to call, and very few of these calls will be of the caliber of those that occur weekly at 9:00 P.M. on the television sets in Las Vegas, Miami, and New York. Within a year, they'll have handled 150 burglaries, 100 domestic abuses, 75 first-degree assaults, 50 armed robberies, 25 recovered stolen autos, 15 child abuse cases, 10 suicides, 5 rapes, 4 search warrants, 3 patient abuses, 2 arsons, 1 fatal fire, and a partridge in a pear tree for every two homicide scenes they process as the lead investigator. Their workload will prevent them from following up on cases, and news that an arrest was made will often come as a surprise when a court summons magically appears on their desk. Even then, they will probably have to root through the case file to refresh their memory since all the calls they handled in the past months will start to run together.

The new female CSI will soon discover that the heels, skirts, and long face-flopping hair flaunted by the investigators on television don't work well when you're climbing inside trash dumpsters in the search for evidence or going up in the fire department's cherry picker. It won't be long before Fruit of the Loom long johns replace the Victoria's Secret water bra and matching panties and the skull cap equipped with a wind liner make the curling iron one of the most unnecessary appliances in their home. The new male investigator will see that a necktie dangling precariously over a gooey dead body is an accident waiting to happen, and starched white shirts and smooth-soled dress loafers are recipes for disaster. The uniforms hanging in their closets are testaments that fashion has been sacrificed for practicality.

The new CSIs will find themselves working outdoor scenes on the hottest of hot and the coldest of cold days and struggling as they try to photograph and sketch evidence before a torrential downpour washes everything into a nearby storm drain. They'll accept the risk of catching lice, scabies, poison ivy, and other gross things from victims, suspects, and crime scenes but learn not to complain because bugs and bumps are nothing compared to the threat posed by daily contact with biohazardous materials. It's only a matter of time before an array of gadgets from the Galls police supply catalogue finds their way onto their Christmas list.

It won't be long before new investigators realize that there really is very little overlap between their job and the position as it is portrayed on television. Within weeks, they will have seen firsthand the awful things that grown-ups do to kids, and kids do to grown-ups, and people do to animals, and animals do to people, and people do to themselves. They'll start each shift wondering what unimaginable tasks await them and if they'll get off on time. Will they go up in the helicopter again to take aerial photos? Perhaps they'll have to collect another fetus from an abortion clinic for paternity testing in a case of alleged rape? Maybe they'll photograph another two-year-old who is about to receive skin grafts because he was scalded as punishment for drawing on the wall with a crayon. Will they have to follow another tow truck bringing a car with a dead body inside back to headquarters? Hopefully, the woman who scalped herself and cut her face off is still locked away because one self-mutilation every ten years is more than enough. Where does it end? . . . or doesn't it?

Despite the differences between the real world and television, working in a crime lab takes the cake as being one of the coolest places to spend forty hours or more each week. It pains me to think that some poor souls out there sit behind a desk all day. Without bodies, evidence, search warrants, and the morgue to discuss, what do desk-job people like that talk about at the dinner table? The results of their Norton Antivirus scan?

While in graduate school at the George Washington University, I took a law class where the instructor, a federal prosecutor, defined evidence as "stuff we use to prove things." It wasn't until I started working as a CSI that I realized that evidence truly is all kinds of *stuff* that provides detectives with investigative leads, links a victim to a suspect, links a suspect to a crime scene, or corroborates/disproves the statement of victim, suspect, or witness. Evidence isn't always in the form of a gun, a knife, or a DNA sample—it can be as bizarre as a Styrofoam egg carton, a Big Mac container, a Hooter's T-shirt, a package of tennis balls, a map of Wyoming, or a leather dildo, all of which contributed in one way or another to the resolution of cases that I was assigned.

Locard's theory of exchange is the guiding principle in forensic science and provides the fuel that keeps investigators hungry in their never ending search for *stuff*. At its very core is the notion that whenever a person comes into contact with an object or another person, something is taken and something is left behind. In other words, when a bad guy enters a house with the intent of committing a burglary, he leaves something behind (he might cut himself and leave blood or walk in mud and leave a shoe impression) and he takes something with him (there might be soil from the victim's flower bed imbedded in the sole of his shoe or paint from the victim's freshly painted windowsill on his jacket). Determining what *stuff* a suspect might have left behind, and what he could have taken away from a crime scene sometimes requires thinking outside the box. The ability to think about the *stuff* in a creative manner is what separates a CSI and a detective from a *good* CSI and a *good* detective. It was precisely this resourceful thinking by Canadian investigators and the willingness of scientists to apply their skills in a nontraditional manner that resulted in the conviction of Douglas Beamish in the murder of his estranged common-law wife, Shirley Duguay. While searching for the body of the missing thirty-two-year-old mother of five on Prince Edward Island in 1994, the Royal Canadian Mounted Police discovered a plastic bag containing a bloodstained coat with adhering strands of white-colored hair. Laboratory tests indicated that the hairs did not come from the suspect, as initially thought, but from a cat. It was no coincidence that the bloodstains on the coat were of the same type as Shirley and that Douglas's parents owned a white fuzzy feline appropriately named Snowball. With no other evidence to follow up on, the strands of hair were sent to the National Cancer Institute's Laboratory of Genomic Diversity (LGD) in Frederick, Maryland, which was in the process of mapping the feline genome. The LGD established a genetic match between Snowball and the questioned hairs recovered from the jacket. Beamish was subsequently convicted of second-degree murder and sentenced to fifteen years in prison. This case set a legal precedent, as it was the first time that animal DNA analysis was allowed in a Canadian court.

Since Snowball's debut, prosecutors in the United States have been following Canada's lead and presenting animal DNA in cases involving poaching, animal cruelty, and Endangered Species Act violations. In Gainesville, Florida, state game officials regularly rely on animal DNA to pursue illegal poachers. It isn't uncommon for game officers to send confiscated venison for DNA testing if it is suspected that it came from does that were killed out of season. Cattle DNA was used in a California theft case, llama DNA in a Florida animal cruelty case, and big horn sheep DNA in a Montana poaching case. The first-known case involving the presentation of canine DNA evidence in U.S. courts occurred in Seattle, Washington, and revolved around the 1996 shooting deaths of a pit bull mix named Chief along with his humans, Jay Johnson and Raquel Rivera. Prosecutors maintained that the defendants, George Tuilefano and Kenneth Leuluaialii, forced entry into the crime scene after being denied a request to purchase marijuana and killed Chief and his owners. DNA was used to show that blood on the defendants' jackets matched that from the dead dog, with only one chance in 350 million that the blood belonged to a dog other than Chief.

But why stop with animal DNA? In 1992, the body of a woman was discovered in the Arizona desert. A pager left at the crime scene was eventually traced to Mark Bogan, a man who owned a white-colored pickup truck similar to that reported to have been seen speeding away from the location. Bogan stated that a female hitchhiker stole his pager after an argument, but he denied ever having been at the crime scene. A search of Bogan's vehicle yielded two seed pods from Arizona's state tree, the paloverde. Detectives determined that if they could match these seed pods with trees at the crime scene, they could, by extension, place Bogan at the location of the murder. This process was complicated by the fact that genetic variability of paloverde trees had not been previously studied and it was unknown if the seed pods contained enough DNA for a genetic analysis. Once the validity of the test was established and researchers determined that it was in fact possible to identify individual paloverde trees, the process was undertaken. The results placed Bogan at the scene of the crime and he was convicted of first-degree murder.

The utilization of nonhuman DNA in the forensic sciences has tremendous potential. Will it one day be possible to match leaves on a suspect's clothing to nursery-raised bushes in front of a victim's home? Can we match wood fibers on a suspect's jacket with the damaged window frame at a burglary scene? Will we be able to do DNA on leather to place a pair of gloves on a suspect's hands, or a torn piece of a shoe left at a crime scene with a pair of shoes in a suspect's closet? I am not a forensic botanist or a forensic serologist—and I don't know the answers to these questions, but I am thinking outside the box, and that, after all, is all that matters.

With developments in the forensic sciences, we are also taking a new look at some old cases. Take, for example, Lizzie Borden. Did she really give her mother forty whacks and when she saw what she had done, surprise her daddy with forty-one (by the way, those numbers are way off)? Several forensic scientists have revisited this case, and it has even been retried, albeit by a Stanford Law School class a century after the fact. While some remain convinced that Lizzie was indeed the hatchet-wielding maniac she was made out to be, forensic pathological evidence used to reevaluate the time of her stepmother's death (i.e., the rate of food digestion, algor mortis, and the degree of blood coagulation) supports the original jury's "not guilty" verdict. U.S. Supreme Court justices William H. Rehnquist and Sandra Day O'Connor served on the Stanford bench during the time of the mock (re)trial where Lizzie was once again acquitted of the charges against her.

Forensics also played a role in the identification of the Romanov family of Russia. On the night of July 16, 1918, Tsar Nicholas Romanov, Tsarina Alexandra, their five children, Olga, Tatiana, Marie, Anastasia, and Alexei, as well as the royal physician, a nurse, and two servants were executed by a Bolshevik firing squad. In 1991, the bodies of four males and five females were exhumed from a clandestine grave in Yekaterinburg, Siberia. Although the presence and quality of dental restorations suggested the decedents were wealthy, and perimortem injuries were consistent with those sustained by the Romanov family, it was mitochondrial DNA (mtDNA) that established their identities. Since mtDNA is passed along the maternal line, the fact that Tsarina Alexandra's great-nephew, Prince Philip of England, shared the same sequence as four of the female skeletons, a common familial origin was established. For Tsar Nicholas, his mtDNA sequence matched that of his great-nephew, James, Duke of Fife. The sequence of one of the females and three of the males did not match those obtained from the tsar's or the tsarina's maternal relatives and it was concluded that these bodies were most likely those of the physician, nurse, and two servants. The bodies of the two youngest children, Anastasia and Alexei, remained missing.

The investigation did not end with the recovery and identification of the Romanov family burials. In 1921, a woman who had been placed in a German mental hospital after attempting suicide claimed to be Anastasia Romanov. Going by the name Anna Anderson, she resembled the missing Anastasia, but some suspected she was in fact a Berlin factory worker named Franziska Schankowska. After her death in 1984, hair and tissue samples were compared to those obtained from the Romanovs. The results clearly demonstrated that Anna Anderson was in no way related to the royal family. The DNA was then compared to Schankowska's maternal grandnephew. The DNA matched and finally established Anna Anderson's true identity.

New information regarding the death of Napoleon Bonaparte has surfaced thanks to our friends in forensic toxicology. Abdominal cramps, weakness, and vomiting had incapacitated Napoleon since the autumn of 1820, and he succumbed to his mysterious illness in the spring of 1821. The physicians conducting his autopsy diagnosed stomach cancer as the cause of death, but noted changes observed in his liver in addition to the well-nourished appearance of his body. This was inconsistent with the significant weight loss that frequently accompanied cancer. Recent reconsideration of Napoleon's symptoms has resulted in postmortem diagnoses of everything from scabies and parasitic schistosomiasis to Foehlich's syndrome and Klinefelter's syndrome. Other theories, however, suggest that Napoleon was poisoned.

After the suspected poisoning deaths of one of Napoleon's friends and servants, Napoleon himself feared he might be targeted and expressed his concerns to those who were close to him. Napoleon's fears may have been justified, as a Swedish dentist named Sten Forshufvud drew a parallel between Napoleon's symptoms as documented in his memoirs, and those reported in cases of arsenic poisoning. Samples of Napoleon's hair were subsequently tested and the results revealed a higher-than-normal level of arsenic, and it appeared it had been administered in small doses over a lengthy period of time. It is unknown if Napoleon's death was the result of a conspired murder plot or if his exposure to arsenic was accidental, but several researchers in the case point to the Scheele's Green pigment used to tint the green wallpaper in Napoleon's home. It is possible that mold growing on the home's damp walls could have released arsenic in the form of a gas to which he was chronically exposed. It is also possible that medications ingested by Napoleon contained arsenic that, in combination with the wallpaper, could have resulted in the elevated levels.

I could write an entire book on the role of forensic science in the resolution of some of histories greatest mysteries. DNA technology put the name of Michael Blassie to the remains interred in the Tomb of the Unknown Soldier, it subsequently settled the rumor regarding the escape of France's Louis XVII, and put to rest a century's worth of gossip regarding the supposedly faked executions and burials of outlaws Wild Bill Longley and Jesse James. With forensic technology, we have identified the body of Josef Mengele, established the forgery of the Adolf Hitler diaries, taken a new look at the Shroud of Turin, and put away Dennis Rader for the crimes he committed as the BTK serial murderer. Forensic evidence utilized in a recent reexamination of the Jack the Ripper case indicates that a man named Walter Sickert might be responsible for the series of slayings, and undermines Albert DeSalvo's claim that as the Boston Strangler he sexually assaulted the victim Mary Sullivan. High lead levels found in the bodies of members of the Franklin Expedition, presumably from the solder in their tinned food, may have contributed to the deaths of these sailors during their ill-fated journey to chart a Northwest passage from Europe to Asia. There has been an anthropological analysis of trauma to the victims killed and reportedly cannibalized as part of Alfred Packer's prospecting expedition through the Colorado Rockies and we currently await the forensic anthropological findings of bone recovered from a Donner Party camp to see if science supports history's accounts of starvation and cannibalism.

Advances in forensic technology and the ability to solve contemporary cases and reexamine older ones have come this far because of astute CSIs, unrelenting detectives, well-trained analysts, and the occasional history buff—all of whom spend their days and nights thinking outside the box. They all dream of cat hair, dog blood, seed pods, lead solder, green wallpaper, and all the other little things that the rest of us just regard as *stuff*. In the forensic sciences, one man's trash truly is the CSI's treasure.

CHAPTER 2

A Sucker's Born
Every Minute . . .

As a <u>real</u> CSI, you learn a lot of things through firsthand experience that can't be taught in a classroom, read in a book, or seen on television. In my case, I learned the most from my mistakes. It took me a few months and half a dozen bloody crime scenes before I figured out why my dogs were so eager to lick my boots when I came home from work. I wished someone had told me that I'd start a fire if I put my flashlight bulb-side down on a 1970s-era, mustard-yellow shag carpet, and I should have been warned not to place my pepper spray on a warm radiator unless I was in the mood for it to deploy on Christmas Day while the house was full of company. It only took one call before I realized that when a man and a train get into an altercation, the train always wins. I learned that *wheps* were welts, *ramshackled* was ransacked, *hackers* were unlicensed taxi drivers, and *40s* were big strong beers. *Commitment* turned out to be a word reserved for Harlequin romance novels, and both men and women referred to their significant others, not as their girlfriend or boyfriend (or, God forbid, wife or husband), but as their baby's mama or their baby's daddy. Only once did I make the embarrassing mistake of asking a victim what he meant when he said he was out looking to "score a nickel of rock," and within a week of working, I knew where I could pick up a do-rag and a hoodie for a big night out on the town.

One thing that I quickly learned was that dead people weren't as pleasant as I initially thought they'd be. They certainly weren't the friendliest bunch and many were inconsiderate and chose to break on through to the other side outdoors in the middle of a thunderstorm or on the coldest and windiest night of the year. Some made the break right at the end of my shift and caused me to work unwanted overtime and almost all of them emitted some foul odor but didn't excuse themselves. A few didn't even bother to put on clean socks before my visit and stunk up my van as I drove their clothing back to headquarters.

Despite my aversion to these people that I didn't even know, my acceptance of the position in the Crime Lab confirmed my readiness and willingness to look at them, smell them, touch them, and roll them. I knew that I would have to listen to the wet sounds of happy little maggots with full tummies slithering through rotten flesh and understood that I might be occasionally asked to assist in the removal of nipple and belly button rings. Although I didn't like the idea, I acknowledged the fact that I'd need to hold their hand as I rolled their fingerprints and shove my hand deep into their pockets as I inventoried personal effects. I agreed to make regular trips to the morgue to witness autopsies and watch as the pathologists bagged up organs and packed them inside canoed torsos kind of like how Frank Perdue hides the bag of giblets inside an Oven Stuffer Roaster. I was willing to do a lot of things that I never envisioned myself doing, but I had to draw the line somewhere. I crossed that line the day a dead man's hand ended up in my mouth. Never suck a dead man's hand was just one more of the many lessons that I had to learn the hard way.

My midnight shift began at 10:30 P.M. and once I left Crime Lab headquarters for my first call of the night, I didn't return unless I had to. I handled all crime scenes that occurred in roughly a 300-square-mile area; a region that was distributed across five of the department's nine precincts. I found it senseless to leave headquarters, drive twenty minutes to a call, then twenty minutes back to headquarters, only to get dispatched to another call in the area I had just left. I don't know why I cared. It wasn't my gas. One thing was certain: I *never* returned to the Lab between calls on the nights my supervisor worked. She was one of the nicest people I knew, but she had a lot to say at 3:30 in the morning. By that hour, I was usually struggling to stay awake and was at the height of my grumpiness. She'd chat, chat, and chat. She'd tell me about her furniture, and her car, and bingo, and her ankles, and coupons, and Salvador. I felt sad when Salvador died and wondered if she'd ever get a new parakeet.

On this bitter night, I planted my van in one of my favorite spots, which was in an empty lot adjacent to an old cemetery. I had grown to like it here because I couldn't be seen from the road and was reasonably assured of being left alone. I had tried dozens of other hiding places, but patrol cars always seemed to find me. In my mind, if a police car was parked out in the middle of an open lot, the cop was saying, "Come talk to me!" But if the car was tucked away behind a building, the driver was saying, "Leave me the hell alone!" The problem seemed to be that I was the only person who had studied this version of Emily Post. I say that because when I was in *my* "leave me alone" spot, officers didn't hesitate to pull up alongside me, roll down their window, and start to chat. They were just being friendly, nosey, or both. They usually wanted to know if I happened to have any nasty crime scene photos with me. Sometimes, they wanted to hear about the latest gross calls I handled or if I knew any details on crime scenes across town that had made the evening news. Then there were those who had friends who wanted to get into forensics and wondered if I had any advice or better yet any connections.

If I did have photos with me, I knew there would be a steady stream of invaders taking over my quiet, solitary space. It wasn't that I minded talking; I actually liked it when the officers and I tried to top one another's stories. But there were nights like this one when I simply hoped to be alone. The last thing I wanted to do was roll down my window and give the wind permission to bite at my face as I engaged in idle chatter. It was just that cold.

I flipped off my headlights and the interior dome light hoping I would disappear into the night. The heat was cranked and it stung my face, but my feet were still cold. The ever-present chill from the back of the van crept forward as soon as I turned the blower down. I closed my eyes as I fumbled with the heater, trying to find a happy medium. The silence of the police radio was a rare but welcome pleasure. The bad guys didn't seem to like being wet or cold, so bad weather usually meant a slow night for Crime Lab. I prayed that I had handled my last call of the shift. The wind howled at my van and the swaying branches of the oak trees around me seemed like long fingers extending down from the night sky, reaching for the gravestones.

The sound of the wind and the sensation of the heat blowing on my face were hypnotic. Relaxing even more, I pushed my seat back but grumbled when it was abruptly stopped by the cage that separated the van's passenger and equipment compartments. I had brought this curse on myself because I had argued for the installation of these cages to protect us from flying sledgehammers, cameras, shovels, electrostatic lifters, and print kits in the event of an accident. The ability to adjust, or more important recline, the seats was a comfort absolutely essential to a midnight shift that never seemed to be properly rested. On nights like this, I welcomed the idea of getting hit in the head with a flying sledgehammer if it meant that I could maneuver my seat into a more comfortable position.

I untied my boots, loosened the laces, and propped my feet on the dash. I didn't like my Rocky boots even though they were supposed to be some of the better police boots out there. They dug into the tops of my feet and I untied them whenever I could. I turned up my radio's volume, closed my eyes once again, and rested my ear on the lapel mike that dangled from my shoulder. In the years that I had spent on midnight shift, I nodded off only once, but I was paranoid it would happen again. By placing my ear over the mike and turning up the radio's volume, I knew that if I did happen to doze, the blaring sound of someone transmitting on the radio would wake me up faster than an extra large espresso.

This is exactly what happened a few minutes later.

"Eighteen ninety-six Dispatch, can you have Crime Lab go to tac?"

I flew out of my seat and scrambled to turn down the volume. *Goddamn it!* I had gone from a pseudo-reclined to a fully erect position in a fraction of a second. My heart was thumping out of my chest. I rubbed my left ear and wondered if I'd ever hear again. I said every curse word I knew. Hearing the radio suddenly blare was worse than being awakened by a beeping alarm clock after a late night on the town. I was glad that I didn't have a big cup of Dunkin Donut's coffee sloshing around in my bladder because it would have been all over the seat.

I grabbed the microphone and without pushing the talk button pretended to berate the officer who raped me of my tranquility. *What the hell's your problem, jackass?*

"'Twenty-two fifteen," dispatch was calling my number, "can you switch to tac for eighteen ninety-six?"

I wrinkled my face, rolled my eyes, and mimicked her nasally tone. *2215, can you switch to tac for 1896?* I knew it wasn't the dispatcher's fault that it was cold, that my volume had been turned way up, that I wanted to be done for the night, that my boots hurt, that the seats didn't recline, that my supervisor had a dead bird, or that I wanted a sledgehammer in my head—but since I couldn't see her I could blame her. "Switchin'." My voice came across as nasty.

The department consisted of ten precincts and each precinct had three dedicated radio channels: the main channel, a tactical (tac) channel, and a restricted channel. Calls were dispatched and received on the main channel, but if someone had something more informal to say or wanted to engage in conversation that would otherwise tie up the main channel's air, both parties switched to tac. When the conversation was complete, both radios were switched back to the main channel and normal operation resumed. The restricted channel was the "secret" channel and Crime Lab didn't have access to it. 1896 was a Crash Team unit and the fact that he asked me to switch to tac suggested he had a question or a favor to ask of me.

I reached down and toggled my radio to tac. "Twenty-two fifteen here." I sounded anything but enthusiastic.

"Eighteen ninety-six, twenty-two fifteen." I recognized the voice. It was Officer Evarts. "We need you to slide by our location to print our victim at this fatal before he goes downtown. Is that something you'll be able to do for us?" Since Evarts was on the Crash Team, I knew his use of the word *fatal* referred to someone who had died in a car accident or had been hit by a car. *Downtown* was the jargon used to refer to the morgue.

"Uhh," I groaned. I hated requests like these. It wasn't that I didn't want to help, although there was a bit of truth in that considering the weather. This situation was one of Crime Lab's catch-22s. We couldn't do anything to alter a body before it was autopsied unless we had the express permission of the Medical Examiner, and that included putting fingerprint ink on the victim's hands. They rarely gave permission.

This all translated into a situation where it is the middle of the night and there is an unidentified dead person who, under ordinary circumstances, will not be autopsied until the following morning, possibly late in the morning. Only after the autopsy has been conducted can the victim be fingerprinted. Once printed, the fingerprint cards have to be relayed from the morgue to police headquarters and entered into the fingerprint database. Then investigators wait to see if the computer makes a "hit." If there is a hit, the fingerprint examiner must confirm it by comparing the actual prints lifted from the victim with those on file. All of this has to be done before the victim's family can be notified of the death. In the mean time, the family is probably pulling their hair out and calling the local hospitals because dad never came home from bowling last night. However, by printing the victim at the crash scene, investigators can get the identification process started immediately.

I knew Evarts wouldn't like my answer. "I'm direct on that, but I can't ink your victim unless the ME says it's okay. Are they there yet?" ME is the acronym for Medical Examiner but we used it to refer to anyone from the Office of the Chief Medical Examiner (OCME).

In our jurisdiction, it was unusual for the forensic pathologist (a licensed physician) to respond to a death scene. In most cases, he or she dispatched a forensic investigator. These highly trained individuals assess the scene, examine the body, and collect historical, medical, and forensic information that they call in to the on-call pathologist. Based on the information received, the pathologist determines if the body needs to come to the OCME for autopsy or if it can be released directly to a funeral home.

If it was determined that Evarts's accident victim was going to a funeral home, then there wouldn't be any reason that I couldn't fingerprint him or her. But accident victims always went downtown and if the body arrived at the morgue with gobs of black ink on the hands, I'd have a lot of explaining to do. Crime scenes are the jurisdiction of the police, but dead bodies are the jurisdiction of the ME. Therefore, unless the pathologist or forensic investigator is present on the scene, the police can do nothing that will disturb a body. Among other things, they can't move it, roll it, search it, or poke it. Every time I tell my two-year-old, "look but don't touch" and "see with your eyes but not your hands," I think of dead people.

When the body arrives at the morgue, the pathologist's initial assessment consists of a review of the information collected by the forensic investigator as well as photographs of the undisturbed body at the scene. An external examination of the body and photographs of the victim and injuries are also an important, early phase of the autopsy process. Fingerprint ink applied to a victim's hands at a crime scene might obscure small injuries, such as defensive wounds, or compromise evidence in his or her palms or beneath the fingernails. This ink would also appear in the photographs of the body taken at the time of autopsy and no one wants these photos to fall into the hands of a defense attorney, who will be prompted to ask in court, "So, Miss Crime Lab, *what else* did you do to the body before it went to the morgue?" The implication being that the CSI caused some of the other visible injuries to the body, planted evidence, and so on.

"Negative. The ME's seventy-six [enroute]. We really need this guy printed." Evarts yelled over the drone of the fire engine motors running in the background. They sounded like generators. The fire department was probably out there illuminating the accident scene with its powerful floodlights. "If we don't print 'em now, it's not gonna happen till later this morning. We don't have an ID [identification]. Can you come out here and give us a hand? There's nothin' at all suspicious about this accident." The bounce in his voice told me he was walking.

I looked at my watch. He was right. If I didn't print him, Evarts wouldn't have an ID for the victim until after lunch.

He piped in again. "I understand that you were out on a scene last week and printed a guy without using ink. Whatever you did there, we need you to do here."

I threw my head backward onto the seat, which made the cage rattle. It was true, but how the hell did Evarts find out about it? I was learning not to do people favors anymore because somehow whatever you did for them would be translated into a new job responsibility. Recovered stolen autos, for example, presented a similar situation. The patrol officers had to fingerprint these cars themselves unless they were used in the commission of another crime. In that case, Crime Lab would take on the responsibility of vehicle processing. On a few occasions, however, we would slide by the location anyway to offer a hand, even if the car didn't meet Crime Lab's criteria for response. Before long, we were being requested on all recovered stolens and the same officers who we had helped a few weeks back would become irritated if we didn't or couldn't help them again.

I shook my head in disbelief. "Ten-four [okay], I'll try. I'm seventy-six. Gimme about twenty [minutes]." I sounded perturbed.

I toggled my radio back to the main channel before Evarts could even reply. I tied my boots and headed off.

I thought about my conversation with Evarts as I drove to the scene. It was obvious that another officer at his location told him about the John Doe I printed the preceding week. I would have been justified if I refused Evarts's request, but on a death that was not at all suspicious, I didn't see any harm in helping.

There are three types of fingerprints: patent, latent, and plastic. A patent fingerprint is a print that is visible to the naked eye, such as one made with blood, chocolate, grease, or fingerprint ink. The opposite of a patent print is a latent print, or a print that is invisible to the naked eye unless it is treated with chemicals, powders, or viewed under special lighting. The third type of fingerprint is a plastic print. These are three-dimensional in nature, such as prints pressed into a soft material like putty or gum.

The residues on an individual's fingertips responsible for the deposition of latent prints primarily consist of oils and water, which are transferred from the fingertips to a surface when it is touched or handled. If there is reason to believe that a smooth and shiny surface could contain latents, the easiest method of visualizing them is to lightly dust the area with a small amount of carbon black fingerprint powder. If a print develops, it can be photographed or physically lifted from the surface. Lifting a print is simple and doesn't involve any high-tech equipment. The sticky side of a piece of transparent tape is laid over the print and when it is peeled back, the powder sticks and the tape is then affixed to a white glossy card. This card is transported back to the Lab for subsequent examination.

When I was at the death scene the previous week and was asked to print the body, I initially refused because of the ink issue. But then it occurred to me that if I gently pressed the victim's fingertips onto a print card, thus depositing the latent residues, and then dusted the shiny card with fingerprint powder, I might be able to get the victim's prints. It worked!

As I approached the crash scene, I couldn't help but notice that I wasn't in Kansas anymore. I hadn't passed a check-cashing booth or liquor store with bulletproof glass in the past fifteen minutes and could no longer smell fast-food grease or hear the thumping beat of the rap music blaring from the car beside me. I went from being in an ugly, urban corridor replete with corner hackers and ten-dollar hookers to a serene, rural environment marked by the occasional estate of a professional baseball or football player.

A patrol car blocked the road and the officer, who had to be freezing, detoured the few cars that approached down a side street. He had a red cone-shaped gadget screwed onto the end of his flashlight, which transformed it into a glowing traffic wand. My van was unmarked and I knew that I would be directed to follow the detour. When I didn't turn, the officer snapped his red wand toward the side street. I just stopped in the middle of the road. I could tell he was getting mad because his strokes grew increasingly short and abrupt. A flashlight was yelling at me. When it was clear I wasn't going to turn, the officer stomped toward my van.

I rolled down my window far enough for him to see the uniform patch on my sleeve.

"Sorry, I thought you were just another idiot driver." He backed toward his car. "Let me back up and let you through. Be careful, it's a solid sheet of ice down there."

The asphalt glistened under my headlights as I drove toward the scene. I decided to park in the middle of the street to avoid the icy puddles that had accumulated along the shoulder. I sat there for a moment taking in the last bit of heat I would feel for a while. The wind tore through the open fields and rocked my van like a cradle. I slipped two pairs of glove liners over my hands and then wiggled them into a thick, fleece-lined outer pair. My cap had a wind liner that would certainly come in handy. I tugged it down as far as it would go. The wind was blowing so hard that it was difficult to open the van's door and as soon as I got out Mother Nature slammed it closed behind me.

The loose hairs that missed getting stuffed in my cap lashed at my face like whips and it was hard to walk against the force of the wind. I thought that maybe if I had been a little slower responding, the dead guy would have blown away and Evarts would have canceled me.

I found my way through the maze of police cars and fire trucks and located Evarts, like most other officers on the scene, sitting in his warm car doing paperwork. It always looked like the police and highway workers stood around doing nothing. I didn't know what the highway crew's story was, but I did know that the police had to be some of the most patient people on Earth because it seemed like they were always waiting for someone. In this case, Evarts was waiting for me to print the body. Once I was through, he had to wait for the morgue transport service that would cart the dead guy away. Then he had to wait for the tow truck. The fire department couldn't leave until the tow truck was done, and Evarts couldn't leave until everyone else had left.

There is a protocol in place that establishes the succession of individuals to arrive at a death scene and when they are to be notified. This is done in a specific order to prevent too many people from showing up at once and rushing the work of those before them. Once an officer arrives at a scene and determines that the services of the Crime Lab are necessary, he or she puts in a request. Then the officer waits.

Although deaths are priority calls, Crime Lab's response can be significantly delayed if we are tied up on a search warrant or another death scene. Eventually, we will get there and take pictures, make sketches, record measurements, take notes, and perform specialized processing if necessary. When Crime Lab is ready for the body to be dealt with, we call for the ME. Then we wait with the officers.

Sometime later, a forensic investigator shows up and takes photographs, conducts interviews, and examines the body. The investigator calls the details in to the forensic pathologist, who determines if an autopsy is necessary. If an autopsy is required, the OCME body transport service is requested. If no autopsy is in order, the funeral home of the family's choice is called. Either way, we wait.

But the officers understandably get tired of all the waiting, so they frequently try to circumvent the rules, and when they do, there are problems. Oftentimes, they call for Crime Lab and the ME at the same time. They are under the false assumption that Crime Lab will get there first, do their thing, and just as they are finishing up the ME will arrive. The timing never works out. On more occasions than I could possibly count, Crime Lab arrived at a scene *after* the ME. When this happened, it wasn't uncommon to find the victim pulled from his or her original location, rolled over, with his or her pockets emptied and the room turned over from searching. It wasn't the fault of the ME, they operated under the assumption that Crime Lab had already been there. The impatient officers or their supervisors who directed them to hurry things along were the guilty ones.

I stood outside of Evarts's car for a second, hoping he would see me. I didn't want to have to take my hand out of my pocket to tap on his window. I had been out of my van for only a minute or so and was already shivering. I looked at the jumble of crunched car metal in the grass near Evarts's vehicle. There was no way I could work out in that open field, in that cold, with that wind. I shuttered at the thought of taking my thick gloves off and wearing only latex to print the dead guy. Nursing school, which I absolutely despised, was looking like the good old days.

Evarts was deep in thought and I had to tap.

"Good evenin', ma'am," he chirped while rolling down the window. He sounded too happy for being trapped on the side of the road with a dead guy in the middle of the coldest night in history.

"Gimme hheeaatttt." I hung through his window to snatch up some of the warmth while the wind tore at my back and made the loose fabric of my coat flap like a flag on a pole. I had handled a bunch of calls with Evarts and he regularly found me in my hiding spots. He turned the vents toward me and flipped the blower to high. The heat stung my ice-cold face, but it was a good sting, like the kind you get when you put alcohol on poison ivy.

Evarts took notice of my runny nose. My sniffs couldn't keep up with the drips. "Don't you dare leak on me," he warned as he covered his papers and leaned away from my head.

"Well if your passenger's seat wasn't filled with all your junk, I'd get in!" I couldn't feel my lips move when I talked. I probably looked like a ventriloquist. "You have to be nice because I'm doin' you a favor and it won't take much for me to reconsider!"

Evarts corrected my interpretation of the junk in the passenger's seat. He slapped his hand loudly on the pile of papers. "This is work. Some of us in the department actually do it on occasion, ya know?" I wanted to ask if the 7-11 hot dog container poking out from the console was also work, but I was too cold to form the words.

I pressed my hands up against the vent and watched Evarts fasten the papers in his lap to a beat-up, old metal clipboard. He was always a tad bit disheveled but he was a brilliant investigator. He reminded me of Columbo.

"Not that you asked, but I'm gonna roll your guy's fingers on print cards and then dust them. You'll end up with ten cards, but that's the only way I can do it."

"I was wondering how you planned to do it." Evarts pulled his ski gloves over his hands and readjusted his cap. "And I do appreciate the effort."

"So, where is our little friend?" I was hoping the dead guy wasn't still inside of the mangled car.

"He's over there, under the sheet." Evarts pointed in a direction opposite the car. "He was ejected."

I saw the sheet fluttering in the field. The victim was far from the vehicle, or so it seemed to my untrained eye. I didn't have a lot of experience interpreting accident scenes, although I found them to be one of the more interesting types of calls. If civilians were allowed on the Crash Team, I'd jump on the opportunity.

"What time did it happen?" I was bouncing on my feet as I asked the question to keep my blood moving. Evarts turned down the blower, cut off the heat, rolled up the window, and got out of the car.

"Not sure when it happened 'cuz the only witness won't get

up off the grass and talk to me." We were in such a low-traffic area that the accident could have occurred hours ago and gone unnoticed. It looked like the guy's car might have slipped on a patch of ice. The driver lost control, hit a tree, and then rolled a few times.

Each step toward the scene was one step farther away from the windshield created by the emergency vehicles. As we made our way into the grassy field, it was as if we had awoken the dead. Doors began to open and tired but warm officers and firefighters began to emerge into the cold, windy, floodlit night. Tears streamed out of the corners of my eyes and my lips and nose stung. I pulled my turtleneck up over my face and tugged on my wind-lined cap so there was just a small slit for me to see out of.

I was wearing so many layers that I looked like one of those kids in the toilet paper commercials who stuff their clothes with tissue for padding. I could barely bend, much less contort or twist. I was wearing silk long johns, over which were normal long johns and then my issued cargo pants. On the top, I wore a long john shirt, a turtleneck, my Kevlar vest, my uniform shirt, a uniform sweater, and my issued coat. Departmental regulations prohibited us from wearing turtlenecks, but I wore one anyway—I just made sure it was navy blue like the rest of my uniform and I rolled the neck down during roll call so my supervisor wouldn't take notice of my dress code violation. This would give her something to add to her list of things to talk about at 3:30 in the morning. I suspected she knew, but she never mentioned it. As soon as I was alone in my van, I pulled my turtleneck up around my neck, but had to remember to roll it back down at the end of my shift. It reminded me of putting makeup on as I rode the bus to junior high school and then remembering to wipe it off on the way home so Mom wouldn't see it.

Evarts and I scanned the ground with our flashlights. He was probably looking for evidence related to the crash and I was trying to make sure I didn't step in something gross. As we got closer to the car, I could smell gasoline and something that reminded me of burned rubber. The vehicle itself looked like a crumpled soda can in the recycle bin. It was upside down, and it was quite evident that it had rolled because grass, mud, and branches were embedded in the roof, doors, grille, and undercarriage. The windshield was folded like an accordion and the side windows were smashed out. The front end had obviously struck a tree because there was a deep, U-shaped concavity in the grille, and twigs and bark were embedded in the crumpled metal. Glass, metal, plastic, and contents from the car's interior were scattered along the accident path and the deep gouges in the frozen earth offered silent testimony to the force of the impact. I shined my light inside the wreckage. There was no way anyone could have survived the crash. The back of the driver's seat was just inches from the steering wheel and the floorboard nearly touched the dash. The airbags had deployed but offered the victim little protection since his ejection indicated he probably was not restrained. The driver's seatbelt swayed in the wind and the buckle clinked against the side of the car as if to emphasize the point. For a second, I forgot about being cold.

"Well," I said matter of factly after taking it all in. I pointed to the Christmas tree air freshener still hanging from the twisted rearview mirror. "That could be a selling point."

Evarts turned and motioned for me to follow him to the body. The yellow beam that emanated from his flashlight indicated that his battery was dying. He provided me with a little more history as we walked. "The car is registered to a seventy-two-year-old guy just up the road. The victim doesn't have a wallet, but he isn't seventy-two."

The white sheet was conspicuous in the black, starlit field and lay close to a tree that showed recent damage. The vehicle's hood was nearby. As we approached the body, I couldn't help but notice the way the sheet danced eerily in the wind. It looked like the victim was trying to get up. Evarts must have noticed it too because he turned to me with a look of consternation and raised one eyebrow. I just had to ask the obvious question, "Think he's fakin' it?"

We stood over the body for a moment as Evarts finished briefing me. Someone had tucked the corners of the sheet under the body and secured the sides with rocks. He or she did a good job because it remained in place despite the wind. "Would you like the honors?" I didn't have any latex gloves in my pocket, so I refused Evarts's offer to lift the sheet. "His face didn't hold up too good," Evarts warned as he kicked a rock away with his foot and pulled a corner out from what I gathered was the head. Within a second, the wind took hold of the sheet and yanked it off the body. I had to duck fast to avoid getting hit in the face with the bloody fabric. I was appalled to see that Evarts hadn't put on latex gloves and watched as he balled up the sheet wearing his ski gloves, which probably doubled as his off duty gloves. "Voila!"

The guy's body appeared to be in pretty good shape, at least externally. His head, however, was another story. This guy was dead all right, really dead. I had a flashback to childhood cartoons. "You know, he reminds me of those *Tom and Jerry* episodes where they'd get flattened by the steamroller!"

Evarts didn't miss a beat. "Yeah, but on *Tom and Jerry* they get back up again."

I was shivering again and my toes stung. "Well, I'll tell ya, if this guy gets up, I'm bailing and you're on your own getting prints! Actually, if he gets back up maybe you can just ask him who the hell he is!" Since I didn't have my latex gloves on, I used my boot to gently jar the victim's arm to check for rigor mortis. His arm was still generally flaccid, but his hands were clenched in a loose fist position. They were definitely in rigor.

The postmortem interval is a term used to refer to the length of time a person has been dead. In determining the time of death, we were trained to look at the dates of newspapers stacked up on the front porch, expiration dates on the milk in the fridge, dates of messages left on the answering machine, and dates of missed appointments. We were also instructed to generally assess the degree of rigor, livor, and algor mortis development. While each of these is undoubtedly influenced by the specific conditions and circumstances of death, together, they nevertheless provide *some* information regarding the time of death.

Rigor mortis is Latin for the "stiffness of death" and refers to the complex metabolic cellular process that causes the muscles of the body to become rigid and inflexible in the hours following death. Rigor is first detectable in small muscle groups of the jaw, face, neck, and hands, but moves throughout the body, generally from head to toe. As a rule of thumb, rigor develops during the first twelve hours following death, stays for twelve hours, and disappears over the next twelve hours as decomposition sets in. Rigor mortis can also indicate if a body has been moved after death, as would be the case if a victim was found lying on his or her back but had his or her knees drawn up to the chest or arms in the air. Gravity would prevent someone from dying in such an unnatural position.

Livor mortis is Latin for the "blueness of death" and refers to the gravitational settling of red blood cells to vessels in the lowest areas of the body, causing a bluish-purple discoloration of the skin. Livor will occur only in vessels that can be distended by blood, so if the body is lying on a firm surface, vessels in tight contact with that surface will be compressed and devoid of discoloration. In other words, if a body is found lying on its back in an extended position, livor mortis will probably not be present on the shoulders, buttocks, or calfs since these areas are in tight contact with the ground. Like rigor mortis, livor mortis can indicate whether a body has been moved after death. If a body is found lying on its stomach, but livor is present on its back, then somebody better start asking questions.

Algor mortis is Latin for the "coolness of death" and refers to the body's loss of heat as it approaches ambient temperature, or the temperature of the surrounding environment. Like rigor and livor mortis, the development of algor mortis is highly variable and influenced by external factors. The fact that the body temperature wasn't even recorded by the forensic investigator in my jurisdiction spoke volumes.

I turned to Evarts, "Okay, I'll be right back. Let me go get the tools of the trade." There was an unwritten Crime Lab rule that you first survey a scene with only your eyes, make an initial assessment and develop a plan of action, and only then do you grab your equipment. As I walked back to my van, I heard Evarts cursing and I turned to see him flailing around with the sheet. It looked like he was trying to put it back over the body, but the sheet was flapping over his head like a sail. I thought about helping him, but only for a second.

The wind pushed at my back and sped up the pace of my walk. If I extended my arms I probably could have flown. My hands were numb, my lips were frozen, my eyes were watering, and my nose was dripping. For some unknown reason, probably force of habit, I had locked the van when I arrived at the scene and now fumbled with the keys as I desperately tried to get inside. After what seemed like an eternity, I heard the joyful sound of the lock click. I sprang inside of the van, frantically started the ignition, blasted the heat, and pressed my hands against the vents.

At first the air felt cool, really cool, but I kept my hands in place armed with the knowledge that the heat was on its way. I started to regain sensation after a few minutes and rummaged through my satchel for one of the many chemically activated hand warmers my brother bought me for Christmas. These things worked fabulously and I didn't waste a second breaking the seal and vigorously shaking the packet so it could start to generate heat. As it warmed up, I searched behind the seats for small- or medium-sized latex gloves. I could only find extra larges. It annoyed me to no end when other investigators would use the last of something and fail to replace it. But I also had to share the blame since I hadn't done a careful equipment and supply inspection before I took the van on the road. I grabbed a handful of extra large gloves, my hand warmer, and my print kit, enjoyed one last moment of warmth, then shut off the van and headed back into the night.

The walk back to the body was worse than I expected it to be. My brief rendezvous with the heater only teased me and made the wind scouring my face and screaming in my ears seem all that much colder. I bowed my head and stared at the ground as I walked. I was miserable. I hated my job on nights like this—but my self-pity was put in check when I thought about the family that would receive the worst imaginable news in the upcoming hours.

A small crowd of police officers and firefighters had gathered around the body. I dropped my print kit to the ground and pressed my hand warmer against my face. As I stood there, desperately trying to warm my frozen cheeks, I had to chuckle at the sight of the exposed body and the balled up sheet stashed beneath a pile of rocks. Apparently, Evarts lost his battle with the wind sail.

One of the firefighters broke the silence. "So, we hear you got some special way to get his prints."

I was sure these guys hated running light details and would have preferred to be anywhere but here. They were doing us a huge favor by illuminating the scene and I had to be nice, even if I was cold, grumpy, and tired. "I have something that I'll try but I don't know if it will work or not . . . we shall see." I opened my print kit and removed tape, scissors, magnetic powder, and my wand. I lined them up on the lid of my kit like surgical instruments on an operating room table.

All eyes were on me and I felt like a tiger in a circus ring expected to jump through a fiery hoop. I didn't blame them though. After all, it wasn't long ago that this kind of stuff used to fascinate me too—but that was before an interest turned into a job. I handed a stack of fingerprint cards to Evarts. "These are gonna blow away. Can you hold 'em and do my writing for me?"

I squatted down uncomfortably in all my layers and only after garnering the nerve did I remove my fuzzy gloves and don the thin, oversized latex pair. I realized immediately that the latex gloves were going to cause problems. Their tips extended about an inch beyond the tips of my fingers and the fit was not snug. This was going to make it hard to manipulate the victim's rigor-laden hands. I also knew that the extra latex was going to get stuck underneath the fingerprint tape and cause the gloves to tear. Torn gloves were anything but welcome on bloody scenes.

"C'mon, tell us how you're gonna print him with no ink," a voice asked from behind me.

I tugged at the gloves, pulling them as far as possible over my fingers to fill the extra latex flapping at the tips. My efforts were in vain. I tucked my hands between my knees to keep them warm. I pivoted in my squat position to see who had asked the question, but the lights on the fire trucks blinded me. I turned back toward the body as I spoke. "I can't put ink on his fingers because the ME won't let us. Instead, I'm going to press each of his fingers onto a separate white card and then I'll dust each one with fingerprint powder. Hopefully, the prints will come up." I turned back toward the crowd and shielded my eyes from the lights by placing my hand over my brow. "I hope it works. This guy is pretty cold though. The guy I did the other day was fresher than this." My choice of words elicited a few snickers and giggles. "We get the best prints from hot and sweaty hands."

I heard someone jokingly ask if the guy I *did* the other day was hot and sweaty. I pretended not to hear him.

I decided to start with the dead guy's left hand because it appeared to be less bloody. More important, if I worked on the left hand it meant my back would be to the wind. I grabbed the hand and could feel its chill through my gloves. I didn't like dead hands because I like living hands. Hands are the first thing I look at on a living person. I really liked beat up hands that showed their owner had been out there hauling wood, mining coal, laying brick, or roping cattle. For me, looking at dead hands was akin to seeing your favorite dessert floating in the middle of a cesspool.

The color of dead people was one of the things that really took me by surprise when I first started doing this job. According to television, dead people are supposed to have blue lips and pale skin. But the only time I saw blue lips was when my brother stayed in the swimming pool for too long—and he was very much alive. The very first time I went to the morgue there was an old man lying on a gurney in the hallway. He was waiting for his turn but didn't look like he was having a particularly good time. He just quietly lay on his back and stared at the ceiling. He must not have been a modest man because he didn't care that he was naked and a bunch of strangers were squeezing past him to get into the autopsy room. I wondered if he ever knew that one day he'd be in this sort of predicament—that is, lying naked on a metal table in a crowded hallway. I was immediately struck by the color of the man's skin. It was yellow and opaque and looked thick and stiff, like a callous on the heel of your foot. He reminded me of a mannequin. I could have propped him up in a department store window with the latest fall fashions on him and no one would have known the difference.

With the crowd at the accident scene anxiously watching me, I tried to extend the dead man's fingers from their clenched position. They wouldn't budge. I pulled and pried and tried to force his hand open, but each time I started to make progress I'd lose my grip in the supersized gloves and his hands would snap closed again, trapping mine in his. I pleaded with him to cooperate. "C'mon, help me out here." He just laid there, ignoring me. I tried and failed again.

By now my gloves were covered in blood, which made it even more difficult to get a grip. I knew that if I could bend his fingers backward and stretch the muscle fibers, I could break the rigor for good and make his hands flaccid. Since his thumb wasn't as difficult to get to as the other fingers, I changed my plan and managed to slip a print card beneath its pad. I pressed down only to realize that the extra latex from my glove was in the way.

My legs were falling asleep because I was squatting in all my layers. Although kneeling in the grass would have been more comfortable, along with it came the risk of putting my knee in some gross thing that broke off the dead man's head. But there came a point when I decided that if I were to get the job done before I froze to death, I just had to go for it. I scanned the ground as best I could for anything that looked wet and pink, and once the coast was clear, I kneeled. I was back in business.

I pulled my gloves down again, got another card from Evarts, and repeated the process. I didn't want to use too much pressure on the thumb because that would obscure the ridge detail in the fingerprint and render it useless. Once finished, I carefully lifted his thumb from the card so as not to smear the print and then let him go.

I turned to my print kit and without even thinking, grabbed my powder and contaminated the bottle with blood. It was for this very reason that I never touched anything inside my kit without wearing gloves. Based on personal experience, I thought that magnetic powder would yield better results than the standard powders that are applied with a brush. I dipped my magnetic wand into the jar and the tiny metal shavings adhered to the applicator like the puffy tentacles on the head of a dandelion. With everyone watching with anticipation, I passed the ball of powder clinging to the end of the wand over the card. A faint print emerged.

I moved the print card back and forth under the light that emanated from the fire truck. Someone behind me was nice enough to shine his flashlight over my shoulder. "Pretty good one, huh?"

The print was horrible. It was faint and there was absolutely no ridge detail whatsoever. All that developed was an outline of the thumb. My pride was bruised and my confidence disappeared. I broke the news. "It's no good." I was disappointed. "I'll try another finger, but I don't think I'm gonna have any luck. I think his hands are just too cold."

One of the firemen couldn't resist, "You mean he's not hot and sweaty enough?"

I was freezing again and my hands were totally numb.

"C'mon, try again," Evarts begged. I knew I wasn't going to have any luck.

"I'll try one more finger." Evarts fumbled through the stack trying to remove a single print card with his big puffy gloves. I knelt beside the body and fumbled with the guy's index finger. My hands barely felt like they were moving. I pulled a felt-tipped pen out of my coat pocket and used it as a lever to lift his finger. I struggled and was finally able to extend the finger just enough to slip a card underneath its pad. Prints were supposed be rolled from nail to nail, but that wasn't going to happen. I was careful to remove the card from his hand in a way that would not smudge my work of art.

"Now for the big moment." I turned back to my print kit.

Evarts crouched down beside me as I passed the powder over the card. Once again, the print barely took the powder and there was no ridge detail at all. I knew he was disappointed. "His hands are just too cold, that's all it is." I had let everyone down.

"Oh well," he shrugged, "at least we tried. I guess we'll name him in the morning."

I changed out of my bloody gloves and as I started to clean up, I thought about my decision to use magnetic powder. I knew it was the right choice. Magnetic powder had several advantages over the standard variety, including the ability to develop rehumidified prints.

Rehumidify! That was the answer! I needed to huff!

"Evarts, wait a minute!" He had started back to his car. "I have an idea. The ME's not going to be getting DNA from his fingers, right? I mean, do you see any reason why they'd want to take nail clippings or swab his hands?"

He looked puzzled. "No . . . why?"

"Just hold the cards for me." I was shivering and wanted nothing more than to get away from this God awful scene, but my conscience wouldn't let me leave without trying once more—even if that meant freezing to death. I pulled the hand warmer out of my pocket and sandwiched it between my hands while Evarts grabbed the cards. When he was ready, I tucked every last flyaway hair into my cap, put on the latex, and knelt down next to the guy like I had before, but this time I scooted as close to him as possible. "Evarts, get down here next to me and have a card ready." I wiggled my jaw back and forth and repeatedly opened my mouth as wide as I could. Evarts just stared at me. "I'm stretching."

I pulled my gloves down so my fingers were slid all the way up into the tips and then began my fight to extend the dead guy's index finger. Using the pen as I had done the last time, I was finally able to pry his finger up from the palm of his hand and once I had a grip on it, I attempted to straighten it by pushing down on the knuckle. It was far from straight but I couldn't push any harder.

I opened up as wide as I could and slowly leaned forward

until the top joint of the dead guy's finger was just inside my mouth. I prayed that he wouldn't get the urge to touch my lips, teeth, tongue, or gums. So there I was, sitting in a field in the middle of the winter with a bunch of people that I didn't know and a dead man's finger in my mouth. My mother would have been proud, even if I wasn't wearing a dress to work.

Evarts sounded like a broken record. "What the hell? What the hell? What the hell?" He just stared.

I firmly held the finger inside my mouth and prepared for the next step. I inhaled deeply and was caught off guard by the musty scent of blood and stale cigarettes on the guy's hand. He must have been smoking right before the accident. I tried not to think about it. Then I proceeded to exhale a deep, long breath from the back of my throat, which was hot and full of humidity. After about five seconds I carefully pulled the finger out of my mouth and quickly pressed it on the card that Evarts had waiting.

Evarts just stared at me with his mouth slightly ajar and his nose wrinkled. It was the did-I-just-see-what-I-think-I-just-saw look.

I turned to my print kit and applied the magnetic powder. With only one sweep of the wand, a beautiful, perfect, dark print filled with ridge detail emerged. Evarts was elated and the firefighters clapped and hooted.

"It's called huffing," I said to Evarts, who was grinning from ear to ear. I covered the print with a piece of tape to prevent it from smudging and asked Evarts to write "Left Index" on the back of the card. "Sometimes prints won't develop very nicely because the oils and moisture that were in them have evaporated. But you can put that moisture back by huffing on the print, then quickly processing it with powder." I nodded toward the dead man. "In this case, his hands are so cold that he didn't have enough moisture to leave a print, so I just added some to his fingertip." You could have heard a pin drop.

Evarts made notes on the card and then proceeded to inspect the print more carefully. When he was satisfied, he circulated it among the firefighters. "And no," he was answering a question that hadn't been asked—at least not out loud. "I've never seen it done like that before either!" Evarts saw that I was in position to print the left middle finger. "Here," he said to the firefighters as he handed them the first set of lousy prints I obtained without using the huffing method. "Compare the detail in these with the print she just got. It's like night and day." Evarts removed another print card from the stack and had it ready for me to grab.

I tugged the gloves down on my fingers to get rid of the extra latex at the tips and then engaged in a struggle to extend the dead guy's middle finger while holding back the bloody thumb, index, ring, and little fingers. When I was sure I had a firm grip, I leaned forward, opened my mouth, inserted the finger, and exhaled. I was careful not to allow it to touch me as it went in and out of my mouth. Immediately, I pressed the finger on the print card that Evarts had waiting. Just like before, I dusted the card and a beautiful, dark print immediately jumped out. I covered it with tape and handed it to Evarts. "That's the left middle."

Despite the cold, Evarts and I got a system going and we were on a roll. Within about twenty minutes I had all but two of the fingers printed and the process had gone pretty smoothly. Since I had moved onto the right hand, my face was toward the wind and the pain was intense. However, as much as I wanted a heat break, I could see the light at the end of the tunnel and it was senseless to stop now.

As we had done with the other eight fingers, Evarts positioned himself with the card while I pried up the right ring finger and straightened it out as best as I could. I opened wide, inserted, and was in trouble before I could even begin to exhale. In a split second, I felt my numb fingers losing grip as the dead man's hand started sliding in my bloody, oversized gloves.

In a flash, the dead man with a squashed head had freed his hand from mine and his ring finger fell to the floor of my mouth before it sprang back to its clenched position and curled over my bottom incisors, locking his bloody hand to my jaw. I could taste the cigarettes and heard Evarts shouting "Oh, God" as I pushed myself back into the grass. But he wouldn't let go! I shook my head back and forth like a dog playing with a toy, but *this* was no game. I shrieked for help but my voice was muffled by the cold stranger's hand that was pressed up against my face.

In what seemed like hours, but was probably only about three seconds, I was finally able to release his grip. I rolled around on the ground gagging, spitting, coughing, and screaming. I was appalled! I was disgusted! I was horror-struck! Suddenly, I wasn't cold anymore. I had blood in my mouth and on my chin and one of the firemen ran to his truck and returned with the only cleaning agent he had: rubbing alcohol. I opened the bottle, filled my mouth and swished, swished, and swished. I did it again and again. I wiped my face down with the alcohol and Windex, and gargled with someone's soda and chomped on about five sticks of gum.

Once I was cleaned up, I walked up to Evarts, who was in the crowd of firefighters probably talking about what they had just witnessed. I could tell they were trying to compose themselves as I approached. I looked at Evarts and then nodded toward the dead guy. "What *the hell* was he thinking?" Everyone just stared at me, not sure if I was joking. "Why do people have to act like that?" At that point everyone broke down laughing, including me. "Listen," my eyes met those of each and every person in the group. "What happened in that field stays in that field." But I knew better than to think they would keep this secret.

I was right. News of the incident spread like wildfire. I heard every sucking up, blood sucker, necrophilia joke in the book. Officers and other CSIs were warned not to leave me alone with a dead man because there was no telling what I might do.

Since the department considered this to be an "exposure," the victim was tested for hepatitis and HIV and thankfully the results came back negative.

The worst part is that I never even learned the guy's name, and he didn't ask for my number. Some things never change and I swear, I'll never suck on a dead man's hand again. Been there, done that!

CHAPTER 3

Gross Anatomy . . .

When I told people I was writing this book, the first thing that they wanted to know was the title. When I told them, their responses were always the same. First came the excuse-me look and then they would repeat it back to me, slowly, inviting me to jump in and correct them at any time. With a book called *Never Suck a Dead Man's Hand,* I felt compelled to give them the abridged version of the hand-in-the-mouth story. Some were amused, some were appalled, and some stared at me waiting for me to tell them that I was just kidding—but they all wanted to know *exactly* what kind of book I was writing. They were suspicious. Surprisingly, I had (and continue to have) difficulty trying to describe it. "Well, it's a memoir, kind of. Not a general memoir, but a memoir of the crazy cases I worked. But it really isn't about the cases—it's about the scenes and the things that go on behind the crime scene tape. It's about all the things they don't show you on television." They didn't get it. Maybe they will now, assuming that I didn't scare them away already.

In case you have the same questions as everyone else, allow me to explain. First, nowhere in this book do I leak investigative details of unsolved crimes that would in any way compromise the resolution of the cases. Although, I must say, I find it peculiar that while police and forensic personnel are tight lipped about what they will tell the general public when a major crime has occurred, any astute busybody can march to the Central Records Division of his or her local police department and get copies of the police reports, Crime Lab documents, and crime scene photographs through privileges granted to them by the Freedom of Information Act. While the information might be free, the reports and photos certainly aren't—but after all, we live in a society where money will buy anything.

Second, in some instances I have tweaked specific details of crime scenes just enough to prevent victims and their families from identifying cases that involved them. It is likely that the green trailer on Main Street has been transformed into a multimillion-dollar home on Investment Lane just like a murder scene at a Chrysler car dealership is now an attempted murder in a 7-11 store parking lot. The last thing I want is for my stories to be at a crime victim's expense.

Third, *most* people's names have been changed. While victims' names are altered for obvious reasons, I made the decision to reference most officers and detectives by pseudonyms because many of the stories involve conversations and jocularity that some may find "inappropriate." I found it easier to change names across the board rather than struggle with each particular situation.

Finally, there is the issue of the obvious emotional distance and gallows humor that I developed while working as a CSI. I had to. I am a sensitive person, really. I cry during long-distance telephone commercials, especially the one where the son calls his mother from across country just to say he loves her. My heart aches for all the kids in foster care whose only wish in life is to have a family, and I hold back the tears when I think of the old people in nursing homes who get all dressed up and spend the day waiting for the visitor who never comes. I find nothing funny about death, crime, or a family's grief.

When I first started making regular trips to visit with the violated, wounded, maimed, and dead, I was revolted at the sheer malevolence demonstrated by some members of my very own community and could not believe the regularity with which intentional emotional and physical pain was inflicted on others, oftentimes by people who claimed to love them. I didn't realize how many people found permanent answers to often temporary situations through suicide, or the number of babies who died unexpectedly. I had been trained, both in school and on the job, to handle the scenes but nobody told me how to handle my feelings. I still remember the first full autopsy that I ever witnessed. It was out of state and involved a young woman who had been the passenger in a fatal motor vehicle accident. She was wearing a red gingham suit, white shoes, and had a string of pearls around her neck. Her work ID hung from its lariat. The ME determined that for whatever reason, she had arranged her seatbelt so it didn't cross over her right shoulder, but instead came out from under her arm. Consequently, when the vehicle in which she was riding was hit head on, her seatbelt failed to restrain her upper body and the forces of the collision whipped her head back and forth so violently that it dislocated and fractured her first and second cervical vertebrae. Death was instant.

I couldn't stop thinking about the girl in the red gingham suit and white shoes. I wondered why she took her arm out of her seatbelt and where she was heading to when the accident occurred. I thought about her mom being handed a plastic bag sealed with evidence tape that contained her bloody pearls and wondered if she had brothers or sisters, or even a boyfriend. I searched for her name on the Internet and found her obituary and a newspaper account of the accident. She had just started graduate school, was one of two kids, and engaged to be married in only three months. She was just like me.

I couldn't go on like that. If I let every victim of crime get to me like the girl in the red gingham suit and white shoes, I would have been a mental train wreck by the end of my first year on the job. Emotionally distancing oneself from the terribly harsh reality of crime scene work is something that happens, *I believe*, unintentionally, unconsciously, and automatically. It is a psychological defense mechanism and a way of dealing with what your brain is telling you to run the hell away from. There is nothing worse than seeing a murdered child, hearing the tortured screams of a mother when she is told that her son has taken his own life, or photographing a girl in her prom dress who was just killed by a drunk driver. Part of this emotional distance involves the development of a gallows or black humor. This spontaneous and context-specific humor is common in circles of emergency workers and serves as a means to deny or suppress "normal" emotional responses to the dire situation at hand. As one mental health worker put it, it's a way of being sane in an insane place.

And what situation is more insane than being in an open field with a dead man's hand shoved in your mouth? You have two choices: you can laugh or you can cry. Although I wasn't eager for it to happen again, or at least in public, I was grateful that I walked away from that scene relatively clean. So, I had a little blood on my chin and a bad taste in my mouth—big deal. Besides, I knew the chances of something like that happening again were remote because most of the time body parts didn't get *in* me, they just got *on* me.

I learned this on my very first body call. Though I had seen the photos, watched the videos, heard the stories, and even processed make-believe body scenes, I was not at all prepared for what the real world held. The four other civilians assigned to the Crime Lab and I had just completed a three-month training session at the Police Department Training Academy. I was the only one new to the county; everyone else had transferred from other county positions. One had been a guard at the detention center, while the other three already worked for the police department; two as tenprint examiners and one as a forensic chemist in the Crime Lab.

The training academy was an old school, or at least I think it was a school. But it didn't look like a school you'd want your kids to go to because there were always a lot of police cars parked out front and people seemed to be screamed at, tackled, handcuffed, and taken down at gunpoint (albeit with fake guns) on a daily basis. There were plenty of police recruits in the building at any given time, but they were about as friendly as dead people and rarely smiled. They looked like they were always scared and were in the odd habit of running over to a wall, pressing their backs flat against it, and staring straight ahead with a stone-cold face and their arms tight at their sides every time anyone who wasn't another recruit walked by. I thought maybe they had something wrong with them—like maybe they were a bit slow or something.

Before we even got to the forensics portion of our training, our primary instructor made certain that we received our Kevlar vests, pepper spray, biohazard safety equipment, face masks, and departmental driver's licenses. He watched as we locked lips and pushed on the chest of an ugly mannequin named Resusci-Annie, learned defensive tactics from an old man who used to be in a gang, and struggled to learn how to run wanted checks on the National Crime Information Center computers that looked like they dated to the turn of the century. We were required to know the departmental rules and regulations inside and out, upside and down, and learn about the department's history, the precincts and their boundaries, and the chain of command. We were tested to make sure we could recite the 10-codes (10-54 is livestock on the highway just in case you ever need to use that one) and the phonetic alphabet (Adam, Boy, Charles, David, Edward, Frank, and so on) in our sleep, and were instructed how and when to fill out each of the department's innumerable forms. A lot was expected from us and we gave every bit of it back to them.

The department was all about numbers. None of the forms were referred to by the big bold name centered at the top of them; that would be too easy. Instead, the tiny number on the bottom right-hand corner referenced them. You didn't ask for a property sheet, you asked for a 15. The narrative reports that we were told we would frequently be writing were 11s, while computer-generated letters to our supervisor had to be printed on a 12L, or we could do a handwritten one on a 12LA. And officers were to be reminded to send up a 106 if they had a suspect in a fingerprint case. You didn't even use the word *form* before the form number; if you asked an officer for "Form 88," you'd sound like a freak. You just said, "Where's my 88?" But it didn't end with the paperwork. An officer on a scene didn't have a name—he or she had a car number; portions of the county weren't referred to by precinct name, but by precinct number; and God forbid you forget to put your ID number on the bottom of your 15—the Evidence Management Unit (EMU) would kick it back.

Then there were the acronyms. There was the FSS (Forensic Services Section) and the CISD (Criminal Investigative Services Division) and programs for kids such as DARE (Drug Abuse Resistance Education), PAL (Police Athletic League) and JOINS (Juvenile Offenders in Need of Supervision).

By the time we got to the crime scene portion of our training, we were ready for a change. After all, the crime scene stuff was our meat and potatoes; it was the reason we were learning how to talk in code, not to mention all the other crazy stuff we were doing. As rumor had it, the five of us were the first civilian CSIs (although one was slotted for a supervisory position) the department had ever hired. Since we were coming into the job as complete novices, a rigorous training program had to be developed and implemented, and Pat was the man to do it. He was a relatively little guy with reddish blond hair and round glasses and he seemed to have a boyish innocence about him. He reminded me of Opie on the *Andy Griffith Show*. Pat was a detective who had spent the past several years assigned to the Crime Lab and it was clear that he was absolutely passionate about what he did, but he was anything but innocent. From the day Pat walked into the academy until the day we were released into field training, he busted our humps, and it didn't take long before words like Dustprint Electrostatic Lifting Kit, phenolphthalein, and cyanoacrylate rolled off of our tongues like poetry and we could recite the proper wavelengths of light required to visualize latent prints treated with an array of fluorescent chemicals in our sleep.

Classroom instruction consisted of lectures, demonstrations, videos, and guest speakers. This was followed by practical exercises that we conducted in the academy's classrooms that had been set up to look like banks, apartments, and bars. Pat staged crime scenes in these rooms and we would spend countless hours photographing, sketching, fingerprinting, spraying photosensitive chemicals, casting shoe impressions, collecting bugs, unloading firearms, packaging drugs, counting money, searching for blood, looking for hairs, and swabbing for semen (we were told it was fake). Pat left no stone unturned, and for our final practical exercise we each processed a mock murder scene and did everything, *and I mean everything* as if it were the real deal. But it didn't end there. After we received our printed crime scene photographs, typed our reports, finalized our sketches, and packaged our evidence, we made the trek to the county's circuit court where we sat before a judge in a courtroom filled with onlookers. A prosecutor questioned us on direct about the work that we performed at the "crime scene" and we then endured cross-examination by one of the public defenders. It was the most scared I had been in years. The humbling part came once we were finished with our testimony—that's when we received the criticism, although constructive, on everything from our photographic skills, to the accuracy of our sketch, the quality of our report, and the effectiveness of our courtroom testimony.

Ten years later I still remember the advice given to me by the prosecutor. "Before you come to court, study your report like you're studying for a test because the less you fumble through your notes, the better you'll look to the jury. . . . Look to the attorney to take the question, and look at the jury to give your answer. . . . Speak loud and sound confident, even if you are scared to death. . . . If I ask you a yes or no question, give me a yes or no answer, don't elaborate unless I ask you to. . . . And don't swivel in that chair!" At the time, I hated Pat for putting us through that experience, but in retrospect, it was probably the single most important part of my training.

Once we passed all our proficiency tests, the final practical, and the courtroom exercise, we graduated to a week's worth of ride alongs with patrol officers in the precinct of our choice. Then we made the much-anticipated transition into the Crime Lab, where we would spend the following months field training on real crime scenes with experienced investigators. The five of us were thrilled to be out of the academy and away from the seemingly slow people who stood up against the walls when you walked by. It wasn't that we disliked it there or did not enjoy our training, we had just been cooped up for three long months and were ready to put our newly acquired skills to use. I wanted to talk in form numbers, spit out 10-codes, and spell people's names using the phonetic alphabet. Most important, I wanted to go to a crime scene. I had still never been to one!

In the months that we were in the academy, or "the compound" as I started to call it, we caught wind that the Crime Lab was in the midst of major change. Besides an upcoming physical relocation, supervision of the Lab had recently transferred from the responsibility of a captain to that of a civilian, and the hiring of the five of us marked the beginning of the Lab's effort to completely civilianize the Crime Scene Unit. However, since we were locked away in the compound and isolated from the rest of the department, we had no clue how much these changes enraged most officers and detectives.

My first real inclination that something was up occurred during one of my post-academy ride alongs with patrol. I had been assigned to ride with a female officer and the look on her face told me she was all but happy to have me strapped into the passenger seat of her car. As we pulled out of the precinct lot at the very beginning of the shift, the first question out of her mouth was, "So how do you feel knowing you're taking someone else's job." I was flabbergasted. *Taking someone's job?*

When we started our field training a week later, Pat put us on the shift to which we would be assigned and rotated us into what would become our permanent days off. I was put on the three-to-eleven shift and my weekend fell on Wednesdays and Thursdays. I was so excited on my first day that I arrived at work an hour early. I sat in my car for fifteen minutes so I wouldn't seem too enthusiastic, but the anticipation of what was to come got the best of me and I rushed into the building. I savored the sound of the door that said CRIME LAB PERSONNEL ONLY unlock as I ran my identification through the card reader. I walked in holding my new clipboard, flashlight, print kit, and the laser distance tape measure that I couldn't pass up at Home Depot. I felt like a scared, but excited kindergartner wearing her new patent leather shoes and holding her box of unused crayons in one hand and unscathed lunchbox in the other, not really sure where to go or who to talk to.

Pat had kept us holed up at the compound for so long that I had hardly met any of my future coworkers. Although a lot of detectives were milling about the Lab, it was Debbie who acknowledged me standing in the doorway looking like a lost puppy. Debbie was the office assistant, but she wanted to (and would) become a CSI. She was friendly, welcoming, cheerful, and went out of her way to make me feel comfortable. Debbie kidnapped me for about forty-five minutes and showed me to my desk, handed me a stack of forms to fill out, and explained the procedures for claiming overtime, comp time, mileage, meals, and all kinds of other things that I knew I'd never remember. Then she introduced me to my sergeant.

The sergeant seemed nice enough. We chatted for a few minutes before he took me around to meet the guys (and yes, they were all guys) who would be conducting my field training. These were the ones who were going to make everything come together for me and I was thrilled to finally get the chance to meet them. As the sergeant introduced me to the first detective, I eagerly extended my hand and tried to commit his name to memory. I was bad with names and was going to have about twenty to learn. But the detective didn't take my hand. He looked up at me, forced out an obligatory "Hi," and then went back to his work. Then I met the detective sitting behind him. I couldn't see his face because it was hidden behind the sports page of the newspaper. He pulled it down only long enough to say hello but never bothered to look at me. We continued to make our rounds and after about the fourth introduction, my enthusiasm started to take a turn for the worse. By the end, it was clear that these guys wanted nothing to do with me. As I would learn in the following days, most would rather get intestinal parasites than participate in any facet of my training.

But I didn't take it personally; I talked to the other new investigators I trained with at the academy and learned that the detectives (also called the "sworn" members of the Lab) were treating all of us wretched job-stealing civilians the same way.

In the weeks that followed, the dectectives, or at least most of them, went out of their way to make us feel anything but welcome. The police, whether they be patrol cops, sergeants, captains, or detectives were also called the "sworn" members of the department. I guess they swore to something, although I still don't know quite what. The detectives must have sworn to be assholes, and they took this oath solemnly. They regularly called us *scabs*, sometimes "jokingly" to our face but usually behind our backs, although they made sure we were within earshot. Each shift started with a brief roll call, followed by the sergeant breaking the bad news and telling which detective would "get" me as a trainee. I had flashbacks to elementary school when I was the last kid up for picks for dodge ball. After the sergeant made the assignment, the detectives would shuffle back to their desks and the one stuck with me would curse, swear, and complain. On one occasion, a detective was so furiously complaining about having to take me with him that I got up and went to the bathroom. I just couldn't listen to it anymore. When I walked back into the room, I overheard him telling the other detectives that if he was going to be stuck with me, he was going to make the best of it. "Yeah, I'll be driving over speed bumps all night long so I can watch those titties of hers bounce around." I was mortified, but held my head up and glared at him the entire way back to my desk. He knew better than to drive within fifty feet of a speed bump that night or I'd be marching straight to the sergeant—who I wasn't convinced was on my side either.

It was obvious that the detectives (or *defectives* as we civilians started to call them) loathed the idea of having civilians replace them as CSIs, not to mention the fact that one was now running the Lab. To make matters worse, we learned that management was forcing the detectives to train the civilians and once we soaked up their years of experience, we would handle the crime scenes and they would be reassigned to other detective units or booted back to patrol. Some of them had been in the Crime Lab for years and loved what they did. In my mind, it didn't make sense to send someone as knowledgeable as Pat into White-Collar Crimes or back to making traffic stops. Their anger, although clearly misdirected, was justified . . . or so I thought.

One of my most memorable training days was when I rode with a nearly deaf investigator named Detective Barber. He was one of the nastier ones and despised having ride alongs—particularly those of the civilian scab variety. He never answered the radio because he couldn't hear it. He never answered me because he didn't want to. We weren't assigned to a call, but he was driving us somewhere. I didn't bother to ask him where we were going because I knew he would ignore me, or just tell me I'd see when we got there. We pulled into an alleyway behind some row houses on the other side of town, and without uttering a word he got out, locked his door, and disappeared inside one of the homes. Although it was only April, it was hot, really hot, and after about forty-five minutes I was on the verge of decomposing. Fed up, sweaty, and needing a drink of water, I banged on the door of the row house. I found Barber sprawled out in a recliner having lunch as he and his mother watched breaking news on television. That was how I learned of the bombing of the Alfred P. Murrah Federal Building in Oklahoma City.

I tried to make the best of field training with the defectives, even though not much of it involved training. One of the first things most of them did before taking the van out of the head quarters lot was disengage the automatic vehicle locater so dispatch couldn't track their movement. At first, I wondered why they did this, but as I sat on a picnic bench with a bunch of strangers at a fiftieth wedding anniversary party for a couple I had never met, I started to get it. I waited patiently while my trainers sat in the barber chair, the dentist's chair, or their kitchen chair, and tagged along as they shopped for cars, tattoos, motorcycles, furniture, and lawn mowers. We even visited some woman in the hospital following her gall bladder surgery. I had no idea who she was, but I told her I hoped she felt better soon.

As we drove through what seemed like relatively safe areas, the detectives would tap their finger on the side window and say, "I handled a homicide there, . . . a robbery there, . . . a suicide there, . . . a homicide there, . . . a rape there, . . . a burglary there . . ." I couldn't wait for the day when I had that kind of experience.

All the detectives had a reputation for something—one was known for taking the supervisor's door off the hinges at night so he could snoop, another liked to jingle change in his pocket as he talked about women in high heels, and another was blessed with X-ray vision and never had to process crime scenes for fingerprints because he claimed he could just look around and tell none were present. Then there was Detective George Cunningham. George, a former homicide detective, outranked the other investigators in the Lab by having obtained the rank of corporal. He was a soft-spoken man who was slightly older than most of the other investigators, and aside from Pat, he was the only detective in the entire Lab who was warm to the civilians from the very first day. George seemed like a sincerely nice guy who really wanted us to do well. While he was angry about the way the changes in the Lab were being orchestrated, he recognized the need for us to be properly trained. After all, we wouldn't be the ones who would suffer from poor training—it would be the victims of crime.

George would invite us into the evidence-processing laboratory if he was working on something interesting, and between calls he would show us how to get to the morgue, the hospitals, the precincts, and the district courts. Each day, I prayed I would get to ride with George. It didn't happen as often as I would have liked, but it did happen the day I got my first body call.

George and I had just cleared a residential burglary and were planning to get some lunch and then mess around with the metal detector.

"Twenty-two fifteen." The dispatcher's voice sounded ominous.

I looked at George. "She said twenty-two fifteen, right?" I was still having trouble deciphering the garbled sound of the voices on the radio. George nodded.

I was nervous using the radio. I tried to sound like everyone else by dropping the first two digits of my car number when I answered her. "Fifteen, go ahead."

"Twenty-two fifteen, ten sixty-three." The 10-codes spun around in my head like the horses on a merry-go-round. I wracked my brain for the meaning of 10-63.

"Ten-sixty-three!" George was smiling. "C'mon—you know what it means. She's telling you to ten-sixty-three." He wasn't going to tell me. George was the only one of the detectives who let us use the radio. Sometimes he even let us drive.

"Uhh," I covered my face with my hand as I thought. "Prepare to make a written copy?" I was asking and telling at the same time.

"Good!" George gave me a thumbs-up. "She wants to give us a call."

I grabbed my pad and pen from my pocket. "Twenty-two fifteen . . ." I unkeyed the mike when I realized I forgot the 10-code for "I'm ready." I fumbled for my cheat sheet.

"Twenty-two fifteen, you okay?" The dispatcher had a giggle in her voice. She had to know I didn't know what the hell I was doing.

"Twenty-two fifteen. I'm ready. Go with it." I wondered if I'd get in trouble for not using the 10-code.

"Twenty-two fifteen, I need you to start up to a suspicious death." I looked at George with bugged out eyes. My hand shook as I numbly jotted down the call information. "Case number is ninety-five, one-twenty, eighteen eighty-three. Unit eighteen forty requested you at seventeen-nineteen hours. You need to respond to two-eighty-seven Wilcox Court, cross streets of Hurley and Madison, map coordinates forty-eight C-six." George turned the van around and started the trek to the crime scene. I hoped it was far away. I guessed this meant we weren't getting lunch.

I was silent for about five minutes. George didn't look at the map book, so I assumed he knew where we were going. I felt a lump growing in my throat. My stomach felt queasy, and my hands were sweaty. I just stared out of the window.

I needed to confess. "Okay, George." I hesitated. "I have to tell you something." My voice trembled and sounded weak.

George looked at me with a sinister smile. He knew. "So, never had anyone ten-seven before, have ya?" 10-7 was the code for "out of service." Normally, it was used when you were temporarily unavailable to handle calls. If you had to run into headquarters to drop off evidence, you'd tell the dispatcher, "Hold me ten-seven at the office for a minute." But we also used 10-7 to refer to someone who was permanently "out of service," in other words, dead.

I took a deep breath and tried to disguise the uneasiness that was apparent in my voice. "No, this is my first one." I didn't know why I was so nervous. I had seen more photos of dead people than I could count and had even been to the morgue, but there was something nerve wracking about seeing a dead person in the original location, in the position the person was in when the person breathed a last breath of air. Just the thought of it gave me butterflies, but not the good ones you get on roller coasters. These were bad ones. My butterflies were more like moths; the kinds of moths that eat holes in your clothes. "I just hope it isn't something too bad, like a decomp or a rifle or shotgun blast to the head. I need to be broken in—slowly."

My reaction to the call surprised me. Fifteen minutes earlier I would have jumped at the opportunity to handle a death. Now that I had one, I was petrified. I changed the radio to the channel of the precinct where we were heading in hopes that its officers would be talking about the call. I didn't hear anything useful. "George, maybe we can ask the officers out there to give us some details. That way we'll know what we're walking into."

George shook his head. "You like Cracker Jacks?"

He had lost it. "What?"

"Do you like Cracker Jacks?" he asked in all seriousness.

"George!" I whined his name loudly. "We're driving to my first death scene and you wanna know if I like Cracker Jacks?"

He looked at me and tapped his fingers on the steering wheel as he waited for an answer.

"I guess so." My tone was suspicious.

He wasn't done. "Why?"

Maybe he was trying to take my mind off the scene. "I like Cracker Jacks because they taste good and, of course, there is the prize."

He probed even further, "And what's so great about the prize?"

Our conversation had turned into a game. "Well, I thought you'd never ask! Let me tell you—the most exciting thing about the prize is that it is different each and every time." I was adding drama by talking fast and in high, exaggerated tones.

George interrupted me. "Well, think of death scenes like the prize in a box of Cracker Jacks. They're exciting because you don't know what you're gonna get. Why ruin the surprise by calling an officer and asking what's in your box?" I just stared at him and wondered when the hell Forrest Gump was issued a permit to carry.

We arrived at the scene far too quickly for my liking. The sight of the police cars rejuvenated the moths in my belly. The address was a single-family home in a somewhat dilapidated neighborhood in one of the shadier sections of town. The street was lined with cars, and most of them were propped up on cement blocks. The ones that had wheels were decked out with bumper stickers of Calvin pissing on Ford and Chevy logos. Despite the fact that it was late spring, many of the houses were still framed in Christmas lights, and there were garden gnomes, birdbaths, plastic deer, and those bizarre gazing balls in unkempt yards as far as the eye could see. George parked the van in the street. The house looked like it had never been painted and the grass was nearly a foot high. A deck extended from the side of the house and it was stacked with black-and-white plastic bags filled with garbage. This was where all the cops were hanging out. I shoved a piece of gum in my mouth to try to settle my stomach. George turned off the ignition and reclined his seat. "This doesn't look good."

I was confused. "Huh? What doesn't look good?"

He nodded toward the group of officers. "It's hot out there. The house is air conditioned, so why are they all standing outside sweating?" This was why I liked training with George. I never would have noticed little nuances like these. "Look, there's the air-conditioning unit." He pointed to the side of the house. "All the windows are closed, so it's gotta be running."

I was taking it all in. "So, what are you saying?" I wasn't sure I wanted to hear his response.

"Well," he hesitated. I stared at him for a second before raising my eyebrows as if to say, *yeah*. George looked at me and then looked away and spoke quickly as if he hoped I'd miss some of what he was saying. "Well, it usually means there are lots of roaches, the victim is rotten, or it's a really messy scene."

"Oh!" I had a fake smile plastered to my face. "Well . . . that's just what I was hoping for." I chomped on my gum. I needed a Rolaid and was certain that I was on the verge of a stroke. I hated six things in life: vomit, drains, heights, brussels sprouts, bugs, and clowns. I had a feeling that my list would soon grow and would include rotten and messy dead people.

The anticipation was the worst part. "C'mon! Let's go!" I said as I grabbed my notepad and latex gloves. When George wasn't looking, I smeared a dollop of Vicks VapoRub beneath my nostrils. I didn't even know if the body was a stinker, but there was something comforting in the smell of menthol. It reminded me of being little with a cold and my mother lovingly rubbing it on my chest. As I looked at the police cars around me, I realized the association was forever ruined. There was nothing loving about this place.

I learned from my limited ride-along experience that the attitudes of our field trainers tended to take a turn for the worse when they were in the presence of other cops. While I trusted that George wouldn't let me down, I couldn't help but worry. I *needed* his help on this scene.

As we made our way to the deck party, the sergeant on the scene walked down the steps and met us in the front yard. He gave me the once-over and then deliberately positioned himself between George and me. He started to tell George the details of the call in hushed tones not intended for me to hear. I was pissed. After all, I was the one holding the radio and the notepad. George grabbed my arm. "This is Dana and she's gonna be handling the scene." The sergeant looked at me coldly and then back to George. "So, if you can give her all the information—that would be great."

The sergeant's demeanor completely changed when he was forced to talk to a scab. He refused to make eye contact and gave me only the watered-down version of what happened. "The victim is a forty-year-old white male found lying on the living room sofa by his kids when they came home from school . . . looks like a self-inflicted rifle blast to what used to be his head."

I shuddered. George called it right—it *was* a messy scene. "Any history on this guy?" I tried to act unfazed by his description of what awaited us inside. I knew he wanted a reaction. George gave me a look that told me I was doing fine, and then he backed away leaving me alone with the sergeant, who still wouldn't look at me. "Yeah. His mother says he's been despondent for quite some time and tried to commit suicide about five years ago." I jotted this all down in my notebook.

"When was he last seen alive?" George was now busy chatting with another officer. I hoped I was asking all the right questions. "Did he leave a note?"

"No note that we could locate, but we didn't want to search too much until you got some photos."

"What about forced entry?"

"Nope. The kids said they used their key to get in."

"All righty then." I closed my pad and put it in my pocket. "Anything else I should know before I start?"

"Yeah. Got a hat?" The sergeant looked at me and smiled for the first time.

"A hat?" I had a puzzled expression.

The sergeant waved his hand as he walked away. "You'll see what I mean in about thirty seconds."

I interrupted George's conversation. "Ready when you are!"

I snapped a pair of latex gloves on my hands as we walked toward the deck storm door. "What happened to the nervous woman I drove to the scene?" George asked sarcastically.

All the people on the scene and the tasks that I had at hand seemed to have put my nervousness in check. Everything felt surreal.

I started to open the door but stopped myself. I turned to George. I wanted to tell him my game plan. "I'll take a look first. Then I'll go get the camera and everything else I'll need, okay?"

"Sounds great!" George was the best. The other detectives I had ridden with handled the scenes and let me watch. By contrast, George let *me* handle the scenes while *he* watched. This was the best way to learn, and like Pat, he genuinely wanted the civilians to learn the job.

I opened the storm door and slowly walked into the kitchen. The room was dark and smelled like grease. The horse-and-carriage motif wallpaper and the avocado green appliances begged for *Queer Eye for the Straight Guy*, but those guys would surely get beat up in this part of town. The counters and the linoleum were off-white with brown flecks and gold glitter. All the place needed was a disco ball and some Bee Gees music. I shined my flashlight around, not sure what I was looking for but knew I found it when I spotted the big jiggley chunk of something gross smeared across the cable bill on the middle of the kitchen table. I inched forward examining it under the beam of my light. George looked over my shoulder and whispered, "Ewww." It was a gooey blood clot. There was more blood and gross things stuck to the floor and walls and as I inspected them, I was startled by a loud *slap* that came from behind me. I spun around to see a bloody chunk of bone slithering down the pages of a wall-mounted girly calendar and let out a shriek as I ran for cover on the other side of the refrigerator. I wondered if the woman in the bikini waxing a red corvette ever knew that pieces of someone's head would be sliding down her toned, tanned stomach.

I cowered behind the refrigerator for a moment, making sure head parts weren't still flying around the room before I dared come out again. When I was sure it was safe, I peeked around and looked toward the living room. The scene was ghastly. "Oh my God." I stared in disbelief.

The living room was sparsely furnished and the metal shelving units stacked with cans of paint and lawn care products (obviously not recently used) gave the appearance that the room functioned more as a garage. Empty coffee cans, beer cans, milk jugs, and plastic food containers awaiting recycling were piled up against the sliding glass door and a rusty old bike hung from a hook in the corner. The only furniture in the room was an old and dusty entertainment stand, a stained brown easy chair, a curio cabinet filled with animals made out of seashells, a beat up coffee table, and a sofa. None of the lamps had shades and some were even missing bulbs. The place was filthy.

There was a headless person on the sofa. It was dressed like a man and it had big feet and a hairy chest. He was on his back and his left arm was on top of his abdomen while the right hung down off the side of the sofa. The stock of a rifle was in between his legs and the barrel lay across his chest with the muzzle near the pulverized mess that used to be his head. A canvas rifle bag was on the floor next to the sofa and a box of ammunition was on the coffee table nearby.

Bone, blood, brain, hair, and skin were spattered everywhere. It dripped down the walls and dangled from the ceiling like stalactites. The floor was an absolute disaster and dodging all the body parts when I went in there was going to take some skill. But that wasn't even the worst part. I was concerned by what was *above* the body. Directly over the dead guy was a ceiling fan, and it was whirring around at full speed. Every now and then, a piece of his blown-up head would break free from one of the fan blades and be flung into an unsuspecting target, like the poor woman in the bikini waxing the Corvette. I knew walking into the living room would be like walking through the woods during hunting season with a big red bull's-eye painted on my back. I scanned the walls for the switch to turn off the fan, but didn't see it. Out of the corner of my eye, I saw another meaty missile go flying by.

One of the officers poked his head in from the deck door. "The kid says the switch for the fan is on the floor behind the sofa." He was laughing. Even George was laughing. I looked at the mess on the sofa and wondered what was worse: hanging over a headless dead guy holding a loaded rifle so I could get to the switch for the fan or just putting on a hat and saying a prayer.

"Who the hell puts a switch on the floor behind furniture?" I thought about throwing the circuit breaker, but I didn't want to cut the power to the other lights—or at least those that had bulbs.

"Apparently, he put the fan in himself and for whatever reason he put the switch on the floor." The officer watched for a minute, but the sound of something else slap against the wall sent him retreating to the safety of the great outdoors.

I motioned for George to follow me to the deck. He spoke before I had a chance. "This is one of the worst ones I've seen. That's about as bad as you can get—especially with the fan spinning. Are you gonna be okay?"

The fear of getting impaled by a piece of some guy's skull made my initial fear of seeing a demolished head or having brains stick to my shoe seem silly. We walked to the van, where George pulled some paper booties out of his personal kit. "Here, these will keep some of that mess off your shoes." The booties were baby blue and looked like the kind that surgeons wear in the operating room. I grabbed my camera, a tape measure, a few evidence bags, and then looked for something to cover my head. I needed a raincoat with a hood.

"George, what should I wear over my head?" He rummaged through his bag looking for a cap, but couldn't find one. There was a fire helmet in the back of the truck, but it was way too big. Besides, its brim got in the way of the flash mounted on the top of the camera. I was elated to find a bright yellow hardhat wedged behind the seat. But I still wanted something to cover my neck and shoulders. I inspected the liner in the trash can, but it was dirty and sticky. George had a similar idea and dumped my lunch out on the passenger's seat and then handed me the blue Wal-Mart bag.

"Well," I was laughing. "I guess that will have to do." I also snatched up my newspaper and sunglasses before heading back to the scene. There was no way I was going to put my costume on in front of all the cops. I'd never hear the end of it. Once in the privacy of the kitchen and in the presence of only George and the lady in the bikini, I tore a hole in the center of the newspaper's Metro section and poked my head through. I adjusted the paper so that it covered my shoulders. Then I tied the Wal-Mart bag around my head, making sure to leave some of the bag hanging down over my neck. Next came the hardhat, booties, and sunglasses.

"So, do I look okay?" I pointed to the hat. "Is the yellow too much? It doesn't make me look washed out, does it?"

George loaded my camera with film and handed it to me. It was time to do it. "Want me to come with you?" His offer was kind, but he wasn't wearing any protective gear and I knew he expected me to say no.

"Nope, I've got it." Some of the cops had started to filter into the kitchen. I knew they either wanted to admire my outfit, or see if the scab could handle a scene this bad. I entered the living room slowly and cautiously, watching the fan for potential missiles. I could hear things dripping and falling. The sound was disgusting and the musty sweet smell of blood made my stomach turn. I chomped down on my gum. All my senses were overloaded. I *had* to keep it together because the cops *wanted* me to lose it.

Examining the scene through the viewfinder of my camera made the sights before me a little more tolerable. It made me feel a step removed from the reality of it all. Without pulling the camera away from my face, I started my photographs. I began in the corners of the room and circled around, gradually moving closer to the fan and closer to the man without a head. The nearer I got to the sofa, the bigger and more numerous were the chunks on the floor and I reached a point where I could no longer avoid stepping on them, no matter how hard I tried. I swore I'd never complain about having toilet paper stuck to my shoe again.

As I approached the sofa, the breeze from the ceiling fan rustled my newspaper bib and plastic scarf and I felt the splat of something land on my shoulder. I looked over long enough to see that it contained curly brown hair and had to look away and pretend it wasn't there. I never envisioned the day when I'd be dressed in a hardhat and a Wal-Mart bag, walking around a stranger's house with a hairy piece of a dead man's scalp teetering on my shoulder. I felt another thump on my hardhat and wondered what little gem was now perched on the top of my head.

I moved in closer to the body. The site was appalling. There was nothing left of the guy's face or the top of his head. What did remain was caved in and completely disfigured. It was clear that he had either put the muzzle of the rifle under his chin or in his mouth. I don't think you're supposed to harbor any ill feelings about the dead, but this guy was a jerk for pulverizing his head knowing that it would be his kids who found him. They would never be the same. I didn't even know him and I would never be the same. I took some close-up photographs of the weapon, the rifle bag, the ammunition, and the body. And then I cautiously moved around the sofa, knowing that the rifle was probably still loaded.

"Hey George." I inspected a small hole in the wall near the body. "I think I found a projectile hole." George peered around the corner. "Can you look outside to see if it went the whole way through?"

"Good eye!" He went outside to see if the projectile exited the house. I photographed the hole and prayed the projectile went entirely through because I didn't want to tear down the wall in search of it. Crime Lab policy required us to make a reasonable effort to collect all fired projectiles. George returned a few minutes later. "Yep. There's a big hole in the aluminum siding. I poked around in there and it's gone. God knows where it ended up."

Once finished with the photos, I handed George the camera. I called out a few quick measurements to him and with the fan still whirring above me, I slid the weapon out from beneath the rigor-laden arm of the headless dead guy. I unloaded it and handed the rifle and ammunition to George. Several of the cops as well as the sergeant watched intently from the kitchen. I felt like this was a test and I had passed. I was confident that I had proven that I knew what I was doing and that I could handle a gross scene as well as a loaded firearm—even if I was a lowly civilian and a scab to boot.

Just as the officer had told me, I found the switch for the ceiling fan haphazardly mounted on the floor behind the sofa. The whole contraption looked like a fire hazard. I kicked a chunk of hair and bone off the toggle and then turned it off with my boot.

Since this was clearly a suicide and the projectile had exited the body, the ME determined that an autopsy was not necessary. Shortly thereafter, two men dressed in dark suits arrived from the funeral home to recover the body. I thought it was odd that they were so formally dressed for such a dirty job. They donned their latex and started throwing the larger chunks of the guy's head in plastic bags. Then they slid the dead guy into a body bag, strapped him to a gurney, and draped it with a piece of purple velvet.

"Hey, come here!" Officers had garnered the nerve to enter the living room and were looking under the sofa. "Wanna see something you don't see every day?" I was suspicious, but curious. "Shine your flashlight under there and take a look."

I did as I was told and was horrified to see a big blue eyeball staring right back at me. As the guys from the funeral home bagged up the eye, I headed out of that little shop of horrors.

I don't like Cracker Jacks anymore.

After wading through a sea of head matter, I was silly enough to ask myself how much grosser things could get. I hadn't yet learned that by asking such questions I was doomed to discover the answers.

My field training ended the following week and I was overjoyed at the prospect of handling crime scenes all by myself. The decision to cut me loose came just in time. I had endured about as much as I could take of most of the detectives and after six months with the department I was ready to assume responsibility for my own scenes. That's not to say my training was finished—I still had a lot to learn and a few kinks to iron out.

The dispatcher had given me my first call of the shift and I eagerly started toward the scene of a hanging. I hadn't experienced one in training and I rehearsed my plan of action as I drove toward the neighborhood located behind the local raw sewage treatment plant. I wondered why people lived there. There were all sorts of equally dilapidated apartments that came without the smell. While the scent of Thanksgiving dinner cooking in the oven and pine needles on the Christmas tree reminded me of the home where I grew up, the people in this complex must have gotten warm and fuzzy memories of home each time they smelled a fart.

My thoughts were rudely interrupted by the shrill sound of three beeps on the radio. The dispatcher sounded these tones as a means of getting everyone's attention.

"Twenty-two fifteen. Dispatch calling Crime Lab unit twenty-two fifteen."

Shit! I fumbled for the radio. *Not again!* I had been lost in my own world and didn't hear her calling me. I hated when this happened. The detectives had assured me I would develop "radio ear" sometime soon, and before long I would soon be able to carry on a conversation with music blaring in the background and still hear the dispatcher call my number. I was beginning to doubt them. "Twenty-two fifteen. Sorry—my volume was down." I lied. "Go ahead."

"Twenty-two fifteen, I need you to ten-twenty-one fifty-five forty-five, ten-eighteen."

What the hell did that mean? I just looked at the radio hoping for an English translation. I was silent.

"Twenty-two fifteen, you direct?" The dispatcher sounded impatient.

"Twenty-two fifteen. Dispatch, you're breaking up. Can you ten-nine [repeat]?" I lied again. She wasn't breaking up, I just didn't know what she wanted me to do.

"Ten-twenty-one fifty-five forty-five, ten-eighteen." I could tell she was frustrated with me by the way she annunciated every syllable.

"Okay, ten-four." I pretended to know what I was supposed to do but I was clueless. I pulled the van to the shoulder of the road and grabbed my mystery decoder. I searched through the 10-codes trying to make a sentence out of the numbers that she just threw at me. After a minute I had deciphered the message. She wanted me (unit 2215) to 10-21 (call), extension 5545, 10-18 (immediately). *Whew!* I grabbed my cell phone and called the number, which happened to be the Crime Lab office.

George answered. "I heard you get that call. Have you had a dangler before?" He didn't say anything about my issues on the radio.

"Nope, this will be my first one."

"Well, gimme a holler if you want me to slide by and give you a hand."

He was kind to offer. "Thanks. I'm sure I'll be okay but I'll call if I get hung up on something!" I giggled at my own joke.

I arrived at the scene about ten minutes later. A bunch of police cars were lined up against the curb in front of the apartment building and I pulled in behind them. A haggard-looking woman scolded me with her cigarette and pointed to a NO PARKING sign. She seemed agitated that the police cars were violating the posted NO PARKING rules and her arms flailed wildly over her head as she screamed at me to move my van. I waved her off, which only pissed her off even more.

I jotted my arrival time in my notepad and looked up to see the woman walking toward an officer who was coming out of the building. I could hear her ranting through my closed window. I felt sorry for her in a weird sort of way. She had definitely circled the drain a few times and looked like she was in her fifties when I was sure she was only in her late thirties. She was thin as a rail, had dark circles under her eyes, and was missing most of her front teeth. Her hair didn't look like it had been combed in days and I doubted she could remember when she last bathed. She could not stand still. She paced, flailed, cursed, and complained. She was a junkie.

After dismissing her parking complaint, the officer walked toward my van. I recognized him from a call earlier in the week but I couldn't remember his name. I rolled down my window and was enveloped by sewer plant fumes. The woman was shouting and kicking the curb. "Mmmm! Is that you I smell or is it her?"

The officer sniffed his armpits. "Oh, that's me! Like it?"

"It's really nice." I leaned forward and sniffed him. "It's kinda spicy, but playful." I waved my hand in front of my face and rolled my eyes. "So, should we move our cars? The sign does say no parking." I looked over at the woman. "I don't wanna piss off any of the good, law-abiding, taxpaying citizens that pay my salary." I was pulling his leg. Every time the police or Crime Lab failed to do what citizens wanted them to do, we were reminded that they, the taxpayers, paid our salaries.

"Don't even get me started. I have been dealing with her all morning. It's gonna be a long day. I locked her up for prostitution before. Can you imagine doin' that?" He looked over toward the woman, and I looked at his name badge: R. H. Chittenden. "Picture driving down the street and seeing her and thinkin', *Oh yeah— I'm gonna get me some of that!*"

"So what am I here for? All I know is that it's a hanging." A crowd had gathered outside of the apartment building. I didn't understand why people felt it necessary to bring their kids to crime scenes. What do they say, something like, "Look, honey, see the nice man splattered on the road? That's what happens when you don't look both ways." It didn't make sense.

"Yeah. He's hanging all right and he's starting to stink." I didn't know how he could distinguish the stench of body rot from that of the sewer plant. The junkie was walking our way again. "The apartment is hot. He'd be ripe for the pickin' by the afternoon."

I got out of the van and walked around to the equipment compartment as Chittenden told the bimbo that we were not moving our vehicles any time soon. She was irate and wanted to talk to a supervisor. They disappeared behind my van while I gathered my supplies. Chittenden soon reappeared. I wondered what he had done with her. "So, what was I saying?"

"Tell me about the call." I slammed the van's door and double checked to make sure it was locked.

"Oh, the call. Here's what went down. The dead guy apparently had an argument with his girlfriend. He pretended he wanted to make good and invited her over for a cookout. The girlfriend also wanted to pick up her dog's leash that she had left in the apartment. Well, she showed up for some grilled wieners but there was no answer at the door, so she just walked in. There he was, hanging in the doorway with the leash tied around his neck."

"Get out!" I was appalled. "He set it up so she would find him?"

"Yep, this is one for the books." Chittenden saw I was overloaded with equipment. I looked like a pack mule. "Here, gimme something." He took my clipboard and camera case. "I'm not even telling you the best part—wait until you see it."

We walked by the junkie, who was now rolling around in the grass, and passed the crowd of thrill seekers and their kids as we headed into the apartment building. Our radios echoed in the hallway. It sounded eerie. I followed Chittenden down to the ground floor and was introduced to Officer Caret, who was stationed at the door. "This is Dana and she's one of the new civilian technicians." Caret recorded my name, identification number, and arrival time in his notebook before saying hello and telling me his first name. He also seemed friendly—even if I was a scab.

"Ready?" Chittenden had his hand on the door. I piled my equipment on the hallway steps.

"Yep." I waited for him to open it. "I'm ready!"

Chittenden hesitated. "Are you sure?"

I scratched my head and pretended to think. "Um, no—wait." I closed my eyes for a second, took a deep breath, and pretended to swallow hard. Then I cracked my neck and knuckles. "Okay—now I'm ready." I hoped the neighbors couldn't hear us.

"You're not gonna puke or faint or anything, right?"

"Open the damn door or I'm gonna give the junkie woman your phone number." That got him moving. Chittenden opened the door carefully so he wouldn't hit the body.

The dead guy was hanging all right. I couldn't imagine being the one to find him. He stunk, too. All this guy's ex wanted was a hot dog and the leash. She'd probably never go to a cookout again.

The dead guy was completely suspended from the ceiling by a

purple dog leash. He was dressed in a pair of jeans, white socks, and a wife beater tank top. The guy's face was a deep plum purple color and was swollen and disfigured from the pressure caused by the ligature. His tongue was distended and protruded and blood-tinged fluid emanated from his nose and mouth. It wasn't a pretty sight. The best part was the note duct-taped to the front of his shirt. It was short and to the point: FUCK YOU!

Chittenden was staring at me waiting for a reaction. "Well," I searched for words. "He doesn't beat around the bush, now does he?"

I walked in to get a closer look at the scene. "Too bad he's dead— I like a man who can just come out and say what he's thinking." I had to swing the guy to the side to get by. He was cool and in rigor. An overturned chair was on the floor next to the body and a foam-ceiling tile was lying on the kitchen counter. "So, you figure he stood on the chair to remove the tile, tied one end of the leash around the water pipe and the other end around his neck, then walked the plank?"

"Yeah, that's what it looks like." Chittenden and the other officer stood at the doorway not wanting to squeeze by the body.

"Did you walk through the scene?"

"Yeah, a few of us did when we got here. We didn't see anything out of the ordinary." I poked around for myself. I loved going through other people's stuff! Nothing appeared unusual to me either. I didn't want to move the dead guy again to get to my equipment so I asked Chittenden to slide it underneath the body.

I ducked down so I could see Chittenden. "Why don't you go ahead and call the ME. This won't take me long. Maybe the timing will work out so they arrive just as I'm finishing."

The radios didn't transmit clearly in the stairwell, so Chittenden left to go outside. As soon as he left, the apartment door began to creak closed and I was about to be left alone with the dead guy. I started to panic. I had never been alone with a dead person before, especially one hanging from a dog leash in a wife beater with a nasty note duct-taped to his chest. I didn't know what I was afraid of, but I certainly didn't want to find out.

"Hey, anyone out there?" There was silence. "Hello!"

"Yeah, need something?" Thank God Caret was still there. He pushed the door open and peeked inside.

"Hell, yeah! Don't let that door close! I don't want to be alone in here with this guy!" I sounded frazzled.

"My sarge told me to keep it closed so the neighbors don't get a look."

I pushed the body to the side so I could see Caret. "Then come in here with me!" Caret opted to prop it open.

Chittenden showed up a minute later and told me the ME had a forty-minute estimated time of arrival (ETA).

Caret didn't hesitate to tell Chittenden I got spooked when the door started to close.

"Soooooo, Dana." Chittenden was peeking around the body. "Just how new are you?" I didn't want to answer him. "How long have you been with us?" I was silent. "C'mon! Tell us!"

"I've been with the department for six whole months." I was working quickly so that I'd be finished by the time the ME arrived.

"How long have you been processing scenes all by yourself?" The tone in Chittenden's voice sounded suspicious. I didn't want either of them to know how new I was for fear they'd think I didn't know what I was doing. He asked again.

"Four days. I was cut loose four days ago."

"Are you serious?" Chittenden sounded surprised, which made me feel better. "Is this your first body flying solo?"

I didn't answer.

"It is, isn't it?" Chittenden and Caret high-fived each other. "Your first body done solo is with us. We're honored!"

"Is this your first hanging?" I poked my head around the body and just smiled and shrugged my shoulders.

"You haven't had one, have you?" They snickered for a minute and then retreated back into the hallway.

I continued about my business taking photos, recording notes, and making a rough sketch. Not long after, the forensic investigator arrived at the scene. I heard Caret and Chittenden talking to him before he entered the apartment. They were all laughing about something.

A few moments later they appeared in the doorway. The forensic investigator was an older heavyset guy with a Fu Manchu mustache. "So, this is your first hanging, eh?"

I shot Chittenden and Caret a look. "They seem to think so."

The forensic investigator snapped a few pictures and gathered some information before turning to me. "Why don't you glove up and hold onto him while I cut him down." He flipped over the chair that was lying next to the body and climbed on top as I wrapped my arms around the dead guy's waist. I didn't like it one bit and he really was beginning to stink, but I wanted to prove that I wasn't afraid or squeamish and could do this job.

He cut the leash and I went down faster than the *Titanic*.

Everything was dark and cold and smelly and I couldn't move. I felt something wet on my neck. *Oh my God, No! Please tell me I'm not pinned under the body!* I managed to get an arm free and reached up only to feel the wife beater. My worst fears were confirmed! I screamed and kicked. The dead guy was on top of me and was drooling down my neck! I heard the three pranksters somewhere nearby. "Get him off! Get this guy off me!"

I couldn't get the corpse to budge but managed to cock my head to the side and free it from the dead guy's furry armpit. "Get him off me now!" My voice resonated throughout the apartment stairwell and I was certain even the junkie in the grass could hear me. The neighbors had to be wondering what the hell was going on. In what seemed like an eternity but was probably only seconds, the forensic investigator, Chittenden, and Caret rolled the body off me and helped me to my feet.

I ran for the sink and started scrubbing with dish soap. I had a big wet spot on my shoulder from the dead guy's dripping mouth and I smelled sour, like an old sock. I was disgusted. That had to have been the grossest thing that could ever happen to me and the smell of my shirt made me dry heave. I scrubbed and scrubbed and heaved again.

They all stood nearby, watching, not quite sure what to say. Finally, Chittenden spoke. "We're sorry, Dana, really." I was silent. "We never thought you'd fall down. We just wanted you to get a good jolt, that's all." I didn't utter a word. "We never intended for you to get trapped under him."

When I was as clean as I could get, the three misfits scurried about, eagerly helping me gather my equipment. On the way back to the van, all I had to carry was my clipboard. It was their pitiful attempt to make amends. I didn't say a word.

I sat in my van packaging evidence, trying to decide just how angry I really was. I became infuriated when Caret drove away without offering a final apology, but he returned a few minutes later with Slurpees. He handed me a red one. "Here, on us."

"On us?" I pointed to the 7-11 logo on the cup. "Nice try. How 'bout on Seven-Eleven?" I sucked it down until I had a brain freeze. "Thanks."

I saw the same forensic investigator on a hanging the following week. I told him, "Mama didn't raise no fool," as I reached for my knife and cut through the rope. This time *he* held the body.

Although I might have learned a lot from Pat at the training academy, there are just some lessons that need to be learned the hard way, and my learning curve continued until the day that I quit the department. After these unpleasant experiences, my family wondered why I didn't just quit. I tried to explain that somebody has to empty Port-a-Pots, somebody has to taste-test dog food, and somebody has to investigate gross dead things. I had a job that 90 percent of the population probably found interesting but most likely couldn't handle. Even some of the CSIs couldn't deal with the things they saw and burned out after only a year or two. My dedicated cohorts and I were society's weirdos who actually enjoyed this line of work. We could find humor in life's darkest moments and were challenged by all the scenes we handled. We were scabs and we were proud!

CHAPTER 4

Try It, You'll
Like It . . .

My family asked lots of questions about my new job, at least at first they did. But their enthusiasm about my career path soon began to wane as I excitedly told them work stories—like all the things people shove up their asses.

"Then there was the guy who hammered three golf balls onto a straightened coat hanger," I demonstrated the hammering action as Mom dished out the mashed potatoes, "and then shoved the contraption in and out of his ass—over and over again!" I didn't demonstrate that part, but Mom still gave me *the look* from beneath her eyebrows.

"Then there was this other guy who ran an electrical current through a garden hose and shoved it up the back alley." I was really getting the look now. I had to rush to the end of the story before I was stopped, "but there was still some water in the hose and zzzaaappp!" I did a convulsing action and rolled my eyes back in my head. Only my brother Chris looked amused. I leaned over and whispered, "How'd you like Mom to find you with a big green snake hangin' outta your ass? Makes 'up your nose with a rubber hose' not seem quite so bad, eh?"

Needless to say, it didn't take long before the "Have you had any interesting cases at work?" question became taboo. My mother gave explicit instructions not to tell stories involving body fluids (especially those of the non-bloody variety), organs, asses, or sexual acts in the presence of company and non-immediate family members. The list soon grew to include immediate family.

Suffice it to say that trying to get my family to volunteer to do a ride along with me was like trying to get them to have a colonoscopy just for the hell of it. Anyone else would have begged for such an opportunity—but no, not my family.

"You tell me about people with body lice, houses infested with roaches, bloated bodies popping when you touch them, you imitate the sounds of maggots chomping on flesh, and want me to sniff you to see if you still smell like a decomp, and *then* you ask if I want to go to work with you?" Bob had a point. He stared at me for a long time and then shook his head in a way that signaled disbelief. "You have some wires disconnected somewhere upstairs." He stomped out of the room, mumbling something about me being crazy and needing to have my head examined. It seemed like my dogs were the only ones that appreciated what I did for a living—after all, I brought home all sorts of scents for them to contemplate.

Dad's excuse for not riding was that he had "been there, done that" in his years as a cop and later as a fireman. Then there was my brother, Chris; poor Chris. I didn't even bother asking him. Any guy who played with *Star Wars* action figures through his mid-teens and took computers apart just for fun had no business on a crime scene. Mom's chances of signing up for a ride along were about as great as her chances of having Ed McMahon and the Publishers Clearing House Prize Patrol show up at the front door. Bob didn't think that I should have even asked her.

"She already hates you working there because of the shift, the overtime, the fact you work holidays, the biohazards, the bad areas you go into," Bob tapped his finger on the table as he went down the list, "and then you ask if she wants to go to work with you?" He was giving me the what-do-you-have-to-say-for-yourself look again. I hated it. When I didn't respond, he continued his tirade. "And if she does go—she's gonna see all the other horrible stuff you do and its just gonna fuel her fire—and I'll be the one that has to hear about it every time she calls! And God forbid you get a body call, she can't even look at a paper cut!" My mind rewound to the time I was eight and I cut my hand on a piece of weather stripping. Dad heard a thud and came into the kitchen to find me gushing blood on the new wallpaper and Mom passed out on the floor. Maybe it really was best that she stay put.

I dragged myself into work and sulked as my co-workers' spouses, parents, and friends suited up for the local rendition of the *Fantastic Voyage*. My best friend April's mom rode all the time. I was envious. But April's mom was from New Jersey and everybody knew that purebred Jersey moms were tougher than Maryland moms. You didn't mess with Jersey moms.

After resigning myself to the fact that my passenger's seat would be forever empty, I went home one day to find an envelope mailed to me from Mom. I opened it and nearly fell down when I found her completed ride-along request form. I was ecstatic—she was actually going to do it! I dismissed all of Bob's warnings and immediately started to plan the day. I'd start by giving her a tour of the Lab. I had to take her to the Firearms Identification Unit so she could see the rubber ducky floating in the bullet recovery tank, then I'd show her some fingerprinting techniques. Luminol, a chemical that glows a bright blue color in the presence of blood, was always a hit with ride alongs, and then I'd let her see what semen looks like under the alternate light source. If there was time between calls, we'd slide by the Salsa Grill for some cheap paella. They only charged police (and scabs) half-price.

I was careful to pick the date for Mom's ride. For anyone who wanted to see a body, Suicide Sunday was the day to buckle up. I had handled suicides on Sundays for six consecutive weeks and figured that people came home from church after learning that they were doomed to the fires of hell and were beyond saving. Their answer: a rope, a revolver, a handful of pills, and, on occasion, the Amtrak Metroliner. Since Mom wasn't too keen on the dead, I decided she was better suited for Burglary Monday. Mondays tended to be busy because employees returned to work to find their places of employment had been broken into over the weekend.

I submitted her ride-along slip and after my sergeant verified that she had no open warrants, she was cleared for the following Monday. The hour before the ride along was to begin, I got the anticipated phone call. "Dane," I could tell by the tone in her voice that she wasn't coming. "I just can't keep off the toilet. I got a case of the brown water." That meant she had diarrhea. She always had diarrhea. Rain, traffic, gasoline prices, and burned toast made brown water leak from the spigot. My brother and I knew that if we had news that was even in the least bit distressing, we had to make sure she was at home, near the bathroom, and had plenty of toilet paper, paper towels, or even old T-shirts within reach. I rescheduled her for the following Monday. That afternoon she had brown water and a headache. The next Monday her eyes itched because she had some wine the night before. The Monday after that she had a heel spur. After the fourth cancellation, my sergeant put her ride-along request form in my mailbox with a note that read, "If she ever shows up, give the form back to me."

Bob must have pitied me because the day after Mom's report of an aching heel, I found *his* completed ride-along request form curled up inside my coffee cup on the kitchen counter—a place where he knew I'd see it. Bob hated blood and guts as much as Mom and I immediately knew she talked him into going in her place. My suspicions were confirmed when I saw that he had requested to ride on a Monday. I prayed we wouldn't have anything gross and hoped we wouldn't have to go to the morgue. I once recommended that a friend of mine, an attorney, visit the OCME. He did and passed out. I told him he was lucky that the pathologists didn't think he was a corpse that fell off the gurney and scrape him up, saw open his head, peel down his face, and put his innards in a Hefty Cinch Sak.

My sergeant rolled his eyes as he scribbled his signature on the approval line. "I'll believe it when I see it." A few days later, Bob walked into the Lab with me on what would be the most memorable day of my entire career. Memorable, that is, for the calls that lurked in the shadows of that warm September day.

As we walked through the Lab and over to my desk, I could hear the detectives joking among themselves. They were all hovering around the sergeant's desk, watching as he scribbled something down on an adhesive notepad. A few of them had met Bob previously, and they were quick to wave a hand at him and shout "hello" from across the room. God forbid they say hi to me—but then again, Bob didn't steal their jobs.

Barber, the defective who left me in the van as he ate tuna and watched the Oklahoma City bombing, couldn't wait to tell me I had a call holding. I was glad because I wanted to take Bob on as many crime scenes as possible. He nodded toward the sergeant. "He's got the info." Barber snickered, "So, Bob, ya ready?" His tone told me he was up to something.

"I guess. Depends on what it is." The reservation in Bob's voice was apparent, but Barber didn't hear it. He was nearly deaf. He claimed it was from years of having the overhead siren blasting in his ears. I attributed it to his brain rotting from the inside out.

The sergeant walked over to my desk and handed me a sticky note with what I assumed was the call information. "I'll approve overtime if you want to head out now." My shift didn't start for another thirty-five minutes.

I looked at the call as two of the detectives waltzed out the door without even acknowledging the fact that I had relieved them early. I decided I was going to take their lead and start arriving at work at 2:59 P.M. for a shift that started at 3:00 P.M.—the hell with them! This place was making my screws loose.

I saw that the call was on the east side of the county. Only Detective Joe Rayburn and I were scheduled in. When there were three of us working the shift, we divided the county in thirds: west, central, and east. When two were in, we divided it in half. Those with the most seniority got first pick where they wanted to work and I knew Joe liked east.

I didn't read any further. "Sarge, this won't be my call." I stuck the sticky note on the desk next to mine. "Joe is in today and he always wants to go east." Joe was supposed to be one of the better investigators in the Lab and it was reported he was so good at fingerprinting that he could get latents off rocks. But I wouldn't know—Joe wouldn't talk to me and he certainly wasn't going to help me learn the job. It was unfortunate because next to Pat and George, I knew that he had a lot to offer.

The sergeant peeled up the sticky note and handed it back to me. "Well, just so happens Joe is already here—he came in straight from court and knows about the call. He said to give it to you. He wants west today."

I was furious. Joe never, ever, ever wanted to work west side—never! The little things like this were starting to drive me over the edge. In other words, Joe came in, saw there was a call holding, and decided to work the opposite part of the county because he didn't feel like handling it. While several of the detectives had started to warm up to the civilians, it seemed like others still went out of their way to keep us from settling into a routine, just because they could. It was a stupid childish mind game that effectively pissed me off.

I shook my head. "Fine!" I tried to sound indifferent. Bob was seeing firsthand what I had to deal with every day and why I always seemed to come home from my dream job (that was turning out to be anything but dreamy) an angry, stressed-out wreck. "Well, its gonna have to wait." Now I was the one being childish—I refused the overtime he offered simply because I could.

Before the sergeant walked back to his desk, he patted Bob on the shoulder. "You'll be fine." I saw him make eyes with Barber and both got smirks on their faces.

"What is up with you guys?" Barber didn't answer. I shuffled through the mail that had accumulated on my desk.

Bob picked up the sticky note and read over the call information. Barber watched him. "So, whatcha got waiting?" I glared at Barber, who knew damn well what type of call was dumped on me.

Bob tried to make out the chicken scratch. "Um, where's it say?" He squinted as he tried to decipher the information. "Looks like it says . . . 'suspicious death'?" Bob looked at me with a face as pale as a corpse.

I snatched the sticky note from his hands while never taking my eyes off Barber. "You didn't . . . tell me you didn't!"

Barber looked down at his desk, chuckling, and the sergeant pretended to be busy and unaware of the events transpiring across the room. He was a bad actor. "You didn't!" I looked at the note and I read through the call information. "Well, obviously there is no rush to get out there." I said it loud enough for all to hear. "Crime Lab was requested for this over an hour ago!"

I grabbed my clipboard and radio and turned to Bob. "C'mon, let's get outta here." I motioned for Bob to follow me and walked to the door without uttering a word.

"Hey, Kollmann," one of them shouted just as I was about to leave. "Forgot to tell you, it's a decomp. A pretty bad one!" I let the door slam behind me as I heard one of them telling Bob to have fun.

As we waited for the elevator, I tried to explain what had just happened. "They knew you didn't want to see a body, so when one came in they let it hold over an hour for our shift, then Joe took west so we'd be forced to handle it." Bob just stared at me. "To make matters worse—it's a decomp." It sounded so catty, but it made me furious.

The silence was interrupted by the ding as the elevator arrived. Although I needed to go the basement where the Crime Lab vans were parked, I hit the button for the lobby. When the elevator stopped, we got out, and I handed Bob my car keys. "Just go home. I know you don't want to go to this call and I don't want to have to deal with you having flashbacks for the next ten years." I could tell Bob was in a quandary. "Really—just go. My feelings won't be hurt." I had waited for this day for months and the defectives had gone out of their way to ruin it for me.

Bob slipped the keys into my pocket. "I'll just wait in the van while you process the scene. I won't come inside, but I'll go with you. Maybe you'll have something better later on."

He got back in the elevator and pushed the down button.

We made our way to the garage where I proceeded to load up my van. The vans were already stocked with county-issued equipment, but we all had our own stuff we liked to take along, too. I had my personal print kit and an evidence bag stocked with boxes, bags, film, and additional batteries. I also carried along an extra bag of clothing, my flashlight, and a biohazard kit that contained alcohol, splash shields, a CPR mask, my respirator, and after the ceiling fan scene, Tyvek suits, a hat, and booties.

We were supposed to do a vehicle inspection and an equipment check before we took a van on the road. I always inspected the van for damage—otherwise it could come back on me. I had caused enough damage on my own and didn't want to take credit for someone else's dents. I usually glossed over the equipment check. Most of us did. There was just no way I was going to inspect forty-plus pieces of equipment when there were calls holding. I checked the camera, made sure I had a metal detector and some gunshot residue kits, and that was that.

The garage was where we parked the Crime Lab vans and where we stored seized vehicles pending processing and/or execution of search warrants. Bob knew better than to touch any of these cars, and as I did my modified vehicle and equipment inspection, he wandered around the garage with his hands in his pockets, peering inside the windows. He was looking at a black Acura. I said to him, "Look at the evidence tag and see what offense is listed. That might be from my suspicious death last night."

No sooner did I speak than the phone in the garage started to ring. I could tell by the ring tone that it was someone calling from inside the building. I contemplated not answering it. When I finally picked it up, I heard Joe's voice on the other end. He cut right to the chase. "Homicide is on their way down to look at the Acura. I told them you'd wait for them. They just want to look inside before we process it."

Since everybody asks about Luminol, I'll start by showing these training photographs. This piece of carpet contains faint footwear impressions made with diluted blood. In the "before" photograph, you can see a few suspicious-looking areas, but you'd never guess that the carpet contains at least five shoe impressions. In the "after" photo, Luminol has been applied and the shoe prints are clearly visible.

It ain't parsley! The purple color indicates a positive Duquenois-Levine presumptive test for marijuana.

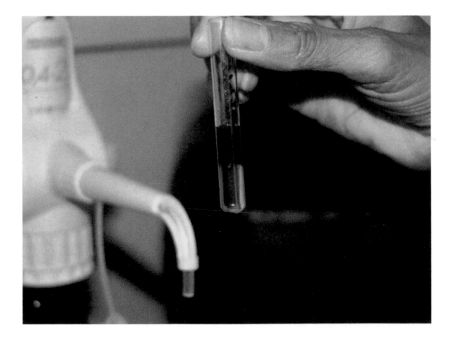

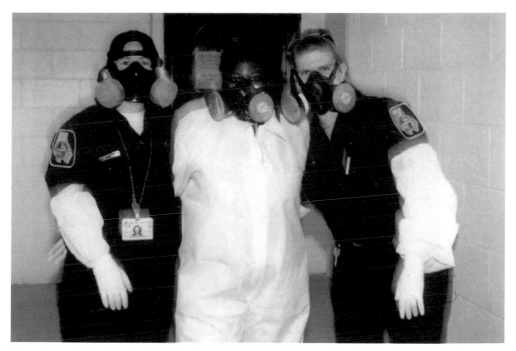

An ominous sight. CSIs April Haddock, Denise Wallace, and Cathy Schene about to engage in some sort of gross act. (*April Haddock*)

A CSI processes the point of entry at a burglary scene, using standard black carbon powder. From the position of the fingerprints, it appears that the suspect grabbed on to the interior of the window frame as he climbed through. The unusual orientation of the fingerprints suggest that they do not belong to the homeowner . . . unless, of course, he is in the habit of climbing through the second-story bedroom window.

CSI Tiffany Ware working hard to package and process evidence before she gets another call.

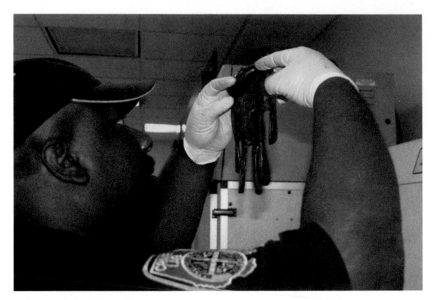

And to think that some people actually retire from their jobs without ever getting to knock down drywall in the search for bullets, collect maggots for time of death determination, or request that the Medical Examiner swab someone's rectum. Here, CSI Keith Johnson finds a sticky old latex glove of great interest. The glove is black because it has been processed it for latent fingerprints.

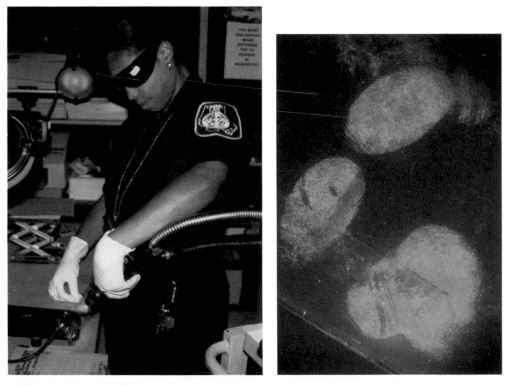

CSI Tiffany Ware using an alternate light source to examine a plastic bag for latent fingerprints. The bag was first processed using cyanoacrylate, commonly know as "superglue," and subsequently dye-stained with a chemical called MBD, which is short for 7-(P-Methoxybenzlamino-4Notrobenz-2-Oxa-1,3-Diazile).

At what other job do you get to say, "*Hey, check out this Mac 10 with an external silencer?*" Silencers, also called suppressors, work by diffusing expanding gases that accompany the detonation of ammunition. Don't try to buy one, though—you'll find yourself wearing a cute little orange jumpsuit and a matching pair of silver bracelets.

Annie, the Crime Lab mannequin that was supposed to be used for training purposes, finds herself in yet another unfortunate situation involving one of the Crime Lab vehicles, as Det. Jack Lingner looks on with concern. (*April Haddock*)

Officers keeping a straight face as they very seriously explain how they believe these "suspected human remains" are related to an explosion. Oddly enough, they are pointing to a dog's toy bones that are still wrapped in plastic with orange price tag stickers. These jokesters borrowed a few props from a nearby pet store and set up a little scene of their own just to see how I would react!

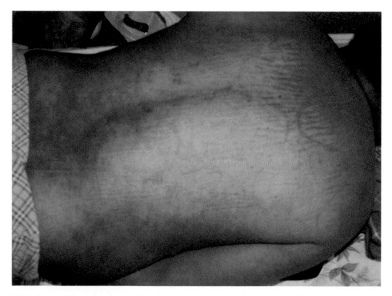

This is exactly why you should always put sheets on your bed. After a long night of drinking, this guy decided he'd forgo the bed linens and now look at him. . . . He's going to be known in heaven as *you know—the guy with the mattress pattern on his back.*"

This homeowner needed to spend a little less time staging crime scenes and a little more time watching CSI. This is supposed to be the point of entry in a robbery; however, all of the damage is to the door-frame—there is no damage to the door itself. It is clear that this guy held the door open as he hacked away at the frame. It didn't help matters that the exterior storm door was still closed and locked!

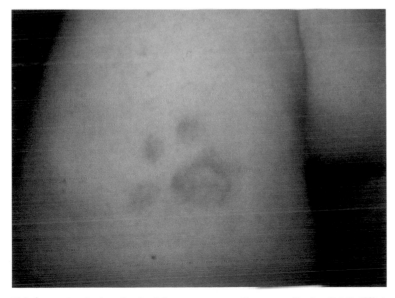

This has to be the best bruise I have ever seen. Can you tell what it is? (*Hint: "Down, boy! Down!"*)

The joys of having a CSI as a mom! We don't bake cookies; we use the UV light to see where the puppy peed! And the puppy is guilty as charged—he *has* been wetting his bed!

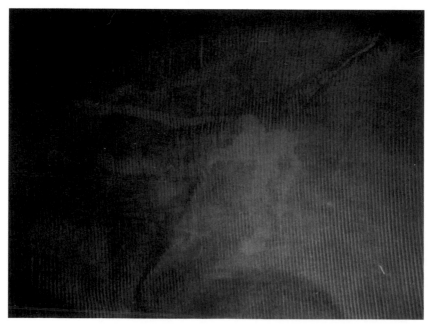

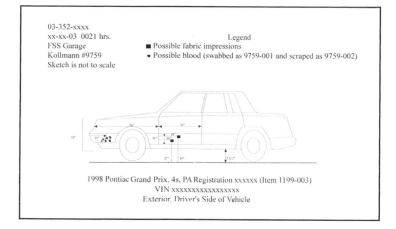

03-352-xxxx
xx-xx-03 0021 hrs.
FSS Garage
Kollmann #9759
Sketch is not to scale

Legend
■ Possible fabric impressions
● Possible blood (swabbed as 9759-001 and scraped as 9759-002)

1998 Pontiac Grand Prix, 4s, PA Registration xxxxxx (Item 1199-003)
VIN xxxxxxxxxxxxxxxx
Exterior, Driver's Side of Vehicle

The CSI rule is: "You don't touch it until you photograph and sketch it." On an involved crime scene, that rule alone makes for a lot of work. This is a rather simple sketch of suspected blood and probable fabric impressions in the dirt residue on the exterior driver's side door of a Pontiac Grand Prix. It is believed that the fabric impressions were left by the suspect's corduroy jacket as he struggled with one of his victim on the ground. This crime occurred in a parking lot. Similar fabric and shoe impressions were identified on the passenger's side of the vehicle parked in the adjacent space.

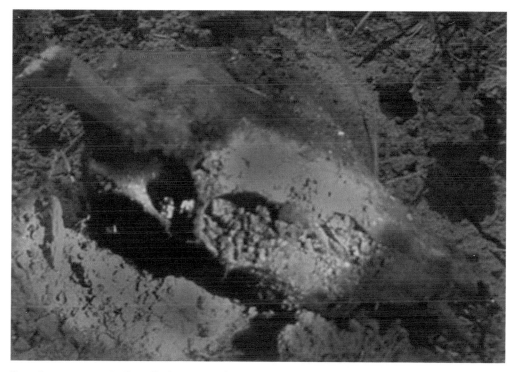

One of many, many similar calls that required countless hours of photography, mapping, measurements, and evidence collection. The smell of something decomposing and evidence of recent ground disturbance led investigators to believe that someone or something was dead and buried in this remote location. Excavation revealed it was just Bambi.

Latent fingerprints on a black trash bag processed with cyano- acrylate (superglue). Rumor has it that if you look into the super- glue tank while your evidence is "cooking," the fumes will for- ever glue your contact lenses to your eyeballs.

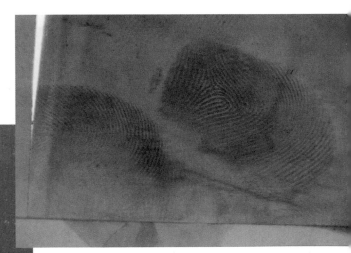

Tape is a potentially valuable piece of evidence because (1) bad guys will often remove their gloves while binding someone, (2) they may bite the tape to tear it and leave their DNA behind, (3) tape will likely collect trace evi- dence from the perpetrators, and (4) the torn edge left on the roll can be matched with the torn piece recovered from the crime scene. The photographs show latent prints developed on the sticky side of duct tape using a process involving so-called "sticky side powder," and prints on the adhesive side of box tape using gentian violet.

Deep in the woods, an encounter with yucca plants is unexpected. But yuccas often served as living memorials in historic-period African American cemeteries, and a closer inspection of these suspicious plantings revealed two headstones.

After traveling all the way to Guatemala City to work on a Mayan skeletal collection, the last things we thought we would find ourselves surrounded by were Idaho potato boxes. They apparently work well for the temporary storage of artifacts.

After knocking down the barricade, my dogs delight in the rare opportunity to smell my collection of roadkill buried in the hedges beneath the pin flags. Once the remains are skeletonized, I'll add them to my comparative fauna collection. Each pin flag is marked with the type of animal and the date of burial. Skeletonization usually occurs in 4–6 months, depending on the season and the size of the animal.

Probing bodies takes on a whole new meaning. This metal rod is pressed into the soil as the investigator checks for differences in soil density, which indicate areas of previous disturbance.

The archaeological discovery of the century! Bob finds that the tripod screen also functions as a makeshift swing when you find yourself in the middle of a cornfield with a toddler who isn't very interested in excavating prehistoric refuse pits. (*Ed Hanna*)

Characteristic soil stain indicative of a prehistoric human burial. In this photograph, the dark-colored topsoil has been removed, exposing the orange-colored subsoil. The dark circular area in the middle was caused when this grave was backfilled and the darker soil on top was introduced to the level of the subsoil. (*Robert D. Wall*)

The nearly complete skeleton of a young adult male, age 24–27 years, recovered from an archaeological site that dates from 1025–1250 A.D. The flexed position of this individual is a common finding in prehistoric Native American burials. He was buried with a variety of shell and bone beads, bone and tooth pendants, and several tools associated with hunting and hide working. (*Robert D. Wall*)

CSIs April Haddock, Laura Ellsworth, and Caitlyn Mingola gaining excavation experience on a prehistoric archaeological site. The data recovery techniques are the same as those used on forensic excavations, but the archaeological ones tend not to smell as bad.

Sometimes Mother Nature does a better job at preserving human remains than the best embalmer does. This is one of several Basketmaker mummies recovered from an archaeological site in Utah.

Human remains (a tibia and fibula in a boot) exhumed from a mass grave in the former Yugoslavia.

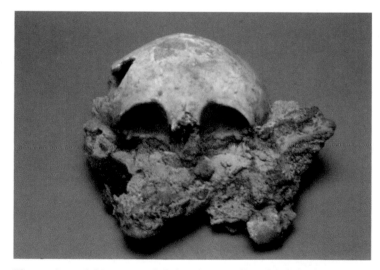

The cranium of this young adult female, as well as the skeletal remains of thirty-five other individuals, was excavated from a limestone cave in Karlovac, Croatia. The high calcium carbonate content in the dripping water caused them to become imbedded in a rock matrix on the floor of the cave, making their removal difficult.

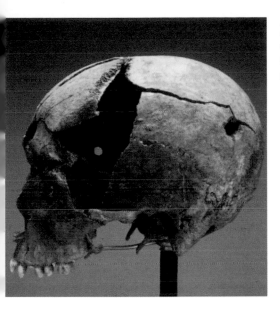

A skull showing an entrance gunshot wound in the right temporal and an exit wound in the posterior left parietal. Note the characteristic external beveling that surrounds the exit wound.

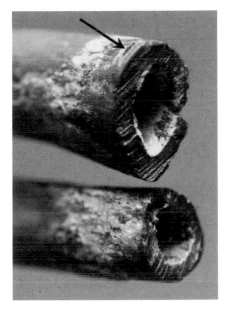

Distal radius and ulna of a 1990s Balkan War victim whose hand had been surgically amputated just prior to his death. Tool mark impressions on the distal margin of the amputation are still visible. The white discoloration is adipocere. Notice the "false start," where the saw blade was pressed into the bone and then pulled back out!

It crumbles like feta cheese, it feels slippery like Ivory soap, and it smells like something that has been hiding in the back of the fridge for far too long. What is it? Adipocere! This guy had been buried in a wet, anaerobic environment for about two years. His head is at the left side of the image, his belt is visible near the center, and his boots are on the right side. The nice thing about adipocere is that it does a fairly good job of preserving internal structures and enables the completion of a limited autopsy.

Probably not the outfit my mother envisioned me wearing to work. Probably not the job she envisioned me doing, either. At this site, construction crews encountered a number of unmarked graves that turned out to be part of a historic cemetery associated with a nearby almshouse. We were charged with the task of going through the construction site to attempt to locate and excavate additional graves. (*Robert D. Wall*)

A victim of the 1990s Balkan War showing a projectile still imbedded in the distal end of the humerus. The white matter adhering to the bone is adipocere.

You can see the devastating, fatal injury to the right femur caused when this individual stepped on a landmine in the former Yugoslavia.

"Joe," my voice echoed in the garage. "I have a body waiting—you know—the one you all dumped on me. Think you could be bothered to come down here with Homicide while *I* go handle a call?"

Joe's tone was indifferent. "The body ain't goin' nowhere." I was silent. "And the car is from *your* call and Homicide wants to talk to *you* about processing."

He was lying. Homicide didn't give a rat's ass who processed the vehicle—as long as it got processed. Sure, I liked to follow my cases through and work on any evidence related to scenes I handled, but that normally didn't happen. By the time a case went to court, as many as ten CSIs could have been involved in different facets of the investigation. After a murder, there was a morgue run, search warrants, evidence processing, reports, sketches, photographing suspects, processing vehicles, aerial photographs, digital enhancements, and so on. Then there was the work done by the examination units such as firearms, chemistry, serology, latents, documents, and computer crimes. Sometimes, when cases went to court, nearly the entire Lab was summonsed.

"Fine, but if they take longer than five minutes, I'm calling you down here." I slammed the phone back on the receiver. If I did call him for help, I knew he wouldn't pick up.

Since the Acura was in the charge of the Crime Lab, a crime scene person had to be present to transfer chain of custody to the Homicide detectives. From the time evidence is collected from a crime scene to the time it is presented in court, investigators must maintain a continuous record of every individual having contact with it. If one of the links in the chain is broken, then defense attorneys could potentially discredit the authenticity of the evidence and present a convincing argument regarding the possibility for outside contamination. As part of the required chain of custody documentation, the person receiving a piece of evidence must sign and date an evidence tag. In most instances, he or she also prepares a written report that provides a detailed description of why he or she accessed the evidence as well as anything he or she did to it, such as process it for latent fingerprints or swab it for possible DNA. Imagine the problems that would arise if we stored evidence recovered from a homicide scene under our beds or in our neighbor's car until it was time to go to court.

I recall one case where a victim and suspect pulled into a parking lot of an apartment complex and an argument ensued. The victim, who was driving the car, was stabbed in the abdomen. He provided police with the name of the suspect. The suspect, however, claimed to not even know the victim (go figure). The officer handling the call requested that Crime Lab respond to the scene and process the interior of the vehicle in the hopes of getting the suspect's prints and calling his bluff. The problem was that the officer decided he had more pressing issues to attend to and refused to wait for me. In doing so, he left the vehicle unlocked and unattended for well over an hour. I eventually responded, processed the vehicle, and got victim's and suspect's prints from inside the car, *but* the first line in my report stated that "at the time of my arrival, the vehicle had no chain of custody. No officer or any other police department personnel were present on the scene." This single statement became a major issue when the case went to court and I cannot help but wonder if this was the reason the jury failed to convict. While I didn't want to see bad guys walk free, it was part of my job to report things as I saw them—even if it was detrimental to a case. The police department might have paid my salary, but it didn't mean that I was biased or partial to its side of the story. I couldn't be—that is what integrity is all about.

Three Homicide detectives knocked at the garage door a few minutes later. I took the search warrant from them and filed it with the other information on the car while they gloved up. Bob was somewhat familiar with this call—after all, it was the reason I was six hours late coming home from work the night before. The abridged version of the story was that someone called 911 and said they noticed a bad smell while they were driving down an isolated road. They went on to say the police should check it out because there could be a dead body in the area—then they hung up. The police responded and found a dead woman in a ditch. It was clearly a dump job, meaning the woman didn't die there but her already lifeless body was pushed from a car. We knew that because she had roadside gravel in the folds of her clothing and we found a torn piece of fabric from her skirt on the shoulder of the road above her. She had sustained injuries from tumbling down the hill, mainly cuts and abrasions, but none of them were bleeding—because injuries inflicted postmortem do not bleed. The 911 caller must have had a case of the "guilties." The caller obviously knew about the body ahead of time because it was too far down the hill for a driver to have seen it. Besides, she was fresh and didn't stink . . . but even if she did stink, the average person would probably assume he or she was smelling a dead animal and not a dead person. Sometime after I had left work, the detectives seized the Acura.

I loaded up my camera knowing I'd need to take pictures of the exterior, and particularly the interior of the vehicle before Homicide started their search. No one had opened the car since it had been recovered and it was important to document its condition while it was still exactly as the suspect had left it. "We'll just take a minute." I watched the detective as he pushed his tie through the gap between his shirt buttons. The other one was coaxing his tie into his shirt pocket. "We just want to look in the glove compartment and see if that stuff in the backseat is vomit."

Vomit???? I hated vomit!

I snapped a few photos of the outside of the car and then carefully opened the front passenger's side door and took a few more. It took only a second for the sour smell of hot summer puke to turn my stomach. I could taste the smell. The Homicide detectives knew better than to step into my field of view while I was busy with the camera. I clenched my teeth and proceeded to photograph the car's interior, opening one door at a time. What was it about the smell of vomit that was so nauseating? I had smelled far worse things—I think it was the familiar association. It was the same reason that I found the scent of blood so appalling—I could relate to it.

The sour odor must have reached the detectives a minute later because one of them let out a loud "Phhheeewwww!" I looked over my shoulder to see them waving their notepads in front of their faces. Bob had disappeared from sight. Once I was finished with general interior shots of the car, I focused on specifics; like the vomit stain, the contents of the ashtray, a purse, some clothing, a pack of cigarettes, and a couple of fast-food wrappers. The disgusting condition in which people kept their cars and houses amazed me. You really can't judge a book by its cover because the cleanest looking people were usually the biggest offenders. I ended by popping the trunk and taking a few more pictures. Ever since another Crime Lab investigator found a living suspect hiding in the trunk, opening it was like being on a game show and looking to see what was behind door number one—I never imagined it could be so suspenseful. I don't know what I would have done if I found myself alone in the garage with a bad guy—at least the other investigator was sworn and had a weapon. Looking in the trunk was a must and if we didn't have keys to the vehicle, we used a crowbar.

Homicide began their search while I took a few notes for the report I would have to write later on. I found Bob on the far side of the garage perusing the names of the investigators on the lockers. He was hiding from the smell. He even wretched when the dogs vomited and I knew that the smell of the dead woman's rancid stomach contents did not go over too well with him. But then again, this was the real-life version of what we watched on *Law and Order*, and I thought his interest in seeing Homicide execute a search warrant would be stronger than his aversion to the smell of old, hot vomit. The look on his face told me otherwise.

When it looked like Homicide was nearing the end of their search, I asked how the car was connected to the scene. Bob stepped up barely close enough to hear. "Well," the detective snapped off his latex gloves and shot them into a nearby trash can like rubber bands. Then he pulled his tie out of his pocket and inspected it to make sure it hadn't dragged through anything objectionable. "The ME found vomit in the victim's nose and mouth. Turns out she was partying with her friends earlier last night. This is a guy-friend's." He pointed his thumb over his shoulder toward the

Acura. "Buddy boy claims he left her at a party around twenty hundred hours . . . says she was fine. But we have witnesses who say that the two left the party together, and now we got yak in the back of the buddy's car. So . . . it looks like we need to have another chat with him and at some point try to determine if that's her yak."

"So," I curled my lip. "Looks like I'll be collecting some vomit, eh?"

"Yeah, that and the purse. We'll also need the car processed for latents."

I told the detectives that I'd probably have to cut the upholstery to get an adequate vomit sample. They just shrugged—after all, it wasn't their car.

Bob was quiet during the ride to the death scene and I felt guilty about bringing him along. I had wanted my family to ride so badly that I selfishly overlooked the fact that they were truly and literally sickened by my job. They were happy that I was happy— and they just wanted to leave it at that.

We pulled into the driveway. It was a single-family home close to the water and the boats, engine parts, and pickup truck with mud flaps containing the silhouettes of nude women told me that the owner of this house was all man. It seemed odd to see squirrels playfully running across the front lawn and hear the squeals of the neighborhood kids splashing around in their inflatable pools . . . and then look toward the house and think that there was a rotten dead person inside. Everything outside seemed so alive and normal.

We could smell death before we ever saw it. Bob was still recovering from the vomit and covered his face with his hand as he caught a whiff. "Oh man!" His hand muffled his voice. "That can't be the body, *can it*?" I hoped he'd be okay. "Oh my God!" He looked over at me. "It can't stink this far away from the house, can it? What the hell *is* it?"

I had to laugh because the smell was really foul. This person was dead and then some. I hadn't even been on the job for a year and was certain that the nerve endings in my nostrils were in the process of burning out from overuse—and I looked forward to it! I never got to smell nice scents, like magnolias in the springtime breeze or warm apple pie cooling on the windowsill—no, my job blessed me with 101 body aromas. If it came from a person's breath, armpits, stomach, crotch, ass, or feet—I'd be there to sniff it, and I have to keep a straight face while doing so.

Even if I hadn't known ahead of time that this was a decomp, I would have known before I smelled the smell. As George had first pointed out, all the officers were standing outside and the fire department was on the scene. Since there was no fire, and no need for floodlights, the fire department guys were most likely there setting up fans to help dissipate the stench. While I appreciated efforts such as these (and I did), having firefighters with big clunky boots traipse through what could be a crime scene and turn on lights and unlock and open doors and windows before I got there undermined the notion of crime scene preservation. I hoped the investigating officer had documented everything before the fire department changed it all. I also hoped I'd win the Powerball. It seemed that the patrol officers and their supervisors often determined if a scene was "really" suspicious from the get go, and before consulting Crime Lab or the ME, *they* would frequently make important and irreversible decisions.

On one occasion, I had had enough of the officers disturbing scenes before Crime Lab arrived, and I became enraged when I arrived at a death and found the apartment completely turned over by the police, the victim pulled from the closet where he died, his body rolled over, and the ME searching his pockets. The officer told me, "We just need you to snap a few pictures." I walked out, refusing to do anything. I drove directly to the precinct and vented to the shift supervisor. I told him that in *no* uncertain terms was it sufficient for me to merely "snap a few pictures," regardless of what his officer wanted. My job duties weren't dictated by patrol; they were sufficiently described in the Crime Lab's monstrosity of a manual, entitled "Forensic Services—Standard Operating

Procedures." According to this book, there were certain things that I was absolutely *required* to do if dispatched to a death. In retrospect, I probably should have let my supervisor handle the situation—but I do have to say that I never had another problem in that particular precinct again.

Bob and I sat in the van for a minute. "You coming?"

He looked at me like I was nuts. His hands were pressed tightly against his nose and mouth and he sounded like Darth Vader when he spoke. "Are you kidding!?!"

One of the officers made his way over to my van. I rolled down the window and invited more of the stench inside. Bob pulled his shirt up over his face and pressed his chin into his chest before covering his face again with both hands.

The officer's nametag said R. G. Royce. "You ready for this one?" He was laughing. "It's *baaaad*. It's as bad as it gets."

I slowly shook my head. My teeth were clenched—the smell was profane.

The Vicks under Royce's nose glistened in the sun as he spoke. "Well, he wouldn't be quite so ripe if Crime Lab got here *when we requested you.*"

I put up my palm. "Stop right there! You can thank the previous shift for the delay."

Royce poked his head around me and gave Bob the once-over. Bob was looking out the passenger's window at some guy running around taking pictures. "So, you got a ride along?"

"Yeah." I sighed. "We just dealt with some dead person's vomit in a car and now this mess. We're not even an hour into the shift."

The guy with the camera had a cigarette dangling from his lips. His shirt was too small and his beer belly blubbered around as he dashed about in his picture-taking frenzy. He snapped a shot of Royce and me talking through the van window and had moved onto Royce's police car. "What the hell?" I quickly asked.

Even Bob looked amused.

The guy maneuvered the camera from the vertical and horizontal positions and twisted the lens as he adjusted his F-stops. He moved from Royce's car to another marked unit that had a person sitting in the backseat. The guy's behavior took my mind off the smell—at least for a moment.

Royce rolled his eyes. "Here's the scoop. The dead guy splits with his girl." I wondered why they always talked in the present tense. It was a cop thing. "The girl tries to call to see if he's okay and doesn't get an answer. Well, this goes on for a few days, so she shows up here today to check on him and finds him ten-seven. She's all flipped out and calls her dad. The dad makes the nine-one-one call and then comes to the scene with his camera. He's been taking pictures for the past two hours. It's a freakin' circus. That's her in the back of the patrol car. She's acting like this is normal!" I watched the dad take pictures of his daughter sitting in the back of the police car. I had seen it all.

Royce smiled as he looked at Bob. "You might want to check to see if he's still breathing. Maybe the ME will give us two for the price of one."

Bob's ad hoc face mask made my mind flash to my respirator. "Damn it!" I banged my fists on the steering wheel. "Damn, damn, damn it!"

Royce stopped midsentence and Bob shifted his eyes toward me to see what was wrong. "I left my biohazard kit on the table next to the Acura." I groaned. "Damn it. My respirator is in it." I got distracted when Joe called down to the garage and I remembered setting it on the table as I answered the phone.

"Man, you're screwed." Royce sounded serious. "I'm not joking. It is bad in there. Can someone drive it out here to you? You gotta take pictures outside anyway, right? Can you do that while someone brings it to you?"

"Yeah, right." I grabbed my clipboard and hopped out of the van. I tossed Bob the keys in case he wanted to turn on the air conditioner. "Hell can freeze over before I ask anyone in that place for a favor. Besides, I don't want to give them the opportunity to say no."

No sooner had I gotten out than Bob was lying across the driver's seat and rolling up my window. I pulled the camera out of the back of the van, violating the Lab's unwritten rule about evaluating a scene before reaching for equipment. I'd evaluate this one as I went.

I nodded toward the fire trucks. "Fan duty?"

"Yeah. Oh, and the ME is already here." Royce anticipated my response. "But before you get all bent out of shape, we started him because you were taking so long. He went in and just took a quick look so he could start his report. We didn't let him touch anything. He said for you to do what you needed to do and when you're done he'll go in for a better look."

It didn't matter to me—after all, the firefighters had already disturbed the scene. I just wanted to get the hell out of there.

With each step toward the house, the smell grew increasingly intense. I stacked my equipment on the side porch steps, loaded film in the camera, and put on latex gloves. I slipped a baseball hat on my head to keep the bugs out of my hair and turned toward the firefighters who were watching intently. "So where's the man of my dreams?"

One of the firefighters looked surprised. "Uh—in the bedroom." He pointed toward the back of the house. "Are you from the Crime Lab?"

"Last time I checked." I guessed they were expecting one of the good old boys.

I tucked my notebook in the back of my waistband. I don't know why I did this—except that everyone else seemed to. I turned back to Royce who was standing next to the firefighters. "Wish me luck." I climbed the side steps that led to the kitchen and stood on the small porch for a moment.

"Hey!" One of the firefighters called. "Don't forget your respirator. You'll need it in there."

I pretended I didn't hear him and disappeared into the hot, humid, gross house. The fire department had set up two huge fans to dissipate the smell: one in the kitchen and one in the hallway just outside the bedroom door. I snapped a picture of each before I turned them off. The whirring sound was distracting and I didn't want fly guts spattered all over me each time I walked by.

The interior of the house was dark and creepy. The maroon

shag carpeting, the gold brocade love seat, and the string art ship hanging on the wall screamed of the Brady Bunch. The smell made my eyes sting and my chest burn. The little test puffs of air that I let through my nose were so foul that it made my brain ache, but when I tried to breathe through my mouth, I could taste the smell. Every second was agonizing. A scene like this would be a perfect challenge for *Fear Factor* contestants.

I set my camera to automatic focus so I wouldn't have to fumble with it. My supervisor could pound sand because there was no way in hell I was going to pull out my bag of tricks and do all the fancy stuff they liked to see on death scenes. It just smelled too bad.

The kitchen was the first room I tackled. I dealt with it early on because it was the room farthest from the body. The fan was positioned to blow the rank air out the opened door. I started with overall pictures, making sure to capture the entire room from all four corners, and then moved onto midranges and finally close-ups of particular areas and items of interest. I photographed the kitchen door and doorframe to show that there was no sign of forced entry, and the three envelopes laid out on the kitchen table. One of them was addressed to "Mom," another to "Carla," and a third to "Steve." I also took close ups of the six empty miniature liquor bottles and the empty vodka fifth in the sink, as well as the eight empty Bud cans that were stacked like a pyramid on the kitchen table. As soon as I depressed the shutter button for the last time, I ran for the door.

As I reappeared on the side porch I noticed that all the firefighters looked at their watch at precisely the same time. It was odd, but I didn't really give a shit. I was dying and found the rancid air outside the house to be refreshing. I lifted my face into the breeze and wiped the sweat from my forehead with my forearm. I felt like that woman on the Peppermint Patty commercial, standing on the top of a mountain letting the wind rush through her hair. What I'd give to smell peppermint.

I took a deep breath and counted to three, then to six, then to eleven. Eventually, I garnered the nerve to go back inside. After I confirmed that the envelopes on the kitchen table were suicide notes, I started on my photographic frenzy—I had never taken pictures so quickly in my life, snapping as fast as the flash would recycle. I worked my way through the living room and dining room and down the hallway toward the master bedroom, photographing each room from all four corners and zooming in on anything I thought to be relevant. The flies thickened as I neared the master bedroom and the drone of their buzzing wings made me dizzy. I could feel them bumping into me and I flinched each time one touched my face or bare arm. I made it as far as the bathroom on my second trip inside. The bathroom was gross and even the unflushed turd in the toilet couldn't take it. The poor thing was gooey, fermenting, and covered with dozens of little maggots that were going merrily about their business and enjoying their boat ride in the toilet's murky waters. It threw me over the edge. I clenched my teeth and ran like hell for the porch.

My face must have told all. Royce looked at his watch, and then came up and offered me some Vicks. "You gonna make it?"

I pulled my notepad from the back of my pants and fanned myself. It took me a couple of tries before I could get the words out convincingly. "Yeah," I swallowed hard, "but that's the worst one I've ever had—and I haven't even gotten as far as the bedroom yet."

I opened up my notepad and scribbled some notes—I was stalling. My tactic was interrupted by the nutty guy with the camera and the beer belly. He spotted me on the porch and started to take advantage of the photo-op. This was enough to send me back inside.

This time, I made it to the bedroom. From the hallway, I couldn't see the body, but I could see that the window was plastered with a black curtain of flies, which reminded me of the *Amityville Horror* scene where the priest comes to bless the house. These flies had stuffed bellies and were basking in the sunlight, much like the way people pass out on the sofa after gorging themselves with turkey on Thanksgiving Day.

The image of Bob in the truck came to mind as I pulled my

shirt up to cover my nose and mouth. It took everything I had to go inside. I finally took a step into the room and felt the temperature rise by what seemed like ten degrees. I couldn't take my eyes off the festering mass on the bed. The site was ghastly and the millions of maggots gave the illusion that the body was moving. From what I could make out, the dead guy was lying on his back. He was covered to the chest with what used to be a white sheet, although his bloated, blistered, rotten left leg was sticking out. He had a tube sock on, the kind with stripes. I hadn't seen anyone wear tube socks with stripes since I was in the eighth grade. What remained of his left arm was extended alongside his torso and his right arm was bent at the elbow, his hand resting next to his shoulder, just beside a handgun. A pillow covered his face. I couldn't help but think of the commercials for the Stick-Up room deodorizers. They usually showed a nicely dressed woman opening the lid to a garbage pail or the laundry basket in her teenage son's room, at which point she'd contort her face and wave her hand in front of her nose as she said, "Now this is a good place for a Stick-Up." They really needed to send that woman to a crime scene like this and have her walk through all the bugs and goop and reach over the body as she affixes the deodorizer to the headboard and cheerfully says, "Now *this* is a good place for a Stick-Up!"

I took a step closer to the bed and shined my flashlight on the body. The heat from my light made the maggots excited and they started to squirm; a few of them popped up in the air like Mexican jumping beans. I yelped when one hit my forearm, but then was mesmerized for a second as I watched a little tiny maggot play peek-a-boo under a flap of skin on the guy's knee while his bigger buddies tunneled in and out of a deep cavern they created in his thigh. The guy's skin was greenish-brown, looked wet and gooey, and was peeling off of his hands and arms. The body was marbled, which meant that the blood vessels were plainly visible and looked like weblike streams of black tar, indicating that bacteria had invaded the circulatory system. The bed sheets were damp and discolored from decomposition juice, and the sticky sound of the maggots slithering through the liquefied flesh started to resonate through my head. I ran.

When I reappeared on the porch, Royce and the firefighters looked at their watches in unison. I didn't get it, and I didn't care. As I recomposed myself, I couldn't help but wonder where the "ashes to ashes, dust to dust" myth came from. The only ashes and dust I ever saw were on fatal fire scenes. Decomposition is a nasty, disgusting event that involves two primary processes: autolysis and putrefaction. The former, autolysis, literally means self-destruction, or the digestion of the body by its own enzymes. In living individuals, acids and enzymes in the digestive system breakdown foods into molecules that can be absorbed into the blood supply and provide the body with necessary nourishment. The digestive system's constant production of mucus provides the requisite defense to keep these destructive acids and enzymes where they belong. Following death, however, mucus production stops and these hungry fellers eventually perforate the esophagus, stomach, and intestine and start melting other internal tissues and organs.

Putrefaction refers to the bacterial, as opposed to enzymatic, breakdown of the body (although much of the bacteria is released into the body cavity through autolytic processes) and causes even the most untrained eye to reach the conclusion that a person is dead. The timing of putrefaction is variable, but the sequence is predictable. It starts with a green or bluish-green discoloration of the body that is first perceptible in the abdomen and groin. As this color spreads, it is accompanied by swelling or bloating that results from the accumulation of bacterial gasses. Bloating is particularly severe in the stomach and intestines, as well as in other body cavities and areas of loose skin, such as the penis, scrotum, breasts, chest, and face. The pressures produced by bloating can cause the tongue and eyes to protrude from the head and force the intestines and other internal organs through the rectum and vagina. As putrefaction progresses, the blood vessels take on the previously described marbled appearance and the skin begins to slough off its epidermis. This gives the body the appearance of having been burned or scalded. Vesicles, or blisters containing gases and fluids of decomposition, form beneath unsloughed skin and burst on contact, while head hair and finger- and toenails slide off with little effort. At this point, the individual is so massively swollen and disfigured that close family members might not even recognize the body of a loved one.

Since I wanted this scene to go away, I stayed outside long enough to catch my breath and then went back into the bedroom to pick up where I'd left off. I shined my flashlight on the pillow and reluctantly leaned forward as I examined a small hole in its center. The hole was surrounded by a faint ring of darker colored residue barely detectable through the staining caused by the decomposition fluids. It *had* to be gunshot residue (GSR).

I put my flashlight back into the holder on my belt and swatted the flies off the camera that was hanging around my neck. I hoped none had walked across the viewfinder, which was now pressed against my face. I walked around the room, snapping picture after picture and stepping on dead bug after dead bug. I tried not to breathe. With the camera up to my eye, I made my way closer and closer to the bed and leaned over as I took a few pictures of the gun, the pillow, and the hole surrounded by the black-colored residue. Each time the flash went off, the flies buzzed and maggots squirmed and jumped. I ran back to the bathroom for more air. The maggots riding on the turd were a pleasant sight for sore eyes.

When I was rejuvenated, I went back in and took a few quick measurements and scanned the scene, making mental notes that I'd transcribe into my notepad outside. There was a wallet on the dresser, which I photographed before searching it. It contained $120. I spread the bills out on the top of the wallet like they were playing cards and took another picture. I looked at the driver's license photograph of a lean thirty-eight-year-old man and compared it to the bloated mess I saw before me. The contrast was frightening. Death is not kind. I headed outside once again.

I stood on the porch for a few minutes as the firefighters and

Royce checked their watches and high-fived each other. They were playing some sort of juvenile game. I was annoyed at Royce, who should have been inside the house helping me—especially with the measurements for my sketch. I'd need to collect the notes, the gun, ammunition, and the pillow as evidence, and I took my time walking to the van to get bags. Bob was still locked away with the air conditioner blasting cold air in his face.

"Don't even ask," I warned as I opened the side door of the van and grabbed an assortment of paper bags. "It's horrible. I'll be done in a few minutes." I didn't even give him the opportunity to respond before I was making my way back to the house.

I walked past Royce and his buddies and called for him to start the ME again. I'd be done in five minutes. In the kitchen, I packaged each suicide note in a separate paper bag. I didn't seal them knowing that the ME would probably want to read them or make photocopies. It appeared that the dead guy got drunk, wrote the suicide notes, then got into bed, covered his face with the pillow, and shot himself in the head. The pillow prevented him seeing the gun as he pulled the trigger.

I headed for the bedroom. The next two things I needed to collect were going to be covered in maggots and slime. The first was the gun. I held my breath as I went into the bedroom and picked it up off of the bed. It was wet and I could feel the warmth of the decomp fluids through my gloves. I carried it into the kitchen where the light and smell were better. Since I didn't want to transport a loaded weapon, I carefully opened the cylinder and used my permanent marker to place a dot next to the chamber that had been beneath the firing pin. I quickly changed my gloves, then took a photograph of the cylinder and made a quick diagram that documented whether each was empty or contained a live cartridge or a fired casing before I unloaded it. Once through, I dropped it in a paper bag.

Since the gun was covered in body sludge, now my notepad, pen, gloves, and even the exterior of the paper bag that I touched were contaminated. This was why I didn't touch anything in the equipment compartment of the van without wearing gloves. I worked with people who saw nothing wrong with propping their nasty boots on the Crime Lab lunch table or on other people's desks—and I was to trust that they had wiped the equipment in the vans free of biohazards? Yeah right.

I changed gloves again and went back to the bedroom for the horrendous task of peeling the pillow off the dead guy's face. I needed to collect it because it appeared to contain GSR and had a bullet hole. As gross as it was, the pillow would be a critical piece of evidence if the question of suicide was ever disputed.

I stood beside the bed for a minute wishing the pillow would magically jump into the bag without me ever having to touch it. When this didn't work, I grabbed a corner of it and started to peel it back, not wanting to see what was beneath it. The pillow made a wet sticky sound as I pulled it away from the guy's face. Strings of face goop connected the pillow to the mess beneath it. Then I saw them. Maggots—millions of them—tens of millions of them! They were swarming in what used to be the guy's face. I gasped for breath, but then smelled the smell. It made me bend over and dry heave just as a fly decided to land on my cheek and wander toward my open mouth. I needed Royce. I needed 911. I needed help!

I flew out of the house and onto the porch only to see Royce and his friends look at their watches yet again. I hung my head over the side of the railing thinking I was going to blow my cookies but somehow I managed to keep it together. I stood there for a minute or two before calling to Royce.

"Hey," I interrupted Royce's conversation with the firefighters. "I need your help inside with something." I sounded breathless. I tried to compose myself, but all attempts failed when I looked down and discovered a family of maggots shimmying down my pant leg and across my shoe. Royce's face drained as he watched me flick my new friends into the grass. "No! You mean I gotta go back in there?"

"It will be fast, I swear. All I need you to do is hold open a paper bag for me."

Royce pulled a pair of latex gloves from his pocket as he

whined, "Oh man! I was already in there, twice!" He grabbed his respirator.

Together, we walked back into the house, down the hallway, and into the bedroom. Royce held up better than most officers I had seen on scenes like this. He got the bag ready as I slowly peeled the corner of the pillow back. The maggots were still swarming. "See what I mean?" Royce peeked over my shoulder to get a peek. "Okay, tell me when you're ready. I'm going to rip the pillow off like a bandage."

Royce counted. "One, two, three—go!"

I pulled the pillow off the face. It felt like it weighed twenty pounds because of the blood, purge, fluid, and bugs. I dropped it into the bag and Royce rolled down the top. It was as if we had rehearsed this. Then we both looked at the guy's face, aghast at what we saw. I quickly regloved and snapped a few final pictures of the mess beneath the pillow. The sight was ungodly. An open casket was not an option for this guy.

Before loading my evidence into the van, I double and triple bagged everything in an attempt to keep the bugs and smell from poisoning us on the ride back to headquarters, but I knew it was only a matter of time. I threw the bags in the back and then climbed into the front compartment.

I was only in the van for a minute when Bob detected it. "Oh my God! Is that you?" He rolled down his window to get some air but soon realized the air outside of the van was about as bad as that inside. He looked frantic, like he was about to pass out. "Oh my God! It *is* you!" He buried his face in his arm. I sniffed myself and the scent of death oozed from my pores. I pulled some disinfectant hand wipes from my print kit and tried to decontaminate my face and hands. I also had some cucumber melon body mist that I squirted on myself. It helped a little . . . until the scent from the back crept forward.

Royce came over to get my name and ID number. I gave it to him, only on the condition that he tell me what was up with the firefighters and their watches.

He grinned. "Well," he seemed embarrassed to tell me.

"C'mon! Tell me!" I was insistent.

"They were taking bets on how long you could stay in there. They actually thought you'd puke. I don't think any of us could have done it without a mask."

"Well, I hope someone made some money off my suffering!" I took it as a compliment. "And be sure to spread the word that the civilian scabs are tough cookies!"

I drove back to headquarters with Bob hanging his head out of the van window like a dog going for a ride. All I wanted to do was drop off my evidence, slide by my house so I could change my uniform, then show Bob the more appealing parts of my job.

No sooner did we pull into the headquarters lot than the dispatcher raised me again. "Twenty-two fifteen. Crime Lab unit twenty-two fifteen."

"*Now what?*" I hadn't even put myself clear of the suicide and back in service yet. "Twenty-two fifteen. Go ahead."

"Twenty-two fifteen, I need you to clear that suicide as soon as possible. You need to start up for a bombing." The dispatcher's voice sounded especially serious.

"Dispatch, Bomb Squad handles bombings, not Crime Lab." She knew that, so I wondered why she requested me.

"Twenty-two fifteen, I'm direct on that. This is a suicide, quadruple homicide. We need Crime Lab out there ten-nineteen [immediately]. Authority of Bomb Squad."

Before I could even acknowledge her, Bob was out of the van and standing at my car with his palm outstretched. I tossed him my keys.

The day of Bob's ride along turned out to be the most challenging day of my entire career—too bad he only stuck around for part of it. He never rode along again. So much for Burglary Monday.

I should have learned from Bob's experience, but no—I encouraged others to ride. One of my students took my advice and participated in a ride along with her local jurisdiction. She got caught up in a car chase and bail out, and subsequently witnessed the suspect fire shots at the officer with whom she was riding. The officer returned fire—killing the bad guy. I gave her extra credit because she wound up being interviewed by Internal Affairs all night.

Other family members may not have ridden with me, or ridden at all, but they certainly took advantage of my skills to solve crimes—especially crimes of the heart. The most memorable case was when my cousin Brian called me one day and asked a rather unusual question.

"So, are you alone?" He sounded serious.

I scanned the Lab, looking at the hoards of people surrounding me. "Uh, not really. Should I be?"

"Listen, I need to ask you something. Don't take it the wrong way." I wondered how he got my work number. He took a deep breath and blurted out the question: "Should women's panties be crunchy?"

I held the receiver away and looked at it for a second before pressing it back up against my ear. "What the hell is wrong with you!?!" I now had the attention of everyone in the Lab.

"No, no—listen! This isn't a joke. Let me explain." He was pleading. "Without going into all the detail, let's just say that I think that Jenny is cheating on me." He and Jenny had been married for about seven years and had two children. Bob and I knew there were marital issues because every time we saw them they were having what we referred to as "sidebars." They'd step away from the group, put on a fake smile, and argue without moving their mouths. They had been seeing a marriage counselor.

"I think she's cheating and I need a way to test her underwear for semen." I was at a loss for words.

"Uh . . . ," I fumbled for words. "Sure, that can be done. But . . . , I mean . . ." I couldn't make a complete sentence. "Tell me exactly what you're trying to prove." Forensics and crime scenes were *never* supposed to involve people I cared about. I was out of my element. "I don't want to pry, but what's going on?"

Brian sounded upset. "Jenny called me at work a few months ago and wanted me to stop and get a bikini waxing kit on the way home. It was the dead of winter and we weren't planning to go on vacation. That question was just *so* out of the ordinary that I couldn't help but become suspicious. She also started dressing differently and wearing thongs. She used to hate thongs. Then came the way-too-short skirts and the go-go boots." I knew the boots he was talking about. They *were* pretty bad. "Since all this thong-streetwalker business started, she's been getting called in to work early and having to work late. That never used to happen, and with the baby and all—it just doesn't make sense. When I call her at work, she's never there, and a few times, her co-workers have told me that she *wasn't* called in early or *didn't* have to work late."

It sounded suspicious to me, too.

"I've been taking her underwear, regularly. Without fail, nights that she goes in early or stays late, she wears a thong and when she comes home, they are crunchy."

Brian paused for a minute. I didn't know what to say. "I know she's cheating, but I need proof. I want to have the undies tested and prove that the crunch is semen and it isn't mine. I need to do this before I confront her. Can it be done?"

I was still hung up on his use of the word *crunchy*. That was a word that I pleasantly associated with fresh, crispy potato chips or a kosher pickle right from the barrel. The word *crunchy* was the epitome of onomatopoeia. This job was forever ruining so many associations that used to be pleasant. "Uh, yeah—sure." It took me a few seconds to regroup. This wasn't the ordinary conversation you had with your cousin. "You could do a few presumptive tests for acid phosphatase."

I could tell he was trying to write it down so I spelled it for him. "Acid p-h-o-s-p-h-a-t-a-s-e. It's an enzyme that's present in seminal fluid. It's in other things too—but if you test the crunchy crotch of her panties and get a positive result, you can say that she either had juices of excitement, a mammalian liver, or a head of cauliflower and a couple of turnips down there." Silence had fallen across the Lab and all were intently listening to me. We had plenty of test kits in the Lab, but I dared not give him any—especially for something like this. "Do a Google search on Lynn

Peavey or Sirchie. They're forensic suppliers and I know you can order the kits from them. And hold onto the receipt because I know she'll say I gave it to you." I didn't want to be accused of misusing county equipment, especially since I got caught freezing nectarines and felt-tipped markers in the vat of liquid nitrogen.

"Okay. This is helpful." I felt bad for him. "Anything else I need to know?"

A thought popped into my head. "Yeah. How are the panties packaged? Are they together or separate and are they in paper or plastic?"

He thought for a moment. "I think they are all in a blue plastic Wal-Mart bag. Why?"

"In the future put each pair in a separate paper bag. The panties are more stable that way."

About two weeks later, I got another call. "The test turned bright purple." My heart sank. It was a positive result. "And I haven't seen any cauliflower or livers lying around. I think I can assume it is what it is." He sounded horrible. Devastated.

I was in disbelief. And there were two children involved: I wondered what kind of person would do this to her kids. "Do you know who it is?"

Brian didn't hesitate. "Oh, yeah. It's her boss."

Now the nosey side of me was interested. "How do you know it's him?"

Brian sounded calm, considering what he was going through. "It couldn't be more obvious."

My mind shot back to the underwear. "So, what's next?"

In terms of the positive acid phosphatase tests, I thought he needed something more conclusive. "I can call a few DNA labs and see if they'll do private cases. I can get the prices too."

Brian had obviously done his homework. "If they aren't using protection, then I bet he's had a vasectomy. Won't that mean there's no DNA?"

"Oh no!" I anticipated this one. "It just means there won't be any sperm—but there will be DNA in any epithelial cells left behind." My mind was racing. "Oh, and I'd also get a few pairs of those crunchy undies out of the house—just in case she realizes that you've been collecting them."

Brian confronted her a few nights later. He was armed with the acid phosphatase tests and DNA results proving it wasn't his crunch in her crotch. It all worked out for the best. They are divorced and Brian has moved on with his life. He is engaged to a great woman with a great kid. Best of all, he doesn't steal her panties!

CHAPTER 5

Animal Instinct . . .

Saint Francis is my favorite. I don't know if it is appropriate to say you have a favorite saint. It might be like saying you have a favorite sibling. I wanted to take Francis as a confirmation name, but my mother said I had to pick a girl saint, or the neighbors would talk. They were already talking. My mother suggested Lucy. I never liked the name Lucy; it's an old lady's name. Besides, Lucy is scary. We had a big statue of her in our foyer when I was growing up. She had blank spots where her eyes should have been and held a plate, in the middle of which were her eyeballs. My mother said that Saint Lucy was executed with a sword in the year 303, but God was good to her and saved her from being set on fire. If God was good to her, I wondered why he didn't stop her from being stabbed and having her eyes yanked out. My mother was quick to add that God was benevolent enough to restore Lucy's eyes. I guess that meant she saw the sword coming. My mother said I shouldn't talk like that in front of Lucy because she was a saint and saints could hear everything. Lucy could probably hear better than the average saint because she was blind and I think blind people have sharper hearing than people with sight.

Saint Francis is the patron saint of animals, ecologists, and merchants, and his feast is celebrated on October 4, which just so happens to be Animal Awareness Day. Saint Francis was born in 1182 to a wealthy family from the south of France, and he was named (actually renamed) after his beloved country. After receiving the word of God during prayer, he abandoned his worldly possessions and donned the poor farmhand clothing that has become the trademark dress of the Franciscan Order he founded. I wonder if Saint Francis knew that he'd come to adorn birdbaths all over the world.

Saint Francis loves animals and I love animals, so I love Saint Francis. I've had my fair share of dogs, including a mutt named Willy, a standard poodle named Chummy (who wasn't so chummy when she bit the neighbors), shih tzus named Chopsticks and Socrates, as well as English springer spaniels named Jade, Mandy, and Sasha. Then there were the reptiles, including an array of chameleons and lizards, and multitudes of rodents along with the babies they consumed, as well as fish, a snake, newts, and Merle the hedgehog.

Growing up, I was always dragging sick, injured, and mange-ridden animals into my house for treatment. Sometimes my father would help me sneak them inside and keep them hidden from my mother while they recuperated. My mother thought all animals had bugs and every critter was going to give me rabies or trench mouth. After being attacked by a stray cat and subsequently ruining my family's vacation as I dealt with rabies shots, I decided I should stay away from God's creatures that spewed frothy spit. As far as trench mouth was concerned, I didn't know what it was, or if it was even a real disease, but every time I got a rash or a pimple Mom would tell me in an exasperated tone, "Now look, you've touched those filthy animals and gone and given yourself trench mouth again." Sometimes she also diagnosed me with hoof and mouth disease too.

I haven't outgrown my desire to help furry friends in need, and when I was at work I seemed to always be involving myself in animal rescue cases. There was the chocolate lab that had been hit by a car. The Wonder Bread man stopped to help and let me borrow his bread rack and use it as a gurney so I could get the seriously injured pooch to the emergency veterinary clinic. Then there was Trax, the possessed dog named after the needle marks on his owner's arms. I wound up taking the poor abused puppy home, and within two hours he successfully destroyed my personal vehicle and shit, peed, vomited, and chewed from one end of my kitchen to the other. He clearly drove his owner to substance abuse. Then again, he nearly drove me to substance abuse.

I invited more stray dogs into my home than I can count and cared for them as if they were my own as I attempted to locate their owners or find them new homes. Bob finally drew the line the day that I picked up a dachshund that had been hit by a car. The veterinarian told me that the poor little thing, which had no tags, had a fractured hip and hind leg. I found myself writing a personal check to pay for emergency surgery. But, as I continue to remind Bob, the story had a happy ending. The owner managed to track me down and paid me in $5, $10, and $20 increments over the following year until I was reimbursed every last penny. We still send each other Christmas cards.

One of the benefits of my job as a CSI was that I had the opportunity to go inside people's homes and see what kinds of animals they cared for. Most homeowners have pets and I know that animal adoption rates would increase if landlords were more lenient in their pet policies. While on duty, I encountered pet squirrels, snakes, raccoons, birds, occlots, monkeys, lizards, tree frogs, piranhas, and, of course, dogs, cats, bunnies, and horses. I saw puppies and kittens being born and had the unfortunate experience of watching two dogs be euthanized. A car had hit one and the police had shot the other. On both occasions, I was so upset that I had to leave work early. I never left work early after handling the death of a person. That's not to say that the death of a human being didn't upset me—I just had not established that protective emotional disconnect with animals that I had in place for humans.

While I got to see a lot of animals at work, they weren't always in the places that you would expect to see them. I hit it off with a burglary victim's three dogs, two ferrets, Macaw, and cat and when I was finished dusting for prints, she asked if I wanted to see what she had living in her basement. The question caught me off guard; most people set traps when they find something nesting or laying eggs in their basement—or they poison it or chop its head off with a shovel. As I followed her down the rickety old stairs, thoughts of child molesters coaxing kids into their homes with the promise of seeing puppies crossed my mind. Within minutes, I was standing in her basement, which had been transformed into a huge playground complete with a series of wooden planks that formed ramps that accessed different levels of a makeshift fort located in the corner of the room. The ceiling panels had been removed and a few of the planks extended up into the rafters. Toys and a tire hung from ropes and there was even a large potted tree, complete with grow lights, and a plastic swimming pool filled with fresh water. Within minutes, I was rolling around on the floor with her two pet raccoons and feeding them animal crackers. She rescued and raised the little guys as babies when they were found on the side of the road next to their dead mother. I couldn't wait to brag to the detectives that they might have found a bad guy in the trunk of a car in the Crime Lab garage, but *I* found two masked bandits hiding in the rafters on an actual crime scene.

Nothing about my job was normal and calls involving animals were of no exception. There was the house that was repeatedly broken into. All the suspect would do was take the parrot cage (containing the bird) and put it on the patio. Then there was the man that committed suicide on Easter Sunday. He did it in a room filled with real live bunnies. I tried not to laugh as a kitten, playing with a cigarette wrapper, fiercely boxed on the face of a dead woman while her grief-stricken family just watched—apparently oblivious to what was going on. There was the one family dog that devoured his owner's face shortly after he died and the other that snacked on a baby. While on the topic of dogs, there was the K-9 officer who responded to a burglary in progress and could see that the suspect was hiding behind a bedroom door. When the burglar refused to come out despite the German shepherd gnashing at his loins, the officer went into the room to investigate and discovered that the guy had been dead for hours. Unfortunately, the dog caused a number of holes that the funeral home had to spackle and paint. Now that is what McGruff the crime dog calls taking a bite out of crime.

Even something as seemingly ordinary as a bunch of chickens on a farm could send me home telling stories. I didn't really care for chickens. I liked cute little yellow chicks but they grow up into big dirty birds that shit a lot and have sharp spurs on the back of their feet and jiggly red things under their chins and on top of their heads.

But Gertrude saw the inner beauty of fowl. She told me to call her Gertie, but I didn't plan to call her anything because after taking a glance at the squalor inside her house, I needed to get the hell out. Gertie was balding on top and had a flaky scalp and long gray whiskers growing from her chin. She was wearing an old stained T-shirt with the faded picture of a cat on the front and her unbridled breasts looked like long, empty water balloons that swayed back and forth as she walked. Her fingernails were black with filth and I watched as she fished a cigarette butt out of an old broken teacup that was on the living room coffee table and lit it. After a drag or two, she spit on her fingers and put the cigarette out and then shoved it into her pocket. She gave me the once-over then asked, "You ain't afraid uh no chickens, are ya?"

I noticed an overturned plastic-mesh laundry basket that confined five small kittens playing on top of urine-soaked carpeting. "Chickens ain't got no teeth, so you don't gotta worry 'bout 'em bitin'." That made me feel safer because Gertie didn't have many teeth and I assumed that meant she wouldn't bite either. She definitely had trench mouth. I followed her down the hallway.

We climbed over a baby gate and into the kitchen. I was stunned and stopped dead in my tracks. The kitchen was covered in crap, feathers, and feed. A big rooster was perched in the middle of the shit-covered kitchen table—the same table that had placemats and dishes on it. "That's Hank. He's a Rhode Island Red." I didn't even know chickens came in types. Several more chickens were huddled together in the corner of the room jiggling their red things, balking, and pecking at gross things on the floor. There were tan chickens, white chickens, red chickens, and black chickens. There were big birds and small birds, and friendly birds and nasty birds. Gertie hugged and kissed Hank and went on to explain that the burglar climbed through the kitchen window and left though the kitchen door, but it didn't appear that he had gone into any other rooms. Nothing was missing. She thought the chickens scared him off. I *knew* the house scared him off.

Then there was Jeffrey. I was a little annoyed driving to Jeffrey's scene because I pulled up the call on my KDT, or my mobile data terminal, and saw that the patrol unit that had requested me had already cleared (left the scene). My response time was only about ten minutes, so I knew that something was wrong. I had learned to anticipate a "bullshit call" when the officer who requested Crime Lab left the scene even though he or she wasn't assigned to another call and knew that I was just around the corner. It was the officer's way of avoiding having to face me.

Little things like this infuriated me. Giving the officer the benefit of the doubt, I pulled up the other calls in the area to see if there was an emergency that required his immediate attention. There wasn't. In fact, this and a traffic stop were the only two calls in the entire precinct. Then I checked the KDT to see what time the officer logged on, thinking perhaps the burglary was keeping him on overtime. I saw that he had just started his shift and this was his first call of the night. There was no excuse.

I scanned the houses on the street looking for the address. I saw 142, 144, 148, and 150. I must have passed 146. I turned the van around and redirected the spotlight as I headed back down the road. 150, 148, 144, 142. The good thing about midnight shift was that there was no traffic. I made another U-turn in the middle of what was ordinarily a busy street and again passed by house numbers 142, 144, 148, and 150.

"Twenty-two fifteen, dispatch." I sounded annoyed.

"Twenty-two fifteen, go ahead." I liked this dispatcher. She sounded young and bubbly. I pictured her being about twenty-five years old, maybe five feet, four inches tall, and about 125 pounds with long curly blond hair and big blue eyes. But voices are often deceiving, and she probably really looked like Gertie the chicken lady.

"Twenty-two fifteen. Dispatch, am I responding to a business or a residence?"

"Uh, let's see." I could hear her typing. "Looks like it is a residence."

"Okay," I was in the midst of making yet another U-turn. "Can you verify the numeric for me? Is it one forty-six? I see everything but one-forty-six."

I could hear her typing again. "Ten-four, twenty-two fifteen, it's one-forty-six. Unit nineteen twenty-six just cleared. Do you want me to have him go to tac so he can give you directions?"

A few minutes later I was talking to Officer Capka. I knew this guy and was surprised that he, of all cops, left. He was quiet and never had much to say, but he seemed to be one of the better investigators and he always waited for Crime Lab.

"Sorry to *bother* you," I hoped he caught the sarcasm, "but can you tell me where this burglary is?"

"Yeah, it isn't easy to find." If it wasn't easy to find, it would have been nice for him to raise me on the radio or tell the dispatcher how to get to the house. "Turn into that old abandoned gas station and follow the road behind it. You'll see a dumpy old trailer. That's where the call is. You can't see it from the road. It took me awhile to find it."

"Ten-four." I heard him start to say something else, but was already switching my radio back to the main channel. It must have been important because dispatch had me switch back to tac for him.

"I just wanted to tell you that the place is a *pigsty*." I heard someone laughing in the background. From the way his voice echoed, I could tell he was back in the precinct. "I would have waited for you—but I just had to get outta there. You'll see what I mean. Oh, and you'll want to talk to one of the complainants before you start processing. His name is Jeffrey. He was home at the time of the burglary." I heard more cackling and what sounded like mooing. His precinct was notorious for playing practical jokes and on more than one occasion, I found my ankles Scotch-taped together and left the bathroom or interview room to find clear fingerprint tape across the bottom of the doorway. If I had a dollar for every time I tripped in that station house, I'd be a millionaire.

I pulled into the old abandoned gas station and drove behind it. It was a creepy place. It was pitch black and looked like the kind of place where midgets with knives would attack unsuspecting travelers in need of gas, eat their organs, and make furniture from their bones. I drove quickly. The trailer came into view—it looked about as scary as the gas station. I parked in the grass because there was no driveway and was greeted by a skinny drunk woman who was missing most of her teeth.

"Watch where you step, baby doll," she warned as I opened the door to my van. I turned on my flashlight and scanned the ground. I had never seen so much shit—and I literally mean shit—in my life! It was beyond words.

"Yeah, baby doll, that's what I mean. Don't want your pretty little shoes gettin' all messed up." I looked down at my clunky police boots. *Pretty?* The turds didn't faze her in the least. I watched in revulsion as her right flip-flop sunk deeply into one of them. "C'mon in. We ain't got no visitors too often." She held the storm door open for me. Only the bottom hinge attached it to the frame.

"So, you were burglarized?" I looked around the living room and saw that the floor was polka dotted with twice the number of turds that were in the yard. The place was a dump and smelled like a sewer. There were about eight roaches stuck in a bug trap in the corner and something was rustling around in a rear room. It had to be a rat. I looked in the bedroom long enough to see that there wasn't an inch of floor not covered by garbage and the amount of scum growing in the bathroom sink and toilet looked like a bad science fair experiment. A stack of 7-11 napkins on the vanity next to the toilet obviously functioned as toilet paper and I had to laugh at the tube of lipstick next to the flypaper and beer cans. I didn't see a toothbrush or toothpaste—but as long as the woman had her lips on, she'd be all right.

I couldn't resist. "Well . . . those burglars certainly made a mess of the place, didn't they?"

"I was out with my boyfriend." I watched in amazement as her entire face caved in when she puffed on the cigarette she had just lit. The boyfriend must have been a real catch. If I woke up in the morning with my arm under her, I'd rather gnaw it off than wake her up! I imagined the boyfriend French kissing those toothless smoky gums and I wondered what it felt like not to have any teeth. The woman was talking to me but I wasn't hearing a word she was saying. I was mesmerized. I was sick.

I zoned back in just in time to see her dig in her ear and then inspect the pickings under her tar-stained fingernails before grabbing my forearm to break her fall as she teetered forward. "I come back and find my stuff's missin'. None of them doors or windows 'round here lock, so they coulda come in anywheres." She took another drag off of her cigarette. "Baby doll, all they stole was a fan and TV that I just bought at a flea market. They was sittin' right next to the door, right where your foots at. They didn't do nothin' else."

There was no way I was going to get any prints. The only thing to process was the filthy storm door because the burglars took everything else that they touched. I sprinkled some PR powder just to appease her and then called it quits. PR, for Public Relations, powder was what we called it when we made a half-assed effort to process a scene just to satisfy the victim. In other words, it was our attempt to make it appear that we tried to get prints when we were really just trying to get out of there. I wanted to go! "Ma'am," I said as I started to feel itchy. "I need your name and date of birth." I pulled out my notepad.

"Sure, baby doll. But I ain't the owner of this place. I'm here keepin' it tidy while my brother is in jail." *Keeping it tidy?* "I'm up here from West Virginia." That explained the twang. "I'm also takin' care of Jiff-ray."

I had almost forgotten about Jeffrey. Capka reminded me that I was to talk to him. Since Jeffrey needed some taking care of, I suspected he was retarded or something was wrong with him. Or maybe he was one of the misfits who came out of the garage on dark nights when the moon was full. "Ma'am, I'll need to have a few words with Jeffrey before I leave." I wondered where he was because I didn't see him in the trailer.

"Jiff-ray?" She look surprised. "You wanna talk to Jiff-ray? I don't think Jiff-ray gonna like you. He don't like people much."

This was like a bad remake of *Deliverance*. I was afraid to look at the gas station for fear of seeing Burt Reynolds on the roof playing the guitar and Jeffrey hiding behind a stack of tires picking the banjo.

"Well," I explained, "I understand Jeffrey was home at the time of the crime and the officer who initially responded suggested that I have a few words with him. It will only take a minute."

She drew a long puff on her cigarette, which made her face cave in again. Just as I was sure it was stuck, it would pop back out. Smoke leaked from her nostrils and she looked like an angry dragon. Finally, she put the cigarette out on the bottom of her flip-flop. "Well, okay then; if you insist. But he ain't gonna say much." She rooted through a bag of trash on the living room floor and pulled out an old, greasy carton of McDonald's french fries. "Here, hold these. Jiff-ray will like you so long you got food." There were hardly any fries left and the ones that were there were soggy from old ketchup.

I didn't get it, but before I could even contemplate Jeffrey's condition, the woman was on the front porch, screeching at the top of her smoker's lungs, "Jiiiiiiifffffff-ray! Oh, Jiiiiiiifffffff-ray! Get cho' ass in here, Jiff-ray! Nice lady here wanna have a word with you!" She stood there with her hands on her hips. "Jiiiiiiifffffff-ray, I be talkin' to you. The police is here and wantin' a word with you. . . . You get out from under there and get cho' ass in the house."

Under there? Under where? This was just too weird to be true.

She continued her yelling. "Yeah you! Don't pretend you don't hear me, Jiff-ray. You get out from under there. You can go back when the lady's done with you." I waited patiently for Jeffrey to come out from his hiding spot and my mind wandered. What if he was half human–half animal from years of inbreeding in the garage. Visions of what might crawl through the door filled my head: a hunchback, a one-eyed mutant, a naked little gnome, a centipede with a human head? Then I heard him. He sounded horrible. He grunted and rustled through the leaves outside as he approached. He sounded like he walked slowly. That was good for me.

"Thatta boy, Jiff-ray. Now don't you go bitin' the nice lady, you hear me, Jiff-e-boy?" She turned to me as she shoved the unlit cigarette back into her mouth. "'K—you ready? Jiff-ray's a-comin'. You best have dem french fries ready."

My heart was pounding and I could hear my pulse in my ears. I had one hand full of french fries and my other hand on the radio mike. I wanted to leave, but it was too late. I was directly in Jeffrey's path.

And then I saw him. He was vile—worse than what I ever imagined. His nose was smashed in and he was naked and covered in shit. His skin was pink and scaly and a few coarse hairs stuck up from his back. He was grossly overweight, his teeth curled out of his mouth, and his chin dripped with slimy drool. As soon as he saw me he charged and grunted like a madman. The lady with the caved in face yelled, "French fries. He wants french fries! Give him french fries or you're gonna get hurt!"

Holy shit! I frantically reached into the nasty carton and pulled out a handful of old, cold, greasy fries. "Okay, okay—take him away! I don't need to talk to him!" I held out the fries, but was afraid Jeffrey would bite off my fingers—he groaned and snorted. I threw them on the ground and Jeffrey ate them all in a single gobble. Then he gave me a pissed off look.

"I told you he don't like people! You gotta keep feeding him!" The woman rummaged through the garbage for another delicacy.

"Please, make him leave!" I was begging. "Please—get him outta here." Jeffrey was nudging me for more fries and I tossed the entire carton on the ground. He pushed the carton around the living room floor trying to fish out the contents, which were glued to the side by the old ketchup. This bought me the precious time I needed to make my escape. I flew out the door to find Officer Capka in the yard. He was bent over, laughing hysterically. He could hardly breathe, and tears streamed from the corners of his eyes.

"Capka!" I was screaming and laughing at the same time. "You're gonna pay for this!" Even the lady with the caved in face was laughing. She steadied herself on the side of Capka's car and told him, "I was wonderin' why she was so insistent on interviewin' a two-hundred-twenty-pound farm pig that don't even know how to talk!"

I was licked and humped a lot at work. This violates departmental rules and regulations and you aren't supposed to do it while on duty, but as long as I was the lickee and humpee and not the licker and humper, I thought I was probably safe. Some people seemed to attract ticks, others mosquitoes, but I attracted the horny dogs who saw me as a big blow-up poodle. On one homicide scene, it was a little disconcerting to know that the news cameras were recording my every movement while a little fuzz ball of a dog firmly latched onto my ankle and feverishly thumped and jiggled his hips in a way that would have made Hugh Heffner envious.

It wasn't just other people's puppies that could be ornery though—even the department's very own K-9 dogs were known to get involved in a little mischief from time to time. The K-9 Unit is comprised of several officers partnered up with utility dogs. These pooches are the officer's coworkers, companions, and pets, and at the end of a long shift, the four-legged friends go home with their handlers where together they unwind and relax until it is time to go back to work.

Brutus was one of the K-9 dogs, but unlike the shepherd that attacked the dead man because he was *told* to, Brutus did what he did because he *wanted* to. You can send a dog to the best obedience school, feed him Gravy Train from a crystal bowl, dress him up in an aviator hat and a matching bomber jacket, and spend $100 having his ears unmatted, but when it comes right down to it, he's still a dog that humps, licks himself, and sniffs other dogs' asses.

Brutus and I were introduced at the scene of an industrial explosion. I had been on the call for about fourteen hours and was taking a much needed break. I leaned against my van and sipped a hot cup of coffee thinking about how disgusting the day had been. First, there was a morgue run to fingerprint a decomp, then a rotten suspicious death, and now this. I looked down at the cuffs of my shirtsleeves and saw that they were stained with something gross. I inspected my hands again to make sure *they* were at least clean. That's when Officer Stanlos approached me.

"So, are they all there?" I had never met him before. He had his German shepherd at his side.

I pretended to count my fingers. "Looks like all ten of 'em!"

He stared at me for a second. "Man! You look the way I feel right about now." I didn't think it was a compliment. I wondered if I looked that bad.

I changed the subject. "It's been a long day and I'm ready for bed." I looked down at the stains on my shirt cuffs again.

"Ewww." Stanlos had a way with words. "That doesn't look good."

I knew what it was—and it *wasn't* good. There were several dead people, and the blast caused devastation to the bodies that was akin to what you would see in a plane crash. The scene was littered with scraps of metal and human flesh. It was nearly impossible to walk from point A to point B and not step in something offensive. I realized the magnitude of this when I was ordered to climb a fire department ladder to access the roof of an adjacent building containing possible evidence.

The problem was that I was scared to death of heights, but I didn't want anyone else to know. I took off my gloves so that I could get a better grip on the rungs of the ladder and hugged it tightly as I ascended. I followed about ten other firefighters and police officers to the roof, but when I was about a quarter of the way up, I noticed my palms felt wet and sticky. By the time I got to the top, my hands and shirt were covered in bits and smears of unidentified human matter that had been transferred to the rungs from the boots of those who climbed up before me. It was yet another lesson learned.

I looked down at the big German shepherd sitting at Stanlos's feet. "Can I pet him?" I wasn't sure if Brutus was in mean mode or knew he was taking a break and didn't feel the need to eat me alive.

Stanlos outstretched his palm as if to say "be my guest."

I held out my hand for Brutus to sniff. At first, he cautiously sniffed from about six inches away, but as he honed in on the location of the junk on my sleeve, he inched closer. His eyes lit up and he twitched his nose back and forth as he snorted and blew wetness from his nostrils.

"Brutus!" Stanlos pulled back on his collar. "Enough!" Brutus looked disappointed.

I patted his head and scratched his ears. "Well, aren't you a handsome boy?" He nuzzled his head into my thigh when I stopped petting him. "Oh, you like that? Is that what you're trying to tell me? You like that?" I scratched the scruff around his neck and then went back to his ears. My tone was animated. "You tell your daddy that you've been working way too long and you wanna go home." Brutus panted and whipped his tail back and forth. "Oh, you're just a big baby, aren't you? You're just a big old baby." I scratched under his chin with both hands and he groaned in delight. "You're not really a mean doggie, are you?" I squatted down and continued scratching. "I need to make my doggies get a job just like you!"

Stanlos poked fun at my voice. "You must have dogs at home." I stopped scratching, but Brutus didn't want me to stop and gave me his paw. When I didn't turn my interest immediately back to him, he lunged forward and took a swipe at my cheek with his tongue. "Brutus!" Stanlos sounded disgusted.

"Oh, I don't care." I really didn't. As long as Brutus didn't have his work collar on, which immediately transformed him into bite mode, he was just like the other dogs. A good friend of mine is a K-9 officer with the Florida State Police. His companion was a Doberman pincher named BoBo. The dog was trained to tear bad guys into pieces, and any burglars entering his home were destined for the same fate. The problem was that BoBo was afraid of folding television tables, and the day that his home was burglarized, he wouldn't leave the kitchen to attack because a folding tray table was in his line of sight. The burglars cleaned the place out.

As I started to stand up, Brutus let out a loud whine, begging me to stay. Before I knew what hit me, his wet and gooey tongue slithered up my neck, across my cheek, over my eye and forehead, and stopped when he got to my hair. Before I could pull away, he slobbered in my mouth and nose, and then got my other eye. He had me pinned up against my van. No, it wasn't at all threatening but, yes, it was gross.

"Brutus!" Stanlos's tone was intimidating. He yanked back on the leash. "Brutus, stop licking!" Brutus stopped long enough for me to regain my footing and then he lunged forward for more.

I tried to push him away again, gently, remembering what his teeth were trained to do. "Okay, Brutus. Daddy says no more."

Stanlos was laughing. "What the hell did you do to my dog?" I pulled a napkin out of my pocket and wiped my face. "I think Bruty Boy is in love."

I reached down and scratched Brutus on the top of his head as he stole another lick. "You know," Stanlos hiked up his pants and shook his head. "You know, that *really* ain't such a good idea." He was trying not to laugh. "I wouldn't be lettin' him lick you like that."

"I know. I can get trench mouth, right."

He looked confused. "Huh?" It only took a subtle hand gesture for Brutus to jump up and plant himself at Stanlos's heel. Stanlos fished a huge Kong from his pocket and gave it to Brutus to chew on. Brutus looked thrilled.

I could tell Stanlos wanted to say something but was trying to refrain. He looked at me, then Brutus, and back to me.

"What's goin' on?" I hadn't a clue what was so funny.

He hesitated for a second. "Did you see that face over there?" He motioned over his shoulder. When the explosion occurred, the force of the blast peeled the face of one victim off his skull like a Halloween mask. It was in the middle of the parking lot.

"Yes." I sounded suspicious. "I saw it. Why do you ask?"

"Well . . ." Stanlos was trying not to laugh again. "We were over there just a few minutes ago and Brutus"—he hesitated—"Brutus had it in his mouth."

He couldn't be serious! I just stared at him for a few seconds before I realized that he *was* serious! I had just let a face-sucking dog slobber on my cheeks, neck, eyes, mouth, nose, and hands!

All I had was Windex. I just started squirting it on my face and scrubbing with paper towels. I wasn't concerned—after all, I had already gargled with rubbing alcohol when the dead man's hand found its way inside my mouth.

Even though our romance was short lived, Brutus kept me in his thoughts and from time to time, he would send me *Thinking of you*—or actually *Thinking of licking you* cards. Some people say that a dog's mouth is cleaner than a human's mouth. Those people haven't met Brutus.

While I wasn't really interested in Brutus's advances, I certainly took advantage of the opportunity to bait Bob with the news of my other suitors. Not all the county's hounds took a liking to me though—and now that I think about it, not all the crime victims did either. When you put a vicious dog under the same roof as a scorned woman, you have the makings for yet another dinnertime story.

I arrived at what would be the scariest call of my career late on a Saturday night, or early on a Sunday morning—you decide what 3:00 A.M. is. Several dogs acknowledged my knock on the door. I waited, listened, and waited, wondering if I had the right address. It wouldn't be the first time I was banging on the wrong door in the middle of the night. Once I nearly got whacked with a tire iron when the dispatcher accidentally sent me to the incorrect location in the wee hours of the morning.

I could tell by the snorting and scratching and the frantic tap of the claws that someone was approaching. "Back up—back up!" The porch light flipped on. "Sit. I said sit!" The man's voice inside sounded angry. "Get outta here—go! Go!"

The doorknob turned and the door slowly cracked open just far enough for me to catch a glimpse of the man's face. He had a goatee. "Can you hold on for another few seconds while I put them away?" I assumed he was referring to the dogs. Just then a big black wet nose pushed through the crack in the door and tried to catch a whiff of me.

"It's okay." It looked like a nice nose. "You don't have to put them away as long as they're friendly." I reached through the crack in the door and scratched the nose that was attached to an old black lab with a gray face. The man with the goatee held onto the dog's collar as I slipped inside. As I said my hellos to the four pooches of varying shapes, sizes, and breeds, I couldn't help but notice something writhing on the living room sofa. It was covered with a blanket. The goatee man caught me looking at the sofa and stared in that direction.

He tried to change the subject. "Looks like the burglar got in through the basement, but I want to see what you think." I watched him watch the Thing on the sofa. It continued to move, slowly, like a giant serpent.

"What the hell is that?" I pulled my flashlight from my belt and lit it up. The Thing didn't appreciate that. It made some groaning sounds and started to rear its ugly head. The goatee man ordered it back to sleep.

The Thing lay back down for a minute, but then started to flail as it tried to free itself from the blanket, which acted as a snare. The goatee man walked toward the basement and motioned for me to follow him. I couldn't move; I was fixated by the creature on the sofa. "What is that?" I really thought it was another animal.

He had already started down the basement steps. "It's my wife."

His wife? I started to follow him downstairs. *His wife?* Just as I started to pass by the sofa, the Thing won her battle with the blanket and freed herself from the trap. She revealed her ugly face—and it *was* an ugly face. She looked around the room, apparently confused. Then she saw me. She looked me up and down and up again. Her hair was sticking out on end and old makeup stained her face. The weave of the sofa cushion was imprinted onto her cheek. The Thing stared at me without uttering a word, then reached for an empty glass on the coffee table. She inspected its contents, which there were none before raising it to her lips and thrusting her head back—trying to get one more taste of alcohol. I watched as the Thing scanned the table and the floor next to the sofa looking for the bottle. Unable to find it, she threw the remaining covers off herself and stood up, not at all shy that the twins were falling out of her tank top or the fact that she was wearing only a thong. Giving up, she slurred "asshole" under her breath. I assumed the goatee man had hidden her bottle. The Thing satisfied herself with an unfiltered Camel and glared at me as I petted the old lab that had wandered over for another dose of affection.

The Thing inhaled deeply and smoke came out her nose as she spoke. "We got five." She had the raspiest smoker's voice I had ever heard.

I tried to be polite and put on a fake smile. Her speech was so garbled, I wasn't sure I heard her right. "I'm sorry. Did you say you have five?" I had no idea what she was talking about.

The goatee man called upstairs for the Thing to stop bugging me and to go back to bed. I didn't think he liked his wife very much. This made her mad. She screamed at the top of her voice, "Don't tell me what the fuck to do!" She waved her cigarette around like it was an extension of her index finger and pointed toward the basement steps, "I've had about enough of your shit. I don't wanna hear your damn mouth one more time." I headed toward the basement again trying to get away from her before I got into the middle of a domestic dispute, but she stopped me before I got there.

"Hey, girlie." I figured that was me. "Come back here. We was conversing—you know what I'm sayin'?" She reached back and scratched her exposed butt cheek and then took another drag off her cigarette before sitting back down. I tried not to hurl as I watched her snort a gob of mucus down into her mouth and swish it around like it was a raw oyster before swallowing it. "I was sayin' I got five dogs," she wiped her nose on her forearm, "but you only see four of 'em." I strained to hear what she was saying through the liquor that still coursed through her veins.

I just looked at her, waiting for her to tell me where the fifth dog was. She looked me up and down again. She wasn't going to tell me.

"So, where's the other dog?" I really didn't care.

She flipped her hair back and then picked something gross off her tongue. She got whatever it was and smeared it on her thigh. "That other dog got dingo in 'em. He'll tear you to pieces no sooner then look at ya." With her legs still in the seated position, she flung her upper body back onto the cushions and covered her eyes with her left elbow. "He'll tear you up. He's a dingo and dingoes are wild dogs. Deadly dogs. He's a deadly dog." She continued to mumble something about the dog being her protector as she slurred herself into another drunken slumber. I was embarrassed for her and wanted to cover her exposed parts with the blanket, but I didn't dare get too close to her. I watched the lit cigarette burn in the ashtray and wondered how long it would be before I handled a fatal fire at this place.

I went down into the basement. The goatee man was standing next to the water heater. The basement was dim and smelled musty. "So, is this where the bad guy got in or is this where you're gonna draw and quarter me and make a prom dress from my skin?" I hated basements and it seemed I was always going into them with strangers.

The goatee man laughed. "I only do that to the women who don't tell their dispatchers their exact address and don't have AVL [automatic vehicle locators] equipped vehicles." I didn't tell him the department had removed the AVLs from the four Crime Lab vans because management decided that the unarmed civilians didn't need them.

I looked at all the firefighter's paraphernalia hanging on the walls in the basement. That was how he knew about AVLs and dispatch protocol.

"So, here's the deal." He was talking in hushed tones, so as not to awaken the Thing. "She"—he pointed upstairs—"has some problems, and alcohol is only one of them. She's been calling me at work, night after night, saying there is someone in the house, but refuses to call nine-one-one. She always insists that I come home. When I do, there is never any sign that anyone got in."

He was quiet for a minute and listened intently to make sure she was still asleep.

"She pulled the same antics two nights ago. I rushed home when she called and I finally got the balls to tell her that this was all in her head, or all in the bottle. That set her off. The cops had to come break up the fight. I told her later on, when she was sober, that I wasn't coming home in the middle of my shift again and that the next time she claimed there was someone in here, there better be some damn evidence of it." He rubbed his brow. He looked like he was at the end of his rope. "So, tonight she calls and tells me that she heard them breaking in through the basement door."

I interrupted his story. "Did she call nine-one-one?"

"No!" He was quick to answer. "She wouldn't call the cops, but said that the burglers never came upstairs. After she heard them leave, she went down and found the basement door all busted up. She also found writing on the mirror." He pointed to an old medicine cabinet that was hanging above the laundry sink. YOUR NEXT was written across the mirror in what appeared to be soap.

"I like the spelling." I just had to point out the error.

The goatee man smiled. "Nothing is missing." He pointed toward the broken door. "I know she did this. I know it's her. I think it is an attention sort of thing . . . she did it."

I walked over toward the door, which was closed and bolted. "Have you touched anything since this happened?"

He threw his arms up. "No! Nothing!" He reached under a fire helmet hanging on the wall and handed me a key. "You need a key to lock and unlock that deadbolt. You tell me how the hell they got in without damaging the lock. Better yet, tell me how they left through this door, locked the door back up once they were outside, and managed to put the key back under the helmet?"

I unlocked the door and inspected the door and frame.

"There's no damage to the doorframe or strike plate, just the side of the door." This was the worst attempt at a faked point of entry that I had ever seen. "Somebody obviously opened that door with a key then chopped at it to make it look damaged. The problem is that they chopped at the door and not the frame. They damaged the wrong part!"

"Bingo!" The man with the goatee pointed to an axe that was lying on the floor. "It gets even better. That axe is mine." He picked it up and showed me his initials engraved on the handle. This axe was on the back screened-in porch. If the burglars never came upstairs, how the hell did they get the axe? The storm door to the porch is still locked and it can only be locked and unlocked from the inside."

He paced back and forth while I looked at the writing on the mirror. "Oh!" he said. "Then, to top it off, they knew exactly where we keep the soap." He pulled a stack of Ivory soap from a shelf cluttered with bulk supplies that I suspected he and the Thing purchased from Sam's Club or Costco. It was a pack of twelve bars, but one was missing. It was in the nearby trash can along with its wrapper. The edge of the soap was flattened and it had obviously been used to write the note.

Before I could even say anything, I heard the Thing's bare feet slapping across the floor above me. It was calling for him. "Frank!" Her voice sounded raspier than before. "Frank!" I heard her walk to the top of the basement steps. "Frank! Answer me, GODDAMN IT! Are you down there screwing that whore?" She sounded furious. "Frank!"

I looked at the goatee man. "Are you Frank?" He nodded. "And am I the whore?" He nodded again.

"Frank! Get that whore outta my house!" She was screaming with all her might. Frank said "one minute" by holding up his index finger and excused himself as he slid by me and ran upstairs, skipping every two steps.

Frank laid into her and I strained to hear the conversation. The Thing was yammering something about him screwing me in their own home and how we needed a hotel. Frank tried to calm her down by saying that I was the one who was going to figure out who had been stalking her for so long. The Thing didn't want to hear it. "That bitch needs to be talkin' to me or she needs to go!"

She stumbled her way to the basement steps and started to come down. "Excuse me, whore, we need to chat." I didn't answer. "We have a big problem, bitch." The anger in her voice was frightening. "Okay. I asked you and now I'm tellin' you—get cho' ass outta my house."

I heard a scuffle, then Frank yelling that she better not hit him again. I heard a smack and another smack and something fall to the ground and break. They were engaged in an out-and-out, knock-down, drag-out fight. It sounded bad. I headed for the yellow fire helmet to get the key but it was gone. *Shit!* I had handed it back to Frank after I examined the door and he stuck it in his pocket. Just then Frank ran down the steps. "You better just go." His face was bleeding and his arms were scratched up.

I reached for my radio. "Gimme the key. I'll call for an officer on the way out."

That's when I heard the claws scratching into the hardwood floor above me. Then I heard the snarling. Frank and I realized what was coming at the same time . . . *the dingo!* I ran back to the washing machine and took cover on top just as the dog came tearing down the stairs and around the corner, baring its teeth, snarling, and ready to attack. Frank was busy screaming at the Thing, who was shouting, "Get 'em, get 'em boy!" Frank intercepted the dog, but only for a moment. Its claws scratched at the top of the washing machine with a rolled back top lip; its teeth gnashed at me. Frank grabbed the dog's color and pulled him away, while it continued to growl and snap its teeth. Frank cursed as he got bitten on the hand and on the leg. It was total chaos. I was trapped in a locked basement on top of a washing machine by a dingo and a drunk.

No sooner had Frank taken control of the monster than my radio signed the alert tones. "Beep, beep beep. Crime Lab unit twenty-two fifteen." Before I could even key my mike, she called again. "Dispatch calling Crime Lab unit twenty-two fifteen."

"Twenty-two fifteen." I knew she could hear the growling in the background. "Twenty-two fifteen. Go ahead."

"Twenty-two fifteen, what's your twenty [location] right now?"

Frank was dragging the dog up the stairs. "Twenty-two fifteen. I'm on the top of a washing machine at that burglary on Chevrolet Drive. Can you start additional units? We've got a domestic here."

"Okay, twenty-two fifteen," I could hear her typing. "I need you to clear that location immediately. I have the female complainant on the phone and she's making threats against you. I have officers seventy-six [en route] to your location."

Threats? What kind of threats? I already had a dingo wanting to snack on me. "Ten-four, dispatch, I'm direct."

"Dispatch advising all units, channel is ten-three for Crime Lab unit twenty-two fifteen out at fourteen-sixteen Chevrolet Drive." By putting me ten-three, it meant that nobody could transmit on the radio unless it was related to my incident or, obviously, if another officer was in an emergency situation. This was done to keep the air clear until it was determined that I was safe.

I planned my exit as I listened to Frank and the Thing go at it again upstairs. They yelled and scuffled and I heard more items fall to the floor and shatter. When it sounded like they were in the kitchen, I flew up the steps and ran out the door, praying that Frank had contained the dingo. The Thing heard me and broke free from Frank's grip and followed me out the door. I felt like I was in a B-rated horror movie as I fumbled with the keys trying to unlock my van as the Thing drew in on me. Just as she approached, I heard the lock click and I scrambled into the van, immediately locking the door behind me. The Thing slammed her fists up against the side window as she screamed all kinds of obscenities at me. I tried to throw the van into reverse, but was so shaken up that I kept clumsily skipping over the R on the gearshift panel. The Thing was bleeding from what looked like a cut on her arm, probably from rolling around in broken glass. I was scared to death that she had a gun, although I didn't know where she'd conceal it—maybe in her thong. Just then the gear popped into reverse and I burned rubber out of the driveway. Within seconds, the scene was glowing red and blue with the overhead lights.

I never found out what happened to the Thing. When I drove down that same street in the years to come, I wondered if she still inhabited the sofa and reared her ugly head only when she thought someone was trying to steal her mate. It wasn't too far beyond the realm of possibilities that Animal Control had come out and euthanized her. Had the dog mauled me, I hoped I'd live long enough to see my mom trying to outdo Meryl Streep's masterful performance yelling, "A dingo's got my baby, a dingo's got my baby!"

While I'd like to think that my dogs were the epitome of perfection, I had to face the harsh reality that they, too, caused me grief—even when I was at work. To assume anything in this line of business only guaranteed some sort of disaster, and I already had a dark cloud following me around.

It was late in the shift, and I had been called into work several hours early. Bob was out of town and I knew my dogs needed to go out. Between calls, I made a quick stop by my house. We were no longer allowed to go home between calls because there had been some speculation that some of the technicians had been "processing" each other in their down time. But my situation was an exception, or so I thought. Besides, I knew that if I asked, I'd be granted permission. There were rumors of the supervisors following us around to see what we did and where we went between calls. Once I was certain I wasn't being spied on, I made the quick turn into my driveway.

Our radios were equipped with an emergency button. This little red button is located on the top of the radio housing and is inside of a well, which prevents it from being accidentally depressed. In the event that we found ourselves in an emergency situation and were unable or didn't have the time to key the mike, pushing this button registered us as being in "emergency status." This information would show up on the dispatcher's screen and all the officers on the channel would be alerted to our status and given our current location. If we were not on a call, the dispatcher could get our precise location from the AVL readings. In addition, she could tell if our car was running and if the doors were open or closed—that is, assuming Crime Lab still had AVLs.

I walked into the house and discovered my three English springer spaniels doing what they were made to do—spring! Sasha, the bossy one, pushed Jade and Mandy out of the way and begged for all my attention. *Pet me, pet me, pet me!!*

I reached down and scratched her head as she hooked her claws over my belt. *Don't stop, don't stop, don't stop!* The other two tried to get as much as a sniff in, but soon retreated to wait their turn. They knew Sasha was crazy and when I was finished with her, they would get twice the amount of loving.

"Oh, Sashi Washi!" I spoke in baby talk. "Did Sashi Washi miss da Mommy?" I scratched her head and then pushed her down. I didn't want to get covered in hair. She jumped right back up and hooked her claws over my belt again. "Well, hello, Sashi Washi." She danced with excitement and clawed at my waist for more. "I bet you need to make pee-pee. Do you and your sisters need to make pee-pee and poo-poo?" Sasha fell to the ground and rolled over. "Mommy gonna tickle your belly-welly! Here I come—I'm gonna tickle dat fat wittle belly." Sasha rolled around and Jade and Mandy came over and started licking and nuzzling into me. "Oh, you gonna kiss da mommy? Mommy gonna kiss you back. Mommy gonna kiss all your parts." Just then Mandy started licking Jade's ass. "Mandy, no hiney licking. No lickin' the hiney. Jade doesn't want her hiney cleaned. Mommy gonna schmack you for that." I reached down and gave her a gentle smack on the jowls. We called this game "Schmack in the mouff." With cupped hands I would alternate little schmacks in the mouth. This drove them crazy! I did a few schmacks and they were jumping out of their skin. "Oh, you like it when I schmack you . . . dat get you all excited?"

I was rudely interrupted. Dispatch was clearly laughing. "Dispatch to unit twenty-two fifteen. Check your status."

My status? "Dispatch, am I in emergency status?"

"Ten-four, twenty-two fifteen."

The dispatcher could barely compose himself. "Twenty-two fifteen, you okay?"

I motioned for my dogs to be quiet, like they understood. I took a few steps away from them so I could transmit in quiet.

"Twenty-two fifteen. Ten-four—accidental. Can you tell me how to reset again?"

He tried two or three times to get the words out, but was completely broken up. "Twenty-two fifteen," his voice broke and he unkeyed the mike. A second later he tried again. "Twenty-two fifteen, depress the red button for—" He became unintelligible and I could hear all sorts of commotion in the background.

"Twenty-two fifteen, depress the emergency button for about five seconds to reset." As I did it, I looked over at the dogs, who were ready for more. After I let them out, I returned to my van to find about thirty messages on my KDT asking who was calling me "Mommy" and who I was smacking and letting lick me. Yes, during Sasha's crazy quest for attention, her claw depressed my emergency button. Consequently, my conversations with my pooches were broadcast over the entire precinct. I can only hope that they believed me when I said that I was talking to my dogs—really, I was.

Animal magnetism was turning out to be a thing for the birds. Animals were putting me on a sure course to trench mouth, divorce, and unemployment. But then I stepped in shit and everything changed.

Determining what *stuff* a suspect could have taken away from a crime scene and what he might have left behind sometimes requires some creative thinking. I learned this on the "dog doo on a shoe" case. The victim in this homicide was killed in a grassy area outside the front of an apartment building. This was the same grassy area that was littered with foul-smelling landmines left by the fuzzy, four-legged building tenants. My co-worker April (the one who had the cool mom from New Jersey) and I weren't on the scene for very long before we found ourselves hiding from view of the television news cameras as we scraped shit out of the soles of our shoes. It seems that the news cameras were always capturing me at my worst moment—like the time I was broadcast over the 11:00 edition dealing with a bout of Kentucky heartburn (my dad's term for picking your underwear out of your ass).

On *CSI*, nobody steps in shit. But the shit on our shoes got all of us thinking: we knew that the victim was shot at close range and if we had turds in our treads, there was a strong possibility that the bad guy did too.

A suspect was developed within an hour or so. The Homicide detectives took a look at his shoes and discovered reconstituted Kibbles 'n Bits. We were thrilled—one dog's trash is another detective's treasure. But it came back to haunt us as Crime Lab was soon requested to collect all the crap from the grassy area in front of the apartment building. A veterinarian was subsequently called in to take buccal swabs of all the dogs in the building with the idea of matching each pile of shit to a specific dog via DNA, and then matching the shit on the suspect's shoe to one particular dog. This would disprove the suspect's claim of not having been in the area. The shit, the shoes, and the swabs were eventually sent off to a person in California who traced migratory patterns of mountain lions through their crap, and while the results of his examination were not confirmatory, they provided enough circumstantial evidence to elicit the suspect's confession.

This case would have made Dr. Edmund Locard proud.

CHAPTER 6

Wheel of
Misfortune . . .

I think a lot about death—my death that is. I worry that I'll die of lung disease or a heart attack. That isn't a very exciting way to leave the world. I hope something more electrifying happens to me—maybe literally. I'd be thrilled if I were gobbled up by a big Arctic sea creature that died soon after eating me. How wild would it be if I were found five hundred years later, perfectly preserved, curled in the fetal position in its belly? I want to be like the Ice Man. I want someone to say, "Cool—check this out" when they find me. I want different countries to fight over the right to "own" me. I want the contents of my last meal to grace the cover of *National Geographic*. I want Brad Pitt to narrate a Discovery Channel program on the recovery of my remains. I was never very cool in this life; maybe I'll find my niche in death.

If it isn't in the cards for me to be discovered a few hundred or thousand years from now, I know I'll be found naked in a bathroom with fly eggs in my mouth. That's the way it always happens—people die unclothed, in horrible positions, with their eyes open. They never seem to have vacuumed, dusted, or even made the bed in preparation for the hordes of unknown visitors who will stop by for a look-see. I feel the most vulnerable to the Angel of Death sitting on the toilet and taking a shower. As soon as I get dressed, I know I'll make it through another day.

When I do die, I don't want to be embalmed. I used to think all good Catholics had to stand before the pearly gates looking their very best. But then I encountered the decomps. There was nothing that could be done to restore these people's beauty and something in the back of my head told me that Saint Peter didn't refuse them entry into heaven based on their appearance alone. Besides, embalming is just gross. I had the opportunity to disinter two embalmed bodies and some miscellaneous pieces. The first pickled body was decomposed and the funeral home just laid a purple nightgown over the woman's goop and then packed her in pink crystals that smelled like mothballs. We had to root around in her casket to collect samples of bone, hair, and fingernails in the attempt to prove, through isotope analysis, that she was starved to death. Then there was the guy who died from diabetes and had been embalmed and buried for about seven years. Evidence came to light that he might have been responsible for a series of rapes and murders that occurred across the country, so we dug him up to get a DNA sample that was to be compared with those recovered from the victims. The man smelled like rotten cheese and his skin was wet and wrinkled. He reminded me of a foot that had been in a wet sock for too long. His face was black and furry with mold and his hair had taken on the color of the coffin liner. I had to fingerprint him but, because of the condition of his hands, decided it would be best to make a three-dimensional cast of his fingertips using an agent called Mikrosil. I was disgusted to discover that when I peeled the hardened silicone off his fingertips, his fingernails slipped off too. His hair and teeth came out just as easily. I never imagined the day when I'd be standing in a cemetery, hovering over an open coffin containing the remains of a furry dead man, and picking his fingernails out of a piece of silicone.

I encountered the embalmed body parts in a potter's field—or cemetery for society's poor. Apparently, the cemetery director was "reusing" plots by smashing through graves and coffins as he dug holes for more bodies. As a result, there were preserved hunks of meat scattered about. It wasn't a pretty sight and it convinced me that there comes a time when you and your parts just need to go away and only memories of you should live on.

When you die, the funeral home attendants dress you in diapers and insert butt plugs and other odd sorts of contraptions to keep your juices from leaking when Aunt Martha leans over to bid her final farewells. They put devices in your eyes to keep your lids shut and sew your mouth closed. I don't want someone shoving something up my ass after I'm dead. I don't want it to happen while I'm living either. I won't even wear contacts or my dental retainer—so the attendants can stay the hell away from my eyes and mouth too. I just want to be burned.

When Pope John Paul II died, I wondered if he'd be embalmed. He had to be—after all he was lying in state for a number of days. I asked Mom. She said that you aren't supposed to think of things like that. I told her that someone had to embalm the pope because he'd start to decompose and stink, but she told me that he was the pope and popes don't decompose and they certainly don't stink. I think if my son asked me if dead popes stink, I'd tell him that it wasn't a stink as much as a smell. Stink has a negative connotation, but a smell is an aroma—not particularly good and not particularly bad.

The Angel of Death doesn't always strike at the best time. I'm not sure what the best time to die is. I guess it varies from person to person. I hope I don't die on a Wednesday night because Bob would be mad if he had to miss *Lost*, his favorite show. He'd probably set the VCR before he called 911. It wouldn't be good to die on a *Law and Order* night either, or when the Orioles were playing a home game. But there are people out there who wouldn't even want to miss a stupid game show—even if their sibling was dead in the next room.

It was in the late afternoon on a hot summer day when I was dispatched to a suspicious death. I should have known that I was going to get a body call because I was wearing my "death T-shirt" under my uniform. Whenever I wore this particular shirt, or if a Garth Brooks song played on the radio, I'd surely get a dead person. The coincidence was uncanny.

The area I was going to was in one of the poorer parts of the county, which meant that the dead person wouldn't have air conditioning, which meant that the body would be a stinker. If it wasn't a stinker yet, it would be soon. Many of the people who lived in that area stunk anyway, so I wasn't too concerned. I looked at the address on the call. I knew exactly where I was going, so I tossed the map book to the side. I got a tremendous degree of satisfaction when I could get to a call without looking at the map. It was a sad commentary on crime statistics.

Within a few minutes I was driving down the street, passing the teenage mothers pushing strollers, the young men fixing up their older model Fords, the groups of kids congregating in convenience store parking lots, the junkies snapping their wrists to passing cars in the hopes of hacking a ride, and the occasional teenage boy trying to intimidate passers-by with his pit bull. The street was lined with its usual array of pickup trucks, El Caminos, and souped-up Ford Escorts. Each row home tried to outdo the next with a more elaborate display of windmills, pink flamingos, gazing balls, bird baths, and statues of the Blessed Mother. My favorite was the house whose owners dressed the department store mannequins in their front yard for every holiday. Veterans Day was the best—they staged battle scenes with some of the mannequins poised as snipers hiding behind trees and the less fortunate lying in bloodied positions on the ground. Whenever I had a ride along, I made it a point to drive by this house.

I knew I was close to the call when I crested the hill and saw the police car double parked in the street. There was only one car. That wasn't a good sign. Normally, there are at least two, plus a supervisor's car. My response was pretty quick, so nobody should have left as of yet. The single police car told me that although the call was dispatched as a suspicious death, it really wasn't all that suspicious. If the officers were truly wary about the circumstances by which this individual met his or her demise, there would certainly be plenty more people on the scene. Even if it was a natural death or a clear-cut suicide, officers are nosy like the rest of us and like to slide by their buddies' calls to take a peek. The fact that the officer was alone told me the crime scene was going to be nasty.

I double parked behind the police car and told dispatch I was 10-23 [had arrived].

The location of the call was a middle-unit row house. It looked dirty. Auto parts were strewn all over the front yard and the few bushes that were in the front of the house were overgrown and probably hadn't seen a pair of hedge clippers in the past decade. The area behind the hedges served as a combination compost pile and recycle bin as evidenced by the rotting food, chicken bones, bottles, and trash. Other neighbors had a wooden bench or a few plastic chairs on their front porch, but for this family, an old van seat served the purpose just as well. The plastic pans of motor oil that lined the sidewalk added a welcoming touch, and the red-ware planter filled with old rainwater and cigarette butts gave the house that homey feeling. The front storm door was propped open with a milk crate.

I loaded my arms with all the supplies I thought I'd need and made my way to the front door. Just as I was about to enter, Officer Gorman, whom I had met about two weeks prior, came rushing out the door. He looked hot and anything but happy. He motioned for me to take a step off the porch and back into the yard. I started to put my camera case down before I joined him, but he darted forward, snatching it out of my hand before it even touched the ground. "C'mere," he whispered as he jolted his head to the side, beckoning me to follow him down the sidewalk. He seemed impatient. It was clear he wasn't in the mood for an opening greeting such as a simple "hello" or "how are you."

I reshuffled all the equipment in my arms since Gorman knocked me off balance when he took the case. I followed him down the path, "Yeah?"

His tone was hushed. "Just a simple OD [overdose], the guy's upstairs on the toilet with the syringe still in his arm."

"Okay, is he stinky?" I whispered, not knowing quite why.

"Nah, he's pretty fresh. Warm too. I doubt he's been dead

more than an hour or so." Pearson looked back to the house and then down at the equipment in my hands. "You're not taking all that stuff in there with you, are you?"

I looked down at the equipment cradled in my arms: a notebook, clipboard, latex gloves, evidence bags, flashlight, and tape measure, and he had the camera. "Uh, yeah. I need all of it. Why?"

Gormon shook his head. "You need to either stick that shit in your pockets or give some of it to me to hold. Load your camera up out here and put the case back in your van."

"I don't get it." I shoved the tape measure and notebook into my pants pocket and then started to load the camera. "Why are we whispering and why can't I carry this inside?"

"Unless you want roaches the size of dogs to jump into your camera case and start layin' eggs, you'll wanna keep *all your shit* outta that house." He held his thumb and index finger about two inches apart. "I'm tellin' you—those babies are big!"

I hated roaches.

"The dead guy's brother is in there. He's sittin' right next to that window." Gorman pointed to the window behind the front porch. It was partially open and didn't have a screen. I could see the outline of someone sitting there and could hear the television. "Wait till you meet him. I know it'll be love at first sight."

I looked at the old car tires and hubcaps lining the fence. Clearly, a Martha Stewart–inspired design. "Yeah, too bad I'm married. I like a man in touch with his creative side." I loaded the camera.

"You'll love this one." Gorman lit a cigarette and took a long drag. "The dude in the kitchen lives here alone, but his brother comes and goes." I watched the smoke billow out his nostrils. He had a shaved head. He was hot. He puffed again and was in no rush to exhale. "He comes home and sees his brother's car in front of the house, but when he can't find him, he goes upstairs and sees he's dead on the pot." The smoke slowly leaked out his mouth as he spoke. "He does what any concerned brother would do: he walks to the store around the corner to buy a rotisserie chicken and a bag of chips, then hits the liquor store for his suds. He comes home, greases his chops, and then calls nine-one-one. As a matter of fact, he's *still* got the feedbag tied around his neck."

"That reminds me of the suicide I handled last year." Gorman and I started walking toward the house. "The guy finds his wife dead in the bedroom—GSW [gunshot wound] to the chest. Before he calls nine-one-one he orders a pizza, eats, then cuts the grass. I swear!"

"Yeah," Gorman shook his head in disbelief. "This guy had a chicken and chips."

I got as far as the front porch when I saw the first one. It was little, probably a baby. But where there was one roach, there were hundreds of them. Gorman stepped into the foyer first and subtly pointed to three roaches huddled in the corner. I shivered. The kitchen was to the left of the foyer and a flight of stairs that accessed the second floor was straight ahead. Gorman turned to the kitchen and spoke to the unbelievably obese man seated at the table. He was a corn-fed white boy if I ever saw one before. "This is the Crime Lab girl." I hated being referred to like that. It made me want to put my hand on my hip and bop my head back and forth. "She's going to do her part of the investigation and then we'll call for the Medical Examiner. Once she's done, you and I can talk about a funeral home." The double-gutted guy never even looked in our direction. He was busy gnawing on a greasy-looking piece of meat that he held in his bare hands. A burning cigarette and a Budweiser were within arm's reach. His eyes were fixated on the television set located on the kitchen counter and he seemed to be captivated by Pat Sajak as he orchestrated the events on *Wheel of Fortune*.

I stared at the man for a minute and watched as he used his teeth to rip through the gristle on the end of a drumstick. He wasn't interested in saying hello. I turned to go upstairs and made it as far as the first step when a huge roach scurried out in front of me. Not wanting to step on it and hear the dreaded crunch under my boot, I yelped and jumped back, slamming into Gorman. I was breathless. "Oh my God! Did you see that?" When I realized how loud I shrieked, I looked back to the kitchen, not wanting to offend the big man or say anything that would make him lose his appetite. Gorman didn't seem to care. He followed the roach with the beam of his flashlight as it disappeared behind the overflowing kitchen trash can. The pot-bellied man pointed the remote toward the television and turned up the volume. I had a better view of him now. He was so fat that he had to spread his legs apart to let his abdomen blubber hang down. I called this a front butt because when people like that stood up, you couldn't tell which side was the front and which side was the back. They had a butt on each side.

I let Gorman go up first. He made light of the situation by scanning each step with his flashlight and keeping his palm on the butt of his gun, ready to draw it in a second's notice. The steps were absolutely filthy and I knew they had never been vacuumed or swept. Beer cans, mail, dirty dishes, ashtrays, and soiled laundry were only some of the items that cluttered them and I feared the critters that would jump out if I dared move anything. The house smelled like a combination of grease, stale cigarettes, mildew, and sweat. I wondered how Front Butt could even use the steps without falling over all the mess. When I got to the top, the scene was even worse. The dirty laundry was piled knee high and fast-food bags, beer cans, soda bottles, and other garbage cluttered the hallway. A sour smell permeated the air, a smell that was clearly caused by the living and not the dead. "Gross," I mumbled really not caring if Front Butt could hear me. "How can people live like this?"

"He's in here." Gorman rapped his knuckle on a partially closed bathroom door. "Want your camera before I open it?" He had obviously been around for a while. He knew the routine.

I reached for the camera. "Before I even go in the bathroom, let me get a few pictures of the top floor of this place and steps leading up here." I went back down to the foyer only to hear the man slurp his beer and then let out a huge belch that probably jarred some of Earth's tectonic plates. The woman on the television wanted to buy a vowel. I took a quick picture of the stairs from the foyer to show the condition of the house and then ran back to the safety of Gorman. "Did you hear that burp?"

He was laughing. "I wasn't sure which end it came from!"

My smile disappeared. "Well, I assumed it was a burp! We're gonna be in trouble if it wasn't because hot air rises."

He beat me to the punch. "No, we're gonna be in trouble if that wasn't a burp because there's only one bathroom in this place and there's a dead guy on the toilet!"

I took more pictures of the upstairs. Both bedrooms were overflowing with junk, car parts, trash, and dirty laundry. There were no beds and I figured the brothers must have counted sheep in the downstairs living room.

"All right." Gorman was listening to something happening on the radio. "Okay, let's do this." I just wanted to be done with this scene. He turned the radio volume down and walked toward the bathroom. The door was slightly ajar. I took a picture before he pushed it open.

The bathroom appliances were a dirty-looking mustard yellow color and I wondered who thought it made a nice match with the baby blue tile floor. Surely enough, there was a dead man on the toilet—well, sort of. He was sitting on the lid. This was a welcome surprise because I had handled many deaths where the people received their calling in the middle of taking a dump. They didn't even get a chance to flush.

I snapped another picture from the doorway.

The dead guy was dressed in a pair of jeans and what was once a white T-shirt with a bald eagle carrying the Confederate flag in its claws. He was wearing a pair of biker boots and a blue-and-white bandanna was tied around his right bicep, making a tourniquet for the needle that was still imbedded in his forearm. I could tell that he pulled the bandanna from his head because his hair was smashed flat. A lighter and a spoon with some sort of residue were lying on the vanity and a small empty vial was in the sink basin. As I snapped a shot of the vial, a roach popped up from the drain. This only reinforced my drain phobia. I hate drains. I have always hated drains. Growing up, we had silverfish that liked to hang out in the drains in our tub, and I haven't been the same since.

I took more pictures of the bathroom, listening for the high-pitched whine that signaled the flash had recycled and I could take another shot. As I waited, I noticed that the dead guy's head was arched back and was lying on top of the toilet tank. His eyes were open. All my dead people had open eyes. I didn't like it. Once I tried to close them like you see on television. I gently wiped my hand across the dead person's face, but the eyes felt all cold and hard, and their eyelashes tickled my palm. I didn't like the feeling one bit and the person's eyes were still open when I was done. I never tried to close dead eyes again. As I looked at the dead man's face, a roach slithered out of his mouth and scampered across his cheek, across his eyeball, and disappeared into his hair.

The bathroom was tiny and I needed to stand on the tub ledge to capture the overall scene, but a gnarly, mildew-stained shower curtain was in my way. The dead guy didn't seem to mind as I excused myself and brushed up against him while I wrapped my hand in toilet paper. Once I had created a glove about six sheets thick, I felt safe enough to peel back the rancid shower curtain and step on the ledge of the tub for my photos. No sooner had I grabbed the curtain and slid it open than I felt a drip on my head, followed by another and another. Ignoring what I assumed was water leaking from the curtain, I continued to focus the camera and take my shots, but the dripping was getting worse. I heard a scratching sound in the tub beneath me at the same time that Gorman began shrieking from the hallway, "Crime Lab—get the hell outta there!"

I was stunned for a moment—not knowing quite what to think or what to do. Continuing to feel the dripping on my head, I reached up to wipe away the latest drip. When I did, I felt little legs hop onto my forearm and then jump onto my neck and scamper down my shirt. It suddenly became clear that the drips were anything but water—the drips were roaches jumping onto my head. This realization was enough to send me flying off of the tub ledge, screaming! I leaped onto the floor, but tripped on the dead man's foot and fell to the baby blue tile, only to see three roaches knocked to the ground by the force of my impact. "Ahhhhh! Oh my God!" I was screeching! "Gorman, help me!" I frantically shook my head like a dog shaking water from its ears after a bath. "Gorman!" I begged for him to come. "Call nine-one-one." I gasped for breath. "They're eating me!"

Gorman rushed in and helped me to my feet. "Oh my God! " I shook my head. "Shit, fuck, damn!" He swatted the roaches from me with his clipboard and stomped on those that sought refuge on the floor. As he swatted, I pulled my shirt out of my pants and freed the roach that was trapped inside. He beat on me and I begged for more. "Swat 'em, swat 'em!" After a good two minutes of being assaulted, Gorman assured me that I was free of the 'lil bastards. But I was still trembling. "Make sure they didn't lay eggs." He looked, or pretended to look, through my hair and over my clothes for a few seconds and then deemed me safe.

"Oh my God!" I took a breath and tried to compose myself. "Thank you." I itched everywhere and felt like a heroin junkie scratching the bugs that weren't even there. I was hallucinating.

As I scratched, Gorman and I looked into the bathroom and watched dozens of roaches scurry into the walls and drains and disappear beneath the vanity. When most had gone back into hiding, I got my nerve up, tucked my shirt in, and headed back inside. He looked surprised.

I tried to ignore the crunch of the occasional roach that had an encounter with my boot tread. "I'm taking a few measurements, grabbing the CDS [controlled dangerous substances], and then I'm outta here." I handed him my notepad. "I'll call out my measurements, if you'll write 'em down for me." I measured at lightning speed and when I was done, I grabbed the vial, lighter, and spoon and bolted out the bathroom door. I wrapped the spoon in plastic to preserve the small amount of residue that was still present.

Gorman handed me my notepad with the measurements, and we started down the steps. "I'm gonna go out to my car and get an

ETA [estimated time of arrival] from the ME while you finish up."
I followed him down the stairs and into the kitchen. Front Butt
was still in the same spot watching Vanna turn the letters around.

Gorman called to him, but was ignored. "Hey! Excuse me!
Hello."

Front Butt took a slurp of his beer and then shoved a fist full of
chips into his mouth. He had already eaten the chicken as evidenced by the pile of bones in the middle of the table. The bones
we're picked so clean it looked like a vulture had feasted on the
meal.

"Sir, I don't mean to interrupt your show or anything, but
we're about finished." There was still no response. "The Crime
Lab girl just has to take a few more pictures and then we'll be
waiting on the Medical Examiner. You might want to start thinking about which funeral home you'd like to use because I doubt
your brother will be going to the morgue."

Front Butt just stared at the man who was spinning the wheel.
He reached for his cigarette and took a drag. Gorman shrugged
his shoulders and walked out the door, leaving me alone with Mr.
Friendly, who had remarkably turned his attention from the television long enough to grind a roach into the kitchen table with his
index finger. I watched as he scraped up the mess with his fingernail, wiped it into an ashtray, and then set fire to it using his
lighter.

"Oh, Crime Lab," Gorman appeared in the kitchen window
next to the guy. "Those are the brother's keys and jacket on the
counter there." He was talking loudly to annoy Front Butt. It was
working. "We're gonna wanna search that jacket for CDS before
we leave."

I snapped a few more pictures of the first floor of the house.
Between the newspapers, garbage, dirty clothing, and dishes—not
to mention the smell of old beer, sweat, stale cigarettes, and fermenting trash—I was in sensory overload and needed to get the
hell out of there. I didn't want to touch that nasty jacket that was
lying on the filthy counter and I certainly didn't want to put my

camera down. I draped the camera over my shoulder as I snapped on a pair of latex gloves that I found in my pocket and reached for the jacket. Front Butt sighed loudly because I was blocking his view of the tube. I didn't care. The counter was the only uncluttered place to work and it wouldn't be the end of the world if he couldn't see the woman who was loudly shouting, "C'mon! Big money! Big money!" I patted the jacket down first, feeling for anything that might cut or prick me, and then carefully opened the side pockets and fished out the contents.

Then he spoke. At first I thought his stomach was rumbling, or worse—his intestines were rumbling. Unsure of what it was, I tried to be polite and ignore it. I continued to poke through the matches, change, nail clippers, rubber bands, and receipts in the jacket. Then I heard it again. This time I knew it was a voice. "Mooove." I stopped and stood silently for a second, wondering if the man just told me to move. I heard another can of beer crack open, listened to him gulp, and silently counted to three. On cue, he let out a huge belch and then spoke to me once again. "Mooove." His tone was so low that it sounded more like a growl than a human voice. I slowly turned my head, fearing what I might see. I was closer to him than I wanted to be and could see the grease from the chicken glistening on his face and potato chip crumbs dangled from his beard. I couldn't look anymore. I turned back to the safety of the television.

"I'll be done in one second." I tried to sound nice and rushed through the other jacket pocket looking for any additional drugs or paraphernalia. I heard him screech his chair across the floor as he tried to get a view of the television. I'd turn it toward him, but I was afraid of what might crawl out from beneath it. Gorman appeared in the doorway. "No CDs?"

"Nope!" I was relieved. "Okay, I'm done!" I headed toward the door and turned back to offer my condolences. "Sorry about your loss, sir. If you would like us to call a pastor or grief counselor, Officer Gorman would be happy to assist you with that."

"Ahh," he banged his fist on the table. "It's 'Fun in the Sun,' you idiot. There ain't no *R* in 'Fun in the Sun.'" He was obviously talking to the television and not to me.

Gorman walked me to my van, whistling the "I'm a Wheel Watcher" theme song from *Wheel of Fortune*—we couldn't help but laugh when we heard the kitchen window slam shut.

Family members weren't the only ones who were annoyed when death interfered with their plans. The neighbors could be just as guilty.

"What do you mean I can't park in my spot?" The woman was irate. She had driven right up to the crime scene tape and wanted me to lift it while she drove through the scene and to her space.

"Ma'am!" I couldn't believe I was having this conversation with her. "Ma'am!" I was shouting at her. "You are going to have to park elsewhere tonight, okay?"

She was pacing back and forth, waving her keys at me, and ranting about how she pays for *that* spot and how the apartment complex rules state that you are only allowed to park in your assigned spaces.

"Ma'am," I was yelling over the drone of the chopper flying above me. "Look behind me!" I pointed to a car in the middle of the lot. "There is a dead guy in that car." I looked over at another officer who was laughing at my unsuccessful attempts to reason with this woman. "I think that if you tell the complex that there was a dead guy blocking the way to your parking spot, they'll understand." I walked away from her as she continued to yell. *Unbelievable!*

I didn't have the time or the energy to deal with her. I was still shaken up from the events that had unfolded in the past fifteen minutes and it wasn't Crime Lab's job to deal with freaks of nature in need of a parking space. Only minutes before I had been on another shooting scene around the corner. A bunch of guys had been rolling dice in the parking lot when some badass pulled up on them and fired a few shots. Nobody was hit, but I agreed to go out anyway to take some photographs and collect the cartridge casings. Normally, someone had to be injured for Crime Lab to respond, but I wasn't on a call and I liked the officer who had requested me. He had done me favors in the past and it was time to reciprocate.

While Officer Whispel sat in his car doing paperwork, I made a quick sketch of the scene and snapped a few pictures. I could tell that the car was moving as the shooter fired his weapon from the way the casings were distributed throughout the lot. Just as I started taking measurements, I heard a loud pop, pop, pop, pop, pop, a pause, and then three more pops coming from the other side of a row of bushes that bordered the edge of the parking lot. I spun around, facing the bushes, fearing that the shooter was going to burst through them and meet me face to face. It was nights like this that made me thankful I was wearing my Kevlar vest. I stood there, frozen, unable to move. When I finally garnered the courage, I ran to Whispel. He had not heard the shots over the country music, the chatter on the police radio, and the woosh of the air conditioner.

"Did you hear that?" I was out of breath and talking a mile a minute. "Those shots. Did you hear those shots?"

"Shots?" He turned off the radio and the air conditioner and turned down the volume on his radio. He stared intently at me as he strained to listen.

"There were like eight of them—coming from right there." I pointed to the bushes. "I think it was like five of them, then a pause, then three more." Whispel got out of his car and drew his weapon. I watched helplessly. "Don't go in there alone." I felt like a mother and worried that he'd disappear into the bushes. He keyed up his radio. "Thirteen thirty-six. Dispatch, did you get any calls for shots fired coming from my location?"

"Thirteen thirty-six, standby. They're rolling in now."

I grabbed a bag and scooped up all the casings from the ground. I threw them all into the same bag and didn't even bother to take measurements. Ordinarily, we would record the precise location of each one and package them separately. I was sure my supervisors would understand.

The dispatcher sounded the tones to get everyone's attention. "Thirteen thirty-three, thirteen thirty-four, thirteen thirty-five, thirteen thirty-seven, and any other unit that can start up, respond to the area of Sutherland Place, cross streets of Worthington and Sumner, for a shooting. Caller advises at least one individual has been shot." I could hear her typing. "Nine-one-one has received several calls." Whispel ran back to his car.

"Thirteen thirty-six. I'm seventy-six [en route]."

I tore out of the lot behind him. I knew I'd be requested on that scene, so I just pulled into the 7-11 around the corner and listened to the events as they unfolded. About thirty seconds later, several of the units arrived on the scene. There was all kinds of chatter about blocking off the road, detaining witnesses, checking to see if air was up, and then the words I was waiting to hear. "Dispatch, start Crime Lab and Homicide."

I arrived at the scene within seconds. It was sheer chaos. Normally, Crime Lab responds when a sense of order has been restored, but this scene was still hot. For all I knew, the shooter was among the bystanders. "Dana," one of the officers called. "Do you have any crime scene tape?" I grabbed a roll and roped off the car in the middle of the lot. The driver's front door and hood were open. The engine was running, the headlights were on, and a dead guy sat seatbelted in the front passenger's seat, but the driver was missing. I noticed several cartridge casings on the ground outside the driver's door. Another officer used orange traffic cones to mark their location.

The woman was still ranting about her parking space. "Listen," she was calling to me again. "All I need you to do is just untie that tape for one second and let me drive through. Then that's the last you'll see or hear of me. Okay?"

One of officers on the scene decided to take care of her for me. "Listen," he pointed his finger at her and his voice was stern. "You need to move your car out of the middle of the roadway." She was trying to tell him about the assigned parking, but he wouldn't let her get a word in edgewise. "Ma'am, if you haven't noticed, this is a crime scene and this road is gonna be blocked off *all night*. We have emergency equipment that needs to get through here, so if you don't move your car, we're gonna have it towed. Understand?"

She clearly wasn't happy. "Well, can you tell me where I *can* park?"

The apartment complex contained two groups of buildings, each of which were accessed by separate roads. The officer pointed down the hill to the other group of buildings. "Why don't you park down there and then walk up the path to your apartment. That's the closest you're gonna get. Okay? Go!"

The officer walked away. "Can you believe this shit?" She wasn't talking to anyone in particular. "There's a murder right in the middle of my building, and the damn cop wants me to park down the street and then walk up the dark path all by myself." I looked around. There must have been fifty cops on the scene, plus the medics, hoards of bystanders, and a chopper was lighting up the scene like the Fourth of July. This apartment complex was ironically about the safest place to be right now. I ignored her and she disappeared into the night.

I took a few pictures of the scene and hurried to mark the cartridge casings with evidence numbers. I was worried they would get kicked or even worse, crushed by all the foot traffic. The police had finally started to get a handle on the scene and had moved the gawkers back so they didn't have such a direct view of the bloody body inside the car. I started taking notes and listened to the radio as everyone else looked for the driver of the vehicle. I was sure he had also been shot because I found blood spattered on the ground and on the side of the car. The chopper swept the area with its spotlight, looking for the missing victim from above, while K-9 and other officers searched on foot.

Just when I forgot about her, she was back.

"Um, hello—excuse me." I tried to ignore her. "Hello there, I need to talk to you." I pretended I couldn't hear her. It worked because she found someone else to bother. "Excuse me, officer, I have to tell you something."

An officer who had just arrived on the scene walked over to her, apparently not realizing what a pain in the ass she had been a few minutes before. "Okay, there was another policeman here about ten minutes ago and he told me to park down there," she pointed to the lower complex. "I live right over there, but he said I couldn't park in my regular spot." *Uh—here we go again.* I looked up to see the officer trying to follow her story. "Okay, well, I drove down there where he told me to park. I told him that I didn't like the idea about having to walk back up here by myself because of everything that's going on and I didn't want to risk my safety. I got kids you know and I'm all they have. If something happens to me, well, then—"

The officer tried to cut her off. "Ma'am, go back down there and park your car, and I'll see that someone walks you back up to your apartment."

"No, wait!" I wanted to punch her in the mouth but she looked like she'd give me tetanus. "I did what the other officer told me because he said he was gonna tow my car. Anyway, I drove down there and pulled into the parking spot, but there was a man in the bushes and I got scared. Can someone go down there and see what he's doing?"

The officer was perplexed. "What do you mean there was a man in the bushes."

She seemed honestly scared. "I pulled into the spot head on, and as I pulled in, my headlights shined right on him. He was just layin' there. He was up to something. Maybe it's the man who did the shooting, or a pervert or something. Can someone just run down there and check it out before he leaves?"

The officer broadcast the information on the radio and a few minutes later I was asked to respond to the second location. The body of the driver had been located—no thanks to the chopper, the dogs, or the officers, but to the pesty woman who only wanted to park her car.

I was so quick to criticize others who were inconvenienced by the death of another person, but I soon found myself guilty of the very same crime. It made me feel selfish and horrible, kind of like the way I feel when I get caught up in accident traffic and am running late for a hair appointment. One family's life is thrown into turmoil and all I care about is getting my roots touched up.

I still remember the first time I had this feeling. I hadn't even been on the job a year and got dispatched to the murder of a young man. He was dealing crack on someone else's turf and paid the ultimate price for it. Bob and I were scheduled to make a trip to Connecticut when I got off work so we could pay his family a New Year's holiday visit. We were unable to make it during Christmas since I couldn't get time off; I was the low man on the totem pole and got last pick of vacation. Unfortunately, murders involve overtime, a lot of it, and I was livid when I found myself in another jurisdiction, sitting in a Homicide detectives' car, waiting for the SWAT team to clear a suspect's apartment so we could execute a search warrant. Bob and I should have been on the road six hours before. I didn't care about the search warrant, and I didn't care about the dead guy—I just cared about my plans being ruined.

I should have seen the writing on the wall from the time I accepted the position in the Crime Lab. The training academy was scheduled to start the week I was supposed to travel to Seattle for an American Academy of Forensic Sciences conference. I had to cancel my trip at the last minute. Overtime, court, and scheduling issues would cause me to miss countless bridal and baby showers, retirement and anniversary celebrations, weddings, birthday parties, doctor's appointments, hair appointments, lunch dates, family dinners, and even the cookout that I was hosting. But I got used to it. I had to. Only once did I put my foot down. I flat-out refused to work one Sunday, which was my day off. I had already worked seven hours of overtime that week and had to attend the baptism of my goddaughter. I got written up.

There were also times when the inconveniences were worth it

in the end. I learned this on the robbery of a FedEx warehouse. The suspect in the case obviously had knowledge of the location because he entered through a set of bay doors (not the main entrance) and went straight to the office that contained the delivery money at the precise time it was being counted. It was no coincidence either that an exterior security camera was covered with a towel.

The victim of the robbery stated that the robber was wearing gloves and a ski mask and that he really didn't touch anything other than the office door and a metal bookshelf. There wasn't a lot that I could do, but since there was the possibility that the victim was lying and she had something to do with the crime, I dusted the office for fingerprints anyway.

I cleared the scene shortly thereafter (hitting a police car in the process) and headed back to headquarters since it was quitting time. No sooner had I pulled into the Crime Lab parking lot than the officer assigned to the call raised me on the radio. He needed me back at the FedEx warehouse because additional evidence had been located. I was pissed. I was supposed to swing by a friend's Christmas party when I got off work.

Annoyed that I would be on overtime, I turned around and made the half-hour trek back to the crime scene. When I arrived, I learned that one of the K-9 dogs picked up a scent trail that took him behind the FedEx warehouse and to the edge of the dark parking lot. This was where the K-9 officer noticed a towel draped over the first of a set of two chain-linked fences that separated the rear lot from the interstate. The towel was positioned directly above a hole cut in the links of the innermost fence. Further examination revealed a similar hole in the fence behind it. The view of this area was partially obscured by a delivery truck trailer.

The picture was coming together. It appeared that after committing the robbery, the suspect ran through the dark parking lot to the rear of the warehouse. He knew he didn't have to worry about being captured on camera, and because it would have been difficult to see where the holes in the fences were under the cover of darkness, he ran for the light-colored towel that he had previously placed there. He scampered through the holes in the fences and escaped in a getaway vehicle that was waiting on the shoulder of the interstate highway.

Hoping to still get my hands on some eggnog, I quickly photographed the area, including the trampled vegetation leading toward the interstate as well as the unoxidized and recently cut links in the fence. I snatched the towel and put it in an evidence bag, but hesitated before I drove off.

I didn't want to deal with the hassle of taking evidence from the fences. The more stuff I collected, the longer I'd be on overtime. But my conscience got the best of me and I soon found myself in knee-high weeds snipping samples of the portion of the fences cut by the bad guy. I did this in the unlikely event detectives developed a suspect and wanted to match the tool impressions on the fencing with a particular tool in his possession. I made sure the ends I cut were clearly distinguished from the ends the suspect cut, then packaged my evidence and quickly left work. I got to my friend's just as the party was winding down.

About a year later, I was surprised to get a phone call from one of the assistant state's attorneys wanting to arrange a meeting with me to discuss my role in the FedEx investigation before the case went to trial. I didn't even know an arrest had been made and had long since filed this case into the recesses of my mind. I told the attorney that I just collected a few lousy prints, snapped some pictures, and took a towel. She seemed surprised that I didn't know the rest of the story. "Dana, your decision to take samples of that fence is one of our best pieces of evidence. It links the suspect with the scene." She went on to tell me that on the night of the robbery, another jurisdiction made a routine traffic stop and became suspicious about a mask, gloves, and bolt cutters lying on the backseat of the car. Believing these items could be related to the FedEx robbery, the vehicle was towed into the Crime Lab, where one of my coworkers processed it and collected, among other things, the bolt cutters. Our agency's firearms and toolmark examiner subsequently took the pieces of fencing I collected and compared them to test impressions made with the bolt cutters. He identified them, to the exclusion of any other tool, as having been the implement used to cut the fence. Unlike *CSI*, where all the investigators know details of one another's calls, our Crime Lab was so busy that we didn't have time to follow up on cases and we were usually unaware of the roles each other played in any given investigation.

Over the next few years, I thought about this case a lot, especially when I was feeling tired, lazy, or both. I had to accept the fact that being inconvenienced was part of my job and that being lazy wasn't. It is kind of funny that as I think back, I remember every last detail of the FedEx robbery and virtually nothing about the Christmas party that I was so hell-bent on attending. I received my fair share of inconveniences on the job, but cases like the FedEx robbery made it all worth it—that is, as long as I wasn't forced to miss *Wheel of Fortune*.

CHAPTER 7

Splinters in the Windmills of Their Minds . . .

My mother always said that the pot shouldn't call the kettle black, so before I tell you about some of the nuts that I met at work, let me first say that I, too, have a couple of bats in my belfry. I'm sure they have been flying around in there for years. But as long as I'm not living out where the bus doesn't run anymore, I think I'll be all right.

In my defense, I had virtually *no* chance of growing up normal. The same is true for my brother Chris. It all started when we were small children and Mom told us that she was a little teapot and made us watch as she tipped herself over and pretended to pour the tea out. We watched with curiosity as she washed the leaves of her plants with the milk from the fridge, claiming it made them shiny, and sprayed shellac on bagels that eventually made their way into a rather bizarre centerpiece for the kitchen table. She told us tales of wolves that would blow down houses knowing there were three little piggies inside and of a brother and sister who were abandoned in the woods and lost their breadcrumb trail only to meet a witch in a gingerbread house who planned to boil the boy and bake the girl.

When my brother and I were kids, we were introduced to my

mother's "Ways of the Family." This was a seemingly endless list of peculiar rituals and odd interpretations of daily events that other kids our age didn't have to go through. I'd like to think that most of these oddities stemmed from Mom's Sicilian heritage and had something to do with Old World superstition.

On the first day of each month, before noon, Mom made sure we yanked out one of our head hairs and threw it over our left shoulder while saying, "rabbit, rabbit, rabbit." Then we hit someone; no one in particular—just someone close by. Confused but still feeling compelled to pluck and hit, I calculate I have lost about 438 hairs to date. Bob even plucks before noon now. We also said "rabbit, rabbit, rabbit" as we threw spilled salt over our left shoulder. A dropped comb required us to step on it with our left foot and count to three or Mom said we would be disappointed. She didn't elaborate on the reason for our disappointment, but I figured it had something to do with being bald by thirty caused by years of monthly hair plucking. A dropped fork meant a woman was coming to visit and a dropped knife meant a man was on his way. There was no time frame from the moment of the drop to the moment of the visit, but even the Jehovah's Witnesses knocking on the door to hand out free copies of the *Watchtower* counted as visitors. I asked Mom how they could count as visitors when they really didn't come to visit. The logic in her answer was about as rational as putting onions in our socks when we had fevers, "Because I said so."

If Mom dropped a comb, fork, or knife, my dad would live. If she dropped a pair of scissors, he'd be a dead man before sunset because that meant he was putting his fire boots under some other woman's bed. Chris and I knew better than to shake out a tablecloth, otherwise we'd shake away the good luck that came his way when he spit on his new baseball bat or my way when I found a cricket in the house. Lots of things brought bad luck though, and I still never consider opening an umbrella indoors, wearing opals since I don't have an October birthday, mending a garment while still wearing it, hanging clothing on a door knob, putting on a shirt inside out, placing a hat on the bed, or storing bread upside down, and if I smoked I would never light three cigarettes from the same match. Chris and I kissed countless loaves of moldy bread before throwing them away, gagged down pickled herring on New Year's Eve, made sure Dad was the first to enter the house on New Year's Day, and tried not to go anywhere without a penny in our shoe. When an eyelash fell out, we'd put it on the back of our hand before making a wish and blowing it away, and we didn't want to sing before breakfast unless we wanted to cry before dinner.

We never could tell Mom when we bit our tongue, no matter how badly it hurt because she'd say it was because we were getting ready to tell a lie—even if we weren't about to lie. If she thought we were lying, or lying about not getting ready to tell a lie, she'd make us look her in the eye. She'd stare long and hard, and claimed to be able to see the truth inside. That scared us as much as Jesus putting black marks on our souls.

When her friends moved, my mother made sure they left their old brooms behind and bought them a new one and a box of salt to sweep away the evil. We always had to dismiss personal compliments unless we wanted to get a headache, and we weren't allowed to put our shoes on the table or our feet would burn. When we put our shoes away, they could never be on a shelf that was higher than our head and if my dress hem was flipped up, I had to bend over and spit on it before fixing it. That didn't go over well in church.

It got crazier: we *always* had to leave a room through the door from which we entered it—otherwise we broke the fundamental rule of "crossing the house"—and I guess we *always* had to get out of the same side of the bed each day so we didn't break another rule that was probably called something like "crossing the bed." We had an upside down horseshoe wrapped in red ribbon over the front door to ward off any hexes and Saint Christopher medals tied with red ribbons on top of each of the doorframes to protect us from bad spirits. Just in case something evil did get in the room, we had the palm from Palm Sunday under our mattresses—that is, *all* of the palms we received throughout our entire life. If a princess can detect a pea beneath her mattress, I must be a pauper because I have thirty-six years of palms under mine and I sleep like a corpse.

I came to realize that not all kids my age knew that itching hands meant money, ringing ears meant someone is talking about you, and heartburn during pregnancy promises a baby with a lot of hair. In high school, I'd go nuts closing all the open umbrellas, plucking hairs, stepping on combs, and insisting the cafeteria lady turn the loaf of bread right side up. Most people thought I was a little "off."

I still do most of these rituals, but let me tell you—the one about entering a room and leaving it through the same door is a pain in the ass—especially on crime scenes! I have made some modifications to that rule and nothing too bad has happened to me. Now, if I walk into the front door of a friend's house and see that people are congregating on the back patio on the other side of the sliding glass door, I no longer walk back out the front door and around the house. I'm proud I have overcome that small obstacle.

So, I might not always have both oars in the water, but at least I can blame it on my mother and all her square pizza-making bookie relatives who filled her head with all of that ridiculous nonsense. But in the Crime Lab, I met a met a bunch of people who had their headlights on dim; some were chance encounters, some were victims, some were officers, and some were dead (their lights were really dim). I'd love to hear *their* excuses.

I had one of my close encounters of the odd kind on a cold, rainy winter's night. It had been a pretty slow shift for Crime Lab and I hoped that the bad guys would stay in until it was time for me to go home. It wasn't a good night for crime, but if one had to be committed, I prayed it would be indoors. I had just gassed up my van and was heading to 7-11 to get a coffee.

The streets were unusually quiet for a Saturday night. I was only two blocks away from a university campus and it was normal to see flambasted students staggering back to the dorms after a late night of off-campus parties. At this time of the night, the air was usually thumping with bass coming from the Dodge Neons that the college kids had outfitted with 500-watt Kenwood systems complete with subwoofers and enough speakers to create surround sound. But no one was out this bitter cold, wet, and windy night. Well, almost no one.

As I drove down the dark road, I was startled to see a man and woman walking down the yellow centerline. I assumed they were sloshed students who didn't happen to notice the cement sidewalk paralleling both sides of the road. It was raining, the street was icy, and they were wearing dark clothing—a sure recipe for disaster. The man was loaded up like a packhorse. He had bags, backpacks, and totes hanging from his neck, shoulders, and arms and was pulling two full-sized suitcases behind him. The woman's arms were empty. I slowed down as I passed, looking at them. They stared back at me and continued their trek down the centerline.

What the hell? That was becoming my most frequently used line at work. I made a U-turn and headed back toward them. Not being armed, I knew that I shouldn't stop, but I didn't want to get dispatched to two flattened people with suitcases on the yellow centerline of the road later in the night. I wouldn't mind it so much on a warm summer night, but not in the freezing ice and rain. Besides, I just had to know what they were up to.

I found them still marching, single file, down the middle of the road. The woman took the lead position and walked quickly while the packhorse struggled to keep up, stopping every few paces to reposition bags and pick up the toppled suitcases. They didn't look homeless, like students, or even burglars making off with hoards of valuables—they just looked out of place. They looked crazy! There were no hotels, bus terminals, or train stations anywhere nearby, which would have explained where they might have come from or been heading to. This was the road to nowhere. It just didn't make sense.

I pulled up alongside them and hit my flashers. "What's up?" They just glared at me, menacingly. For a second, I had the "oh shit" feeling as I thought perhaps I really might have rolled up on something criminal. But they didn't seem to fit the part. Crooks tended to be a bit less conspicuous. But then again, there were plenty of criminals who were so dumb they wouldn't take a leak if their pants were on fire.

"Did you break down?" The woman just stood there looking at me while the man took advantage of the opportunity to readjust the bags hanging from his shoulders. "Hello?" She didn't flinch. "You can't be walking down the middle of the road. You're gonna get hit. You need to take your parade over to the sidewalk."

The woman stared at me for a few more seconds before saluting and then called to the man, "Jimmy, it's all right. She's the police." I thought about explaining that I was Crime Lab, and a scab at that, but it was best to just let the comment go. The woman and Jimmy moved from the middle of the road to the sidewalk. Jimmy struggled to get the suitcases over the curb and I watched, trying not to laugh, as the totes and bags he had just so carefully repositioned fell from his shoulder. This caused him to stumble and knock both suitcases into a puddle of water. The woman stood at his side, watching, but not offering a hand.

I moved my van alongside them. "Is everything okay? It's a cold night to be pulling suitcases down the road."

The woman looked back and forth and over her shoulders before approaching my van. She appeared to be in her mid-fifties and was certainly no oil painting. Once she was up close to the window, she looked around inside to see who else might be with me. I got the impression she was afraid of someone. She was shivering. When she was convinced I was alone, she whispered, "We're headin' to York."

I wasn't sure what to make of it. I turned up the heat and pointed the blower toward her. "York, Pennsylvania?"

She cut me off. "Shhh!" I agitated her and she jumped away from the van and looked around again to make sure nobody heard me. "No!" she whispered. She stuck her head inside so her face was about six inches from mine. She spoke so softly that I could barely hear her. "We're heading up to New York. We're going into . . ." she paused and looked around again before whispering in my ear, "witness protection." It was pretty obvious that her belt didn't go through all the loops.

"Oh, okay." I looked at Jimmy who was now busy inspecting yellow dinner plates to make sure they hadn't broken during one of the suitcase toppling episodes. "Well, you need to stay out of the road." She saluted again. "Where are you walking to right now? Are you meeting someone?" I was sure to keep my voice down.

"No," she looked at me like *I* was the imbecile in the group. "I just told you. We're going to New York."

It really wasn't any of my business, but I asked anyway. "Well, how are you getting there?"

"We're walking. I figured if we left in the middle of the night, we'd beat all the traffic." She was as serious as a heart attack and it took everything I had not to burst out in laughter.

"Oh yeah," I nodded. "I hear that foot traffic to New York can be bad, especially during the week, so it's a good thing you're going on the weekend."

"See," she yelled toward Jimmy. "Even the police lady says the traffic is bad in the daytime." He was busy loading himself up with all the bags again.

"But don't you think it's a little cold to be walking to New York tonight?" I didn't want them to wind up in the middle of nowhere and freeze to death. That was a very real possibility given the weather forecast.

The woman rubbed her face with her hands. Her teeth were chattering and she was soaking wet from the rain. "It's a little nippy, but we ain't got far to go."

"Not far?" She really was out to lunch. "Ma'am, if you drove to New York from here, it would take you two and a half hours, assuming there was no traffic." She just stared at me again. Her wheel was spinning but the hamster was clearly dead. "Seriously, if you're going to New York, you need to catch a ride. Besides, do you know that you're not allowed to walk up the shoulder of the Interstate pulling suitcases behind you?"

The woman pointed her finger at me. "Didn't they tell you in the police academy that pedestrians have the right of way? I know my rights."

I changed the subject. "Ma'am, if you tell me where you came from, I'll see that you get a ride back there, okay? Maybe you can make arrangements for someone to drive you in the morning."

Her face lit up. "Okay!" She turned to Jimmy, "Get in, boy. She's givin' us a lift."

Jimmy looked thrilled at the prospect of not having to carry all their crap for a second longer and ran toward the sliding door on the side of the van. He opened the door and threw the luggage in as the woman climbed in the front passenger's seat. Before I could get a word in, I had two nitwits in the van with me; one in the front and one sprawled across the floor in the back behind the cage. I swore I'd never drive around with the doors unlocked again.

"Wait! Wait a minute!" They ignored me. "I'm not taking anyone anywhere!"

I was at a loss for words but the woman certainly wasn't. She broke out into Frank Sinatra's "New York, New York." I interrupted her in the middle of the "These little town blues" verse. "Ma'am, we are not going to New York and you and Jimmy need to get out of my van!"

"That's okay, as far as you can take us will be fine." She was like one of those telemarketers who just won't take no for an answer and won't let you hang up without scheduling an appointment for a free gutter guard estimate. "I'd like to listen to the radio please."

"Ma'am, where did you come from?" I thought maybe they escaped from the funny farm that was less than a mile away. "I'll see that you get back to wherever you came from, but I cannot drive you because I don't have a seat for Jimmy and that is against the law." I had no clue if it was against the law or not, but it sounded good. "So, where did you come from?"

She just looked out the window. She wasn't going to tell me where they came from.

"I'll drive you to a gas station that is about three-quarters of a mile away and that is it. You can call for someone to come get you or I can call, but either way, that's where I'm dropping you off, okay?" I started toward the gas station.

"And we're off!" She cheered and clapped. "Hang on, Jimmy, we're takin' a ride." *Oh my God*, I thought to myself. *How do I get myself into so many messes?*

I tried to change the subject. "So, Jimmy is your son?"

"Yeah, he's my son. He is a stupid boy and entirely deaf." She turned to look at him and then turned back around. "Jimmy, you're deaf, right? Tell the lady how you ain't never heard a sound."

Jimmy sat up. "I ain't never heard a sound." I wished I had a tape recorder because my friends at the Lab were never going to believe this one.

I just had to ask, "And why are you going to New York? What is there?"

"That's what I've wanted to tell you!" She was whispering again. "It isn't what *is* in New York, it's what *isn't* in New York."

"Okay," I whispered too. "So, what *isn't* in New York?"

She leaned close and, in a low voice, said slowly to enunciate every syllable, "Ruthann Aron."

"Ruthann Aron?" I just looked at her. "What does Ruthann Aron have anything to do with you going to New York?"

Ruthann Aron was a U.S. Senate candidate and real estate developer, who in 1997 was charged with conspiring to kill her husband and a lawyer who had hurt her political career. She was sentenced to three years in prison. It was big local news.

"Ruthann Aron has been following us around and we need to get to New York to get away from her." She pressed her face up against the window and cupped her hands around her eyes as if she were looking for someone or something in particular. She looked back toward me. "She has the feds after us now too, so Jimmy and I have to be careful. We've been on the run for years."

We were at the gas station in less than a minute. I put the van in park and cranked the heat. "So, how can Ruthann Aron be after you when she has been locked up for over a year now?"

"No!" That got her all riled up. "No! She didn't serve one

damn day! They got a body double in there pretending it's her, and she's on the loose lookin' for us two." She looked out the window again. "It's another government conspiracy. Just like the JFK assassination and the moon landing."

I didn't want to know why Ruthann Aron would spend so much energy chasing the woman and Jimmy, the boy who never heard a sound. She told me anyway. "She knows that I know about the chili."

"The chili?"

She rolled her eyes. "Don't tell me you don't know about the chili."

I really hadn't followed the case very carefully. I thought I remembered something about her trying to poison her husband's chili. When that didn't work, she hired a hit man. But nothing ever became of poisoning allegations—or at least as far as I knew.

The woman grabbed my arm and whispered, "I know the truth about the chili, and she knows I know. That's why we have to go into witness protection. She wants to silence me."

Just then a female officer keyed up on the radio and called out on a traffic stop. The woman went berserk. "Jimmy," she was screaming. "Jimmy, get out—it's her!" Jimmy, who never heard a sound, obeyed his mother. He scrambled about the back of the van where he had just made himself comfortable and started grabbing the luggage containing all their worldly possessions. "Jimmy, it's her. I'd know that voice anywhere! It's Ruthann!" She was panic-stricken and jumped out of the van and, for the first time, grabbed some of the bags from Jimmy. They started running down the street.

"No," I yelled out the window, "New York is the other way!"

"The other way, Jimmy, the other way!" They both did an about-face and ran in front of my truck, in the opposite direction. I split open with laughter. After I was able to catch my breath, I raised dispatch and told her she might want to draw up a "check on a subject" call. An officer responded a few minutes later and I sat across the street and watched as he interviewed the odd couple. Shortly thereafter, the officer drove away. I snickered as Jimmy, the boy who never heard a sound, loaded down with bags, and slipping on the icy sidewalk, tried to keep pace with his mother as he pulled the rain-soaked suitcases filled with yellow dishes north toward New York. His mother was a fruit loop—but poor Jimmy, if he were any dumber, he'd have to be watered.

Jimmy and I could hold our mothers at least partially responsible for our ships sailing off course. And I encountered plenty of other people with seriously crossed wires who I am sure wished that they, too, had a scapegoat. Frodo was one of them.

I arrived on his street late at night and was immediately set off when I discovered that none of the row houses had their front porch lights on, making it impossible to read the house numbers—that is, assuming the houses still had numbers. It was one of *those* kinds of neighborhoods. I drove back and forth a few times, but couldn't as much as figure out if I was on the right block.

"Twenty-two fifteen. Dispatch, can you have the precinct call the complainant from my burglary and have them turn on their front porch light?" I had been busy all night and the officer was long gone, meaning I couldn't even look for a police car to help me find the call. I still didn't understand why people didn't turn on their lights. It pissed me off to no end!

A few minutes later the precinct raised me on the radio. "Twenty-two fifteen, the complainant advises the porch light has been burned out for over a year and he keeps forgetting to buy bulbs." I could tell they were holding back laughter.

What? I knew I was going to be in for a treat. I parked the van and walked down the pitch-dark sidewalk swinging my print kit at my side as I tried to find the address. I hated shining my flashlight at people's houses in the middle of the night. I was going to get shot one of these days.

Eventually, I figured out where I was going and as I walked up the front path, a chubby little guy with a mop of curly hair that fell into ringlets around his face charged out the front storm door and stopped on the top porch step. Despite the fact that I was only about twenty-five feet away from him and walking up *his* path *toward* him, he witlessly waved his arms over his head like he was directing an airplane into the gate and called through a cardboard paper towel roll, "Crime Lab person! Come this way! Here I am! Come this way!"

Not another one! I shined my flashlight toward him as I approached, making sure all this crackerjack had in his hands was a paper towel roll. That's when I saw them: big, ugly, hairy feet that seemed to be a mismatch for his little body. It was Frodo from *Lord of the Rings*! Now he was directing traffic. As I climbed the three front steps, Frodo stepped out of my way and waved me on with one arm while stopping imaginary vehicles with the other. I made it through the intersection safely and stood next to him as he ignored me and continued to direct, whistle, and curse at the occasional vehicle that didn't follow his instructions.

When I finally got his attention, Frodo bounced up and down and clapped his hands. "I'm so, so, so happy you're here!" He put the paper towel roll up to his mouth and yelled off the porch, "I'm so happy! Happy, happy, happy!" I coaxed him inside before he woke the neighbors, although I had a sneaking suspicion that they were used to these little outbursts.

Frodo opened the door and bowed, inviting me to enter first. The living room was filthy but under the light I could get a better look at his feet. I've never particularly cared for feet, but these things were just ghastly. They looked like they should be attached to the ankles of Sasquatch or some other kind of forest beast that is extinct for good reason. He needed to be in the circus. He needed the name of a good groomer. Even a bad groomer would do.

"So," I had to try hard not to call him Frodo. "Do you know where the bad guys got in?"

"Through the kitchen door." He lunged like a fencer toward what I assumed was the kitchen and pointed with his paper tower roll, pretending it was a sword. "Thataway." I watched as he proceeded to pull his T-shirt over his head. "The policeman said you would fingerprint me." He threw his arms up in the air and his head back. "This won't hurt much, right?" I saw that his stomach and back were also covered with a thick black shag carpet.

"Huh?" My eyes went from the torso shag to the hobbit feet. I had to look away. "Put your shirt back on. I'm not fingerprinting you. I'm here to fingerprint your house."

Frodo threw his shag down on the couch and buried his face in his hands. "But what if I was touched? Can't you get fingerprints off of me?"

He was obviously a few feathers short of a whole duck. I didn't want to go into all the specifics of recovering latents from human skin, but the chances of it working on his hairy body hours after the crime were zero . . . less than zero. Living skin sweats, it secretes oils, and it absorbs latent residues. However, it *is* possible to get a suspect's prints from a homicide victim's skin hours and sometimes days after the crime. This was something that I had been interested in for quite some time and even tried my hand at it on a few cases—but I never had any luck. The most common technique involves supergluing the body and then dusting it with magnetic powder. When heated, superglue (also known as cyanoacrylate) vapors create a polymer with latent residues; particularly the amino acids in fingerprints. Evidence is placed in a chamber with several drops of cyanoacrylate and the resulting latent is not only developed, but affixed to the target surface. Powders, dye stains, and other methods of enhancement can be subsequently applied.

"No, I can't get fingerprints off of you." Frodo sat up and pulled his shirt on, inside out. "Your shirt's on the wrong way." He just looked at me. "That's bad luck— haven't you had enough bad luck today?" He fixed it and then sat down on his sofa and propped one of his big feet on the opposite knee and stroked the hairs. It was foul. "Okay, can you help me out here?"

Frodo jumped up and bowed. "Your wish is my command." *Oh my God, get me out of here!* "So they came in through the kitchen door and then what?"

Frodo rubbed his two hands together. "Let me give you a

briefing." I pretended to listen intently. If he didn't cut to the chase, he was going to get some PR powder and that was going to be that. "I was sitting here on the sofa just like this." He sat back down and showed me the exact position he had been in. "Then I heard a rap rap rap on the kitchen door." He cupped his hand around his ear and leaned toward the kitchen pretending to listen. "And I thought, 'Now who could that be rapping on my door?'" He placed his finger on his chin and acted like he was thinking.

"Sir!" I had to compose myself or I was going to pop him in the nose. "Sir, can you just give me the facts?"

He jumped up from the sofa again and started shaking his fists in the air. "Another *Dragnet* fan!" He grabbed the paper towel roll and yelled upstairs, "Veronica, she's a *Dragnet* fan! Hear that, Veronica! She wants just the facts!" Then he turned to me and put his finger over his lips. "Shhhhh," he whispered. "Veronica is sleeping."

"Okay, so someone knocked on your door, then you went to the door, and it was . . ." I waited for him to finish the sentence. "It was . . ."

His face lit up. "Okay, we're gonna play *Dragnet* and I can be the witness and you can be Joe Friday, right?" He was talking a mile a minute. I glared at him. "Okay, okay. It was Bill."

Now we were getting somewhere. "And then?"

Frodo started pacing, really playing the part. "Well, Detective Friday, do you mind if I smoke?" The look I gave him told him to get on with the story. "Bill said he heard that I had a nice TV and wanted to know if he could come in and watch it." I glanced over at the twenty-year-old set with aluminum foil bunny ears hanging from the antenna. "I invited Bill inside and we watched TV."

Frodo called upstairs through the paper towel roll again. "Veronica! You're missing it! You can play, too." He turned to me and whispered, "We should keep it down. She's sleeping."

"Okay, has Bill ever been in the house before and how did he take your things without you knowing?" If Bill had been in the house before with permission, particularly in rooms where items were reported missing, then his fingerprints could easily be explained away. "Can you sit down? Please."

He moved around too much and it was making me dizzy. He sat on the sofa. "Bill has never been here before and he didn't take my things."

"Well, then wwwhhhooo did?" I was raising my voice, and I didn't give a rat's ass if I woke Veronica. "God! Uhh! Do you understand my question?"

Frodo leaned forward on the sofa. "Now, Detective Friday, have you forgotten why you're here? Isn't it your job to find clues and tell me who took my computer?" There was going to be another crime scene at this location because I was thirty seconds from taking my Leatherman and cutting off his hairy feet with my little knife and shoving them down his throat. This was precisely why I didn't carry a gun.

I started toward the kitchen before I had any other bad thoughts, but Frodo jumped in front of me and directed traffic again. I pushed by him and was whistled at and scolded for jaywalking. The kitchen was gross, the linoleum was tacky from the thick layer of grease that had accumulated over the years, and Veronica sucked at housekeeping. As I dusted the kitchen door for fingerprints, I heard Frodo and Veronica having a conversation in the living room. I guess we woke her. Frodo was telling her about our game of *Dragnet* charades and Veronica sounded disappointed that she missed it. She had a singsong voice that reminded me of a mix between Edith Bunker and the female cop from *Fargo*. "Oohh myy, II'm soo soorry I miissed oout on the fuun." She sounded like a wackjob too—a match made in heaven.

I continued dusting, not even caring that I was using my *dirty* brush. This was the brush I saved for gross things, like powdering toilet seats. I didn't like to use the filthy, germ-laden thing on the counters at McDonald's or inside people's homes, but Frodo had asked for it. I was tempted to cover the earpiece and mouthpiece of his telephone with fingerprint powder so he'd walk around town with a black face just because he annoyed me. I moved about the kitchen listening to the sound of my boots peeling up from the sticky mess beneath them. I was afraid that if I stood in one place too long I wouldn't be able to break free and would become a permanent fixture of the house, subjected to the daily wrath of Frodo and his batty significant other. I'd kill myself first. I gave up powdering the door after about a minute because it was just too greasy, and if Frodo didn't care, I didn't care.

Frodo hid around the doorway, watching me through the paper towel roll as if it were a telescope. I managed to ignore him as I packed up my print kit, which was really a two-tiered fishing tackle box with lots of adjustable compartments. "Okay, I'm done."

Frodo stepped into the kitchen still looking through his telescope, which was about thirty seconds away from becoming an enema and getting shoved up his ass. "Veronica said she wants to play *Dragnet* but she is feeling kind of bashful." He opened the basement door. "Don't you want to see where the stolen computer was?" I really didn't, but I waited for Frodo to direct traffic and let me know when the red light turned green and I could safely cross.

The basement was a sordid mess. It smelled sour from all the mounds of dirty laundry and the floor was wet from a leak in the elbow of the laundry sink. Frodo didn't seem to mind. There was a filthy, wet, stained mattress on the floor at the base of the steps and on top were several stained pillows and a filthy blanket. I wondered what creature slept down here. Probably something that spent most of its time living in tree hollows in the woods.

"The computer was here." Frodo pointed to an empty plastic patio table that was covered with a quarter inch of dust. I ignored him because I was busy looking at something else. In the rear of the basement, there was another door that opened to an outdoor stairwell. This door had been completely busted through and was lying in pieces on the basement floor. I was at a loss for words. Frodo seemed unfazed by it and told me in a very satisfied tone, "Whoever took the computer will soon discover that it doesn't work." I wanted to ask him if he ever tried pressing the "on" button. I wondered if hobbits even knew how to use computers.

"Uh," I was pointing to the door. "*Excuse me!* Did you happen to notice this? Did you think it might be important to tell me your door is broken into fifteen pieces?" My voice was raised again. But I figured it was okay because Veronica was awake.

Frodo was busy showing me that the burglar forgot the floppy disks that contained the computer's programs—they were the archaic five-and-a-quarter-inch variety. He seemed to take delight in knowing that even if the computer worked, it couldn't be used because it had no software. "Oh that. Yeah, that happened about two months ago. I haven't gotten around to fixing it." It must have been on his to-do list right after buying the lightbulbs for the front porch.

I threw some PR powder on the plastic table as Frodo watched through the paper towel roll. Then he transformed it into a microphone. "Ladies and gentlemen, we have as a guest on the show tonight—a Crime Lab person." He spoke in an animated radio voice. "Soooo, let's get right down to it. How long have you been in this line of work?" He tried to hold the microphone to my mouth, but I turned my head away. I didn't want that thing anywhere near me after he and his plaque ridden mouth had been talking through it all night long. I wasn't in the mood and didn't answer.

"Can you repeat that and please speak louder. We have a lot of people out there interested in what you do."

I was ready to kill him. "Six years. Six *long*, agonizing years."

"Hear that, ladies and gentlemen. She's been dusting for six long years. Our listeners want to know if you've ever seen guns get shot before?"

I nodded. "Okay, we got a nod. Can you tell our fans how many times?"

Bob and I went target shooting all the time. He even bought me a pistol our first Christmas together. My mother would say that isn't in the spirit of the season, but I figured that if Joseph had had a gun, maybe Mary wouldn't have had to give birth in a barn.

I gave him one word. "Hundreds."

Frodo looked surprised. "Hundreds? And what does your family think about that?"

I had the mike again. "They don't care."

Frodo just stared at me for a minute and then turned and sprinted up the stairs, clopping his big hairy feet the entire way, calling for Veronica. "Ohh, Veronica, Veronica!" I could hear him dashing across the floor above me. "Veronica!" He sounded breathless. "I have to whisper so she don't hear me, but that Crime Lab lady down there *got shot* hundreds of times and her family don't even care." He couldn't have been talking any louder.

"Ohhh myyy." Veronica sounded concerned. "Nooow thaaat's whaaat yooouuu caaall a braaave laaady. She haaas aaalot of cooourage." No doubt, she was off her rocker, too.

I packed up again, walked up the stairs, and headed out the door. Veronica must have been feeling bashful again because she had disappeared by the time I got upstairs.

When I got back to my van, I raised the officer that requested me on the radio and got the real story. Bill knocked on the kitchen door and distracted Frodo by going into the living room and watching TV with him while Bill's friend entered through the nonexistent basement door. He took off with the computer that Frodo has had since 1986. When I asked about the elusive Veronica, I learned that unlike the magical rings, she lived only in Frodo's imagination. Yep, there was no Veronica. It was just Frodo having conversations with himself.

The cheese surely slid off the cracker for Jimmy, his mom, and Frodo, but they weren't the only ones. There were all kinds of nuts out there. Like the guy who was convinced someone was driving his car at night because he kept waking up to find it parked outside the chalk outline he traced around it on his driveway. Then there was the burglary victim who refused to use her front door. She preferred to enter and exit her home through the bathroom window and claimed someone was breaking in to reset her clock. I can't forget about the burglar who started eating the foam from the sofa cushion when the police arrived. He choked to death. There were also the chance encounters with the town's oddballs, like the woman who drove through one of my hiding spots at precisely 2:30 each morning with a parrot on each shoulder putting food out for all the stray cats. And I have fond memories of the man who proposed to me in a gravel parking lot wearing only a white crash helmet and a matching pair of underpants. There were also those who meant well, but their loose screws fouled up their good intentions—like the guy who did CPR on a bloated, maggot-ridden, slimy decomp because 911 told him to, and the woman who didn't trust hospitals so she treated her diabetic husband's leg ulcers with petroleum jelly and baby powder. He died too.

If I learned anything in the Crime Lab, it is that bad things don't just happen to good people. Bad things happen to all kinds of people—young and old, rich and poor, black and white, skinny and fat, short and tall, smart and dumb, and crazy and sane. It doesn't matter who you are, where you live, or what you do, you're not immune from having a bad day and being visited by Crime Lab. However, a lack of common sense and victimization really seem to go hand in hand for a lot of people. That is not to say that there aren't plenty of truly innocent victims out there. Of course there are. But when you hack a ride with a complete stranger, decide to smoke crack in the woods with your cousin's sister's best friend's boyfriend's neighbor whom you have never met before, invite complete strangers into your living room to make a drug transaction, or show up banging on the apartment door of the girl who's been humping your man—how can you not expect something bad to happen? If more people exercised just a little bit of common sense, the number of Crime Lab calls for service would most definitely be reduced.

Speaking of common sense, it probably isn't such a good idea to tie ropes around your neck while you masturbate either (Mom, you might want to skip ahead to the next chapter). Yes, there are people out there who actually do this. We know this because we catch some of them in the act. The ones photographed with their hands in their cookie jars (notice the past tense) were ordinarily sane, smart, well-educated, young to middle-aged white men who experienced temporary leaks in their skylights and as a result no longer participate in the sport. At least each one went out of the game with a smile on his face.

The practice is called autoerotic asphyxia, and its predominately male practitioners are of the opinion that cerebral hypoxia (depriving the brain of oxygen) accentuates sexual arousal. This hypoxia is usually caused by ligature pressure to the neck, although plastic bags, masks, and tape are among the other items occasionally used. Regardless of the mechanism used to bring on a hypoxic state, the more important thing is the ability to reverse the pressure on demand. The problem lies in the fact that hypoxia not only heightens the sexual experience for these guys but it also can cause poor motor coordination, a lapse in judgment, and sudden unconsciousness, at which point it is too late for the victim to relieve the pressure around his neck or remove the bag from his head, and the result is anything but pleasurable. Pornographic materials, sexual props, unusual clothing for the victim, and binding of the hands, feet, and genitals are not uncommon associations.

I learned about autoerotic asphyxia in graduate school, but I thought that it was a rare occurrence. I hadn't a clue that hundreds of people die each year bound, gagged, hanged, and oddly dressed— all at their own doing and for their own pleasure. If hundreds die a year, I am sure that the numbers of those who engage in this behavior and live are staggering—but the practice is like rolling dice with the Grim Reaper and eventually these people are going to lose. I feel sorry for the family members who have to see their sons, fathers, and husbands not only dead but also in such bizarre states.

When we were in the training academy, we watched videos of two people who accidentally asphyxiated themselves while engaging in this practice. They set their camcorders up on tripods and I suppose they planned to watch their home movies at their own private film festivals at a later time. Little did they know that their movies would become law enforcement training tools. I remember these videos like I saw them yesterday. It isn't everyday you sit in a classroom and helplessly watch someone die.

The first guy was fully clothed and wore a big cowboy hat. He looked like the Marlboro man. He stood on a wooden ladder that extended down from his attic and a noose dangled nearby. He slipped the noose over his head, adjusted it so that it fit comfortably around his neck, and then stepped off the rung and completely suspended himself in the air. When he started to feel woozy, he reached behind him and pulled himself back onto the ladder. He did this about three times without incident. The fourth and final time he stayed suspended for a second too long and as he reached back, it was evident that his coordination was impaired and that he was unable to take hold of the ladder. We watched him die. While his brain may have been dead after a minute or two, his body writhed and twitched for far longer than I cared to watch.

The other man we had to watch die had the ligature tied to a shower curtain rod. He was dressed in women's underwear and had a pair of panties over his face. He squatted to tighten the rope around his neck and stood up to loosen it. On the second go-round, he squatted for a little too long and wasn't able to garner the strength to stand back up. His feet slipped out from under him, suspending the full weight of his body from the ligature. His little tryst turned out to be the thrill of his lifetime.

In my time with the Crime Lab, I handled three autoerotic asphyxias and I know of at least six others off the top of my head. The sad part is that these guys were probably the same ones who told their kids not to put jump ropes around their necks or plastic bags over their heads and made sure the Venetian blind cords were out of the reach of children. *Do as I say, not as I do.* In two of my cases, the men were dressed in women's clothing. The other was entirely nude; that is, if you don't count the broom handle he stuck up his rear end. In all three cases, the ligature was applied differently but it was always padded with women's underwear to prevent it from bruising, scratching, or digging into their skin. One guy hung a chain from a ceiling beam in his basement and fastened it around his neck. Much like the man in the video, he squatted to tighten it and stood up to loosen it. Another man hung a rope from his ceiling, which he then tied around his neck. He sat on a bucket and leaned forward to apply pressure and sat up straight to relieve it. The third man tied a rope to each ankle. He then lay in bed on his stomach, bent his feet up toward his buttocks, and took the slack in the rope and looped it under his neck. To restrict circulation, he straightened his legs, and to release the pressure he bent them back up.

Just to show the creativity of some of these guys, I responded to one scene where the man dressed entirely in women's clothing, right down to a bra stuffed with tube socks, a camisole with matching panties, and thigh-high stockings. But he didn't stop there. To prevent the manly bulge in his panties from ruining such a dainty illusion (an illusion that he apparently didn't think was shattered by the moustache and full beard), he threaded several rubber bands together forming a chain, which he secured around his waist as if it were a belt. Then, he linked about four rubber bands together, making a very short chain, and fastened them to the back of the belt just above his butt crack. He reached through his legs and pulled this short string of rubber bands forward and twisted the first one around the head of Mr. Winky. When he let go, the elastic recoil pulled his manliness backward and he was able to stuff his business between his butt cheeks, making him look all cute and girly in his fancy undies. I called him Mr. Fancy Pants.

When you are on a scene with a rookie cop still wet behind the ears, taking rubber bands off the bird of a dead man who is wearing thigh highs and a bra, you create a certain bond that you probably won't share with anyone else again in your life. Crime scenes were turning out to be great places to make new friends.

But while we are on the topic of common sense, or lack thereof, I can't fairly point the finger at only those outside the department when some of the biggest goons I encountered wore badges and carried guns. While 99.6 percent of the officers with whom I worked were smart, rational, levelheaded, sensible people, there were a few who were all foam and no beer. At the time, these individuals made my life miserable—in retrospect, they made my job fun. Take for instance the rocket scientist who was promoted to the rank of sergeant but couldn't tell the difference between livestock and humanstock.

I happened to be working during daylight hours this sunny spring day and was hiding in a somewhat isolated parking lot where the county parked its schoolbuses overnight. On midnight shift I called this place the love lot because you'd always pull in to find couples bumping uglies, or at least gearing up for the big ride. I didn't get it—big yellow buses didn't do a thing for me.

I had just fired up my laptop to start writing a report from a homicide search warrant that I handled earlier in the week. While most reports could be handwritten, homicides had to be computer generated. Some people did all their reports on the computer, but since I didn't like being in headquarters any longer that I had to be, and using a laptop in the van was awkward since the seats didn't slide back due to the equipment cage, I preferred to hand-write most of mine. Only if an assault victim was badly hurt and might go belly up did I go ahead and type the report. That way, if they died, I wouldn't have to go back and computerize the hand-written version. How dare a dead person cause me more work.

I was interrupted just as Windows popped up on the screen.

"Twenty-two fifteen." It was dispatch. "I'm sending down a call for a suspicious death on Pleasantdell Lane." The name was misleading; Pleasantdell Lane was anything but pleasant. "Be advised, a note attached to the call says you're to respond to the trashcan on the sidewalk in front of apartment building sixty-four twenty-six."

I was confused. "Did you say 'trashcan,' dispatch?" All the apartments on Pleasantdell were dumps, but I never heard them called trash cans over the radio before.

"Yeah. That's what it says." I could hear him typing as he tried to find more information for me. "Twenty-two fifteen," he was speaking slowly as he scrolled through the screen on his monitor, "looks like you are being requested for a fetus in a trashcan. You wanna switch to tac and I'll have the requesting unit talk to you."

I didn't hesitate, "Yeah, ten-four." I switched my radio to tac. I wondered what happened—if it was a miscarried fetus, a back-yard abortion, or a homicide? The closest call to this that I had ever handled was that of a woman who had given birth in the toilet at a strip club. She claimed she had stomach cramps so she went to the bathroom, but was a bit surprised to look down to see a baby in the toilet bowl. She claimed she didn't know she was pregnant. Obviously, she wasn't one of the dancers. Since the baby wasn't moving, she did what any good mother would do—she threw it away and then went about her business.

"Nineteen thirty-two, Crime Lab. You here?" I didn't recognize the officer's voice.

"Crime Lab, nineteen thirty-two. Do I need to bring any fancy equipment with me?" Although the vans were fully stocked, there were a few items that we didn't carry on the road with us. If we needed an alternate light source (ALS), spotlights, or fancy chemicals on major scenes, we had to grab them from headquarters or have someone ferry them out to us. These items were not in the vans because they were both heat and light sensitive, had short periods of longevity (like the chemicals), were expensive (like the several-thousand-dollar Crimescope ALS), or were in limited supply (like the spotlights).

"No, I think what you have in the back of your van will be fine." I wondered how he knew what I had the back of my van. I didn't know what he had in the back of his police car. I shut down my laptop as I talked to him.

"Well," he hesitated. "Looks like we have a possible fetus." Police used the word *possible* as a caveat in case something wasn't what it appeared to be. We took swabs of possible blood, collected bed linens containing possible semen, and packaged gold-colored earrings containing possible diamonds—but I had never heard anything called a *possible* fetus.

"You don't *know* if it's a fetus?" I thought that perhaps it was too small to tell. I was giving him the benefit of the doubt.

"Uh," his voice wavered and he unkeyed the mike. A second later he came back on the air. "No, I don't know."

I started up the van. "I assume the medics have been out there. What did they say?"

It took a few seconds for him to answer me. "They think it's—" he unkeyed the mike again and when he came back on he was laughing about something. "They think it's . . . they think it's *a chicken*!" Someone was clucking in the background. *Bawk bawk bawk bawk Bawwwlllkkk.*

A chicken??? "Can you ten-nine [repeat]? Did you say *a chicken*?"

In a tone as matter of fact as if he were telling me the time, he said again that the medics thought the fetus was really a chicken. "*All righty, then* . . . and you still want Crime Lab to respond out to this dead chicken-baby-thingamajig?" The tone in my voice made it clear that I thought he was an absolute bonehead! How could anyone confuse a baby with a chicken?

"Yeah, my supervisor wants you out here because he says there's always a chance it isn't a chicken." He was passing the buck. Now someone was cockle-doodle-dooing.

I didn't know if I should laugh or cry. "Well, did you check for yellow feathers and a beak?" *If it walks like a duck and quacks like a duck, it's probably a duck, you dipshit!* "What do *you* think it is?"

He didn't hesitate to answer. "A chicken." He changed the subject. "So when will you be here?"

"Give me twenty." I flipped my radio back to the main channel and made the drive to Pleasantdell Lane. In that neighborhood the thing in the trashcan was probably some mutant offspring that developed when two people with too many chemicals coursing through their veins got to feeling all hot and bothered.

I arrived at the scene about a half-hour later and had to laugh at the sight. There were about six police cars parked along the curb and the chopper was flying around overhead. I suspected it was just in the area and not assigned to this call, but its presence made the locals think there was something serious going on. If the chopper *was* assigned to this call, I wanted a tax refund because I was not paying for fuel for that thing to get a bird's-eye view of discarded poultry. A large crowd had gathered behind the yellow crime scene tape that encircled nothing other than a rusty old round metal trashcan in the middle of the sidewalk. Some people had pulled up lawn chairs and one guy even set up the barbeque pit nearby and grilled wieners as he watched us work. Lots of people sipped from plastic cups that I knew didn't contain Kool-

Aid—or at least the straight-up variety—and kids ignored us as they chased each other on their bikes. It was a spring day, the cops were putting on a show, and it was cause for celebration.

I got out of my van and met with Officer Barse, who was keeping vigil over the trash can. When he saw me he grinned from ear to ear. "Listen, my supervisor *made* me call you." I could tell by his voice that he was the officer I had spoken to on the radio. "So don't jump on my shit when you see what's in there. Okay?" A few of the other officers walked over when they saw that I had arrived. I didn't think they cared to see me as much as they wanted to see the expression on my face when I saw whatever it was that was taking up residence in the trashcan.

I pulled my gloves on and flipped back the hinged lid to the can, ignoring the photograph-before-you-touch rule. I had to see if I was even going to waste film on this thing. You could have heard a pin drop. The can was filled almost to the top with diapers, Colt 45 bottles, chicken wing bones, Coke cans, a pair of latex gloves with red-colored hair dye, a shoe, a few plastic bags, cardboard boxes, a couple of cartridge casings (I didn't even want to know what they were about), fast-food bags, and other miscellaneous garbage—but no dead chicken baby.

I looked around at the officers. "Did it fly away?"

Barse crossed his arms over his chest. "And you call yourself Crime Lab? I can see it from here." The other officers were in stitches. I'm sure that the bystanders who had caught wind of a dead baby in the trashcan wondered what they found so amusing.

"Is it buried in here?" I hung my head over the can, trying to ignore the stench to get a closer look. "Do I need to move anything—because if I do, I'll need to take some pictures first?"

"Nope, it's in plain view." Barse stepped forward and looked in. "It's right where we left it." One of the other officers was bawking again while his buddy cockle-doodle-dooed. I hoped they weren't about to mate. Barse filled me in as I continued to scan the garbage for the dead chicken baby. "One of the neighbors called the police and said that the girl who lives next door was pregnant a few days ago. This morning she notices the girl isn't pregnant anymore. She looked really bad and was hunched over, holding her stomach and carrying a plastic bag to the trashcan. After the girl throws the bag away, the neighbor sneaks out and opens it and finds what she thinks is a fetus."

"Well, unless it's the child of the invisible man, I give up." I pulled my head out of the trashcan. "I don't see a chicken—I smell a rat!" They snickered. "Show me! Point to it!"

Barse reached his hand into the can and pointed toward a sandwich-sized plastic bag. I had seen it earlier. "This?" I poked at it. Barse didn't answer. "This right here?" He looked in the opposite direction, but I could tell by the way his body was bouncing that he was cracking up. *What the hell?* "You're kidding, right?" I picked up the bag, not giving a damn that I hadn't even photographed it yet.

"This?" I held the bag up to the light and examined it to make sure it contained what I thought it contained. The bystanders oohed and ahhed. "I'm serious, you're joking, right?"

Barse took a swig of his water but started laughing again, spewing it down the front of his shirt. "Now do you see why the medics thought it was a chicken?" I looked inside at the bloody egg yolk and a few small pieces of shell.

I shook my head in disbelief and dropped the bag containing the egg back into the trash can. Now we were all laughing. I walked to my van and grabbed the camera. When I came back, I closed the lid and snapped a picture and then opened it and took another. "Okay, I'm done. See ya next time." I started to walk away, but then turned back toward Barse. "Oh, excuse the pun, but I'll need the name of that chick?" I pulled out my notepad. "I'll also need her DOB [date of birth]."

For the first time Barse had a serious look on his face. He ignored my name and DOB request. "Before you go, there's one more thing."

I glared at him. "Oh yeah? And *what* would that be?" Barse followed me as I walked back to my van. "Did your supervisor find a gallon of milk in the trashcan across the street? Tell him to keep looking, maybe he'll find some bacon and biscuits and he can cook you all a full breakfast in the morning." I hopped in the driver's side of the van, slammed the door, and started the ignition.

"No wait!" Barse was serious. "My sergeant said that when you were done, for you to take the bag to the morgue."

I was speechless. "What?" I looked at him like he had three heads. "What did you just say?"

"I am totally serious. My sergeant said to have Crime Lab transport the bag to the morgue when they were done." He grabbed his mike. "Want me to raise him so you can hear for yourself?"

I was furious. "Let me get this straight. *He* told *you* to tell *me* to take a cracked egg to the morgue?"

Barse just nodded.

"*Like hell!*" I yelled in disbelief. "Does he know that we are the *Crime* Lab?" I said it slowly and annunciated every letter to further my point. "That means we come out when a *crime* has been committed. Unless the laws have changed, it isn't a *crime* to throw away an egg!"

Barse put his hand up like he was trying to ward me off. "Listen, I'm just following orders." I knew he was right and that he couldn't help it if his supervisor was a few fries short of a Happy Meal. Bob always said that supervisors usually rose to their highest level of incompetence. This sergeant was clearly there.

"Just because a woman used to be pregnant doesn't mean that her baby is now an omelet!" I was dying to know who his sergeant was.

"Well, he made me request you because he said people come from eggs and we're not doctors and don't have the qualifications to determine if that thing is human or not." Barse was laughing again. "Look, I'm with you—it's an egg."

"Listen to me!" I was laughing and yelling at the same time. "Tell him that people don't come in white oval shells with yellow yolks. And—aside from your sergeant—most people don't hatch!" I was all flustered. "If he doesn't believe that, then tell him he can take the damn thing to the morgue himself because I flat-out refuse and I can fall back on the fact that Crime Lab isn't allowed to transport bodies. Period."

"But," Barse was smiling now. He knew it was a lost cause. "But it isn't a body. It's an egg."

"Then why the hell is it going to the morgue?" I gave him a two-finger salute and sped off. A few minutes later I heard Barse request his sergeant on tac. I switched over to eavesdrop.

"Crime Lab just cleared—without the . . . body." I hated to get Barse in the middle of this. "She said they don't do body transports."

"All right, I'll address this with her supervisor. In the meantime, I'll need you to take it downtown."

There was a long silence. "I'm direct."

I would have loved to be a maggot on the floor of the morgue when Barse walked in with the egg, asking them to perform an autopsy. Where the hell would they attach the toe tag? All I can say is that Crime Lab work isn't all it's cracked up to be.

CHAPTER 8

Grave Matters . . .

My mother and her fanatical "Ways of the Family" had me hanging off the side of the turnip truck by the time I was six. But I had other issues that my mother had nothing to do with—I just wasn't like the other little girls. At first, my mother tried to "fix" me by buying me dolls and inviting the neighborhood girls over to play. But Jenny Cruise, Julie Mirarchi, and the rest of those little ladies didn't like to set Barbie's hair on fire, make voodoo dolls of our teachers, or practice the art of ad hoc taxidermy. They were no fun. My mother eventually recognized her efforts were in vain and was forced to accept the harsh reality that her only daughter was anything but a clone of her. I may have counted to three as I stepped on a dropped comb with my left foot and kissed lots of moldy bread good-bye, but I still managed to develop into my own person who was the complete opposite of my mother.

By the time I was in junior high school, Mom stopped trying to change me, but she wanted me to be discrete about my interests, particularly those that involved digging and death. She chased me through the house yelling things that didn't come out of other mothers' mouths, like, "Nature is dirty," "Don't let the neighbors see you burying those things in my flower bed," and "How many times do I have to tell you not to bring roadkill into my house?" My mother warned me that if I caught trench mouth, hoof and mouth disease, or some other infection from the things I dug up, poked, or prodded, she wasn't taking me to the emergency room because that's where Carol Patalon's mother worked. She would tell Carol, Carol would tell the kids at the bus stop, and then high school would be a miserable experience for me. Carol must have found out anyway because high school sucked.

My father took everything in stride and actually shared my interest in archaeology. Sometimes we panned for gold in the stream behind the house and spent hours looking through the gravel in the neighbor's driveway for arrowheads. As I got older, my interests didn't waiver one bit and when I started a bone collection next to the woodpile, conducted my own archaeological investigations of a trash dump in the woods, and poked at the dead animals on the side of the street, I became the source of my father's amusement and my mother's migraines. Her debilitating headaches stopped the day I packed my bags, got married, and became someone else's problem.

Bob got his first migraine on September 7, 1990. I had just started working as an archaeological field technician for the Maryland State Highway Administration and my boss introduced me to a good friend of hers. During our very first meeting I knew I had found Mr. Right. Bob liked everything I liked. We stood in the blazing hot sun digging holes in a plowed field, and we talked about our fondness for animals, our favorite places to scuba dive, exotic lands we had travelled to, and our hopes for the future. We also discovered that we both knew the same guy who had been a suspect in a string of who-done-it murders in Maryland and compared stories about him over buckets full of dirt. Shortly thereafter, the State Police reopened the investigation and Bob and I were both contacted by homicide detectives for possible information. We got a kick out of it.

I eventually started working for the same engineering company that Bob worked for and in the years before we were married, we had a blast digging holes all over the East Coast and Canada on paid archaeological adventures. He was the boss, the big archaeological cheese with a Ph.D., and I was the lowly digger, fresh out of college. Yes, hierarchies exist even in the middle of a cornfield. But despite being on different rungs of the archaeological ladder, we had fun and didn't mind being the topic of streamside rumors.

Strictly by chance, I happened to be sent on a cemetery relocation project that required the excavation and relocation of a number of graves that were going to be impacted by a sewer line. That project was a turning point in my life, and it was clear that I found my niche. Finally, at *one* location, performing *one* duty, I found my interests in archaeology, forensics, death investigations, and human skeletal biology coming together for a common purpose. Within a week, the floor of my motel room was stacked with books I had purchased on forensic archaeology, forensic anthropology, and crime scene investigations. I was overwhelmed with information. I decided that before I went back to school, I needed to talk to some people who were actually employed in the forensics field. One individual with whom I spoke was an FBI agent named William Bodziak. Fifteen years following our chat, I found myself in his backyard in Florida celebrating our class's completion of a footwear-impression-evidence training program. Although the physical anthropologists and the forensic scientists with whom I spoke were guarded in their opinions of the job market, I was not discouraged—but practical in my decision. I decided to apply to the George Washington University's Master of Forensic Science program. That way, I figured, I could still take physical anthropology classes but would be eligible for jobs with law enforcement agencies as well.

After about five years together, Bob popped the question on a vacation to some ruins in New Mexico and the following May, I had my wisdom teeth pulled, got married, and graduated with my master's degree. It was a busy month and I don't recommend getting married right after having four teeth yanked out. We had the big Catholic wedding in the city's cathedral. It was where my parents were married and where Chris and I were baptized. But what wedding would be complete without the ways of The Family?

The night before the big extravaganza, I woke up to the sound of tape being pulled from the dispenser and torn off. *Rip and tear, rip and tear, rip and tear.* When I couldn't take it any longer, I staggered out of bed and found my mother at the kitchen table with all her saint cards spread out in front of her. She was busy taping them to the glass on the kitchen door. Saints Lucy, Peter, Bernadette, Dominic, Christopher, and Valentine were among those already affixed to the glass. When I asked what the hell she was doing, she told me that you had to tape the saints to the door the night before a wedding to keep it from raining. I didn't tell her that Bob and I didn't really mind the rain; after all, we worked in it all the time. Mom must have had the saints facing the wrong way though because I awoke to cracks of lightning and the roar of thunder. She feverishly apologized to the saints and anxiously turned them all around so that they were facing in the other direction. But it was too late. They were offended and made sure it poured all day.

Now that fifteen years have passed since our initial meeting, I have come to realize that Bob and I have a lot of shared interests, but we also have a lot of differences. I don't like it when he cleans his rocks in the dishwasher any more than he liked it when I washed my gnarly uniforms with his underwear. But we have always been supportive of one another, and I try not to make fun of his El Camino while he promises to look the other way whenever I am up to doing something gross. This was particularly true when I was in graduate school and always seemed to have my hand in some sort of ghoulish project.

The first time Bob's mother came for a visit she arrived a little earlier than I anticipated. I was in the backyard dressed in a bloody yellow rain suit lying atop a fresh and gooey cowhide holding a knife, a razor, and a can of shaving cream. I was shaving the hide for a range of gunfire experiment for school. The snow around me was covered in blood and hair and it looked like someone had been butchered. As Bob distracted his mom in the living room, I tried to cover the mess I made with fresh snow and tossed the hide and rain suit into the bushes. I was successful, at least until the dogs discovered something better than the mother of all Milk-Bones stashed beneath the azaleas.

I finished that project only to start a low-, medium-, and high-velocity blood-spatter experiment. This one required a baseball bat, a crossbow, a couple of guns, and a trip to a slaughterhouse to get cow blood. I felt like a freak standing at the deli counter asking for two jugs of blood and giving instructions on how to add the Heparin to keep it from coagulating while the people next to me ordered sausages and roasts. I felt better when one of the customers was handed a huge freezer bag filled with eyeballs. He had a medical school bumper sticker on his car, which seemed to validate his order for thirty large eyes. I wanted to be validated too.

The blood-spatter project was messy and everything got covered in blood. I was afraid we would have a lot of explaining to do if the police pulled us over on the way home. Bob soon realized that this was nothing compared to the maggot project that I called "Got eggs?"

At the time that I did the maggot project, there wasn't a lot of literature that documented the conditions required for a fly to oviposit, or lay eggs, at night. In forensics, fly larvae (maggots) can be ground up and tested for drugs to see if the person on whom they were feasting was under the influence of something funky at time of death. More frequently, however, they are used to calculate how long a person has been dead. If flies do in fact lay eggs at night, then the time of death interval could potentially be off by as much as twelve hours. So, for the next few months, I took it upon myself to try to get flies feeling all hot and bothered so that they would oviposit during the hours of darkness. As soon as the sun went down, I'd traipse around the block hiding rotten pigs feet in dark, semidark, and artificially illuminated areas. I hid them under street lamps, in sheds with the lights turned on, and in dark corners of the yard. Every hour I'd go outside and monitor heat and light levels and check the feet for eggs or larvae. There's nothing like waking up to an alarm at 3:00 in the morning to go check the neighborhood for fly eggs on rancid meat while you are wearing pajamas that have cows decked out with Santa hats. But it was all worth it when I got eggs. They appeared one night in the shed when the light was on. I tenderly cared for these adorable little larvae until they turned into flies, which I then lovingly sprayed with Raid so I could have the species identified. Although that project was nasty, it was interesting and my dead flies enjoyed their moment in the spotlight when my findings were cited in a paper given at the annual meeting of the American Academy of Forensic Science.

But cowhides, jugs of blood, and maggots were better than the project that required me to start a finger- and toenail collection. The width and spacing of the vertical striations present on the upper and lower surfaces of nails are determined by the dermal papillae; the same structures that create the dermal ridges of the friction ridges in fingerprints. These are unique to the individual, making it possible to match a piece of a torn fingernail found at a crime scene with the suspect in the crime. I wanted to know to what degree nail fungus affected these striations and once the fungus was treated, if the striations were at all changed. For weeks, I received envelopes containing nail clippings in different stages of rot from strangers all over the United States. Suffice it to say that if there is "fungus amungus," the striations are affected—let's just move on.

The days of those projects are a thing of the past. Now, the only gross thing I do, I do with Bob. We scrape up dead animals from the side of the road and bury them in the hedges out front. My mother has as much of a problem with it now as she did when I was eight and doesn't seem to care that we do it in the name of science. She just thinks that it is wrong. She says that we should let sleeping dogs lie. I say that if the dog isn't going to wake up again, there's no good reason it can't go in the bushes. We really do this for a worthwhile cause though—or so I think. On archaeological sites, animal remains are an abundant but frequently under-utilized source of information. They shed light on prehistoric and historic ecology, hunting practices, diet and dietary preferences, processing and butchering techniques, methods of food preservation and storage, seasonal variation in food supply, animal domestication, and so on. To realize the potential of these remains, it is essential to be able to identify species from the bones we recover on sites. That being said, Bob and I have been busy building a comparative collection. We do this by collecting road kill, burying the remains, and then digging them up when they are skeletonized. We have the process down to a science now. We carry tarps and hefty bags in our trucks just in case we spot something that looks good. Then we bring the stinker home, wrap it in window screen, and bury it in the hedges in the front yard. (We learned the hard way that the dogs have a late-night snack if we put it out back.) We mark the spot with a pin flag that contains the name of the species and the date it was buried, and then we dig it back up anywhere from four to eight months later and collect the bones. We have deer, foxes, rabbits, mice, birds, fish, snakes, squirrels, chipmunks, and a horse. Digging a hole for the horse created some problems, but he's all bones now—that's all that matters. One of Bob's friends who works for the Department of Natural Resources pulled some strings and got us a black bear that had been hit by a car. He's not quite as big as the horse, but he's buried off the property anyway.

Despite what happens in our yard, I must say that we live in a quaint neighborhood with cherry trees, white picket fences, slate roofs, and lots of poodles. The neighbors around here handpick the clover from their grass, resurface their driveways the first warm day of spring, sweep the street in front of their house, and shine spotlights on their front door hangings. Families come to our neck of the woods for weekend yard sales and bring their kids here to trick-or-treat (although most avoid the house with pin flags in the bushes that say SQUIRREL, CROW, DOG, CHIPMUNK). Crime in my part of town is usually minor in its severity. The local paper reported a burglary about three miles away just last week. The article went on to say that the suspects entered the home and took a frozen stuffed flounder. It's usually pretty safe around here.

I had only been in the police academy for a week when two Homicide detectives walked into the classroom and called me out. At first, I thought I was in trouble, like in high school when the principal always used to come get me and march me down to his office for "a chat." But I wasn't in trouble; instead, I listened as the detectives started filling me in on the details of a case. A young girl was riding in the car with her uncle and reported that he drove behind a shopping plaza, got out of the car, and told her to wait—he had something to do. He disappeared into the woods. After twenty minutes had passed and the uncle didn't return, the girl went into the woods looking for him. From a distance, she witnessed him on his knees crying and praying over a mound of loose soil. Frightened, she ran back to the car and waited for him. When she finally arrived home, she told her parents what happened and they called the police. For whatever reason, the Homicide detectives were afraid that the uncle was praying over a grave. Knowing that the department had just hired an archaeologist with cemetery and grave excavation experience, they called me out. I poked around, but it was clear that the crime scene guy had been digging through undisturbed soil for the past two hours.

Being an archaeologist at heart, my most exciting crime scene calls always involved using a shovel and trowel. I hoped that if they killed them, they'd at least bury them. I didn't want to see anyone die, but I did like using the dig kit that the department purchased at my request. Among the items in the kit were two shaker screens. These contraptions are balanced on two legs and have handles that surround the screen basin. By grabbing the handles and vigorously shaking or rocking the screen back and forth, soil falls through the mesh revealing potential evidence. The main screen has quarter-inch mesh and there is an eighth-inch mesh insert that is used to find even the tiniest of hairs, fibers, and projectile fragments.

The kit also included trowels. These weren't just any trowels; they were Marshalltowns. An archaeologist who shows up on a dig with anything other than a Marshalltown or a Goldblatt will probably find his or her excavation unit down in the swamp with the West Nile mosquitoes. But worse than showing up without one of the big names in trowels is coming to your first dig with one of those big gardening trowels with the curved blade; it reminds me of the time Mom sent me to tennis camp with a badminton racket. She said it would be fine. She also told me that if my pet frog was hungry enough, he'd eat the carrots and lettuce she gave me to feed him. The badminton racket broke and the frog died.

No dig kit is complete without a tube-sampling auger and a probe. Both of these instruments are used to test for subsurface soil disturbances (as would be the case if someone dug a hole, buried a body, and then backfilled it). The auger provides a visual means of checking the soil while the probe allows one to monitor soil density. The theory behind the use of these instruments is the fact that soils naturally develop in a layer cake sort of arrangement. A dark, highly organic layer ordinarily characterizes the uppermost region. Beneath this is lighter colored, orangey, denser subsoil. Much deeper gravels and finally bedrock follow the subsoil. When a suspect digs a grave to bury a body, he or she messes up Mother Nature's carefully designed soil stratigraphy and the layers, particularly the shallower dark topsoil and the underlying subsoil, become commingled, or mixed up, when the grave is backfilled. The auger is used to remove a plug of soil, which is then examined to see if the dark topsoil is on top of the subsoil, or if they are mixed together. If the former is found to be the case, it's time to grab the Marshalltown and investigate a little further. If the latter is present, the diggers are sent on their merry way.

Just as former excavation disrupts soil stratigraphy, it also permanently alters the degree of soil compaction. Soils that have been dug up and then backfilled will never regain the same density as the surrounding undisturbed soils, never, never, ever. The probe is a stainless steel rod that measures about four and a half feet in length and is the instrument used to monitor differences in soil density. A perpendicular steel bar soldered to the top of a central rod serves as the handle, and a small ball at the base of the rod prevents significant damage to anything that may lie below the ground surface. The probe is pressed into the ground at regular intervals and the operator feels the degree of resistivity afforded by undisturbed soils. Once a frame of reference is established, it is easy to detect the comparatively softer, disturbed soils.

I'm proud to say that I have probed for more bodies than I can count. I hope frequent probing doesn't imply I'm easy. In one par-

ticular instance, my services were requested by an adjacent jurisdiction. The investigators felt that a missing woman was the victim
of foul play and that there was the possibility she was buried in a
shallow grave on a several-acre lot containing an abandoned
house. I arrived with the probe in hand and got busy at work. I spent
hours testing the property and flagged several "suspicious" areas,
which I later investigated using a shovel. While I was unable to
turn up the missing woman, I successfully found the former occupant of the home's pet cemetery. The little that remained of Fifi
and Snickers was placed in plastic bags and again laid to rest.

The probe also came in handy when I traveled to Croatia as
part of a research team whose trip was funded by the Department
of State, the National Museum of Natural History and the Croat-
ian Academy of Arts and Sciences. The purpose of this trip was to
promote the development of forensic anthropology in Croatia
through instruction and the demonstration of the techniques, instruments, and methodologies used in the identification, excavation, and analysis of human remains. The individuals we searched
for and subsequently examined had been killed during the Balkan
conflict that began in 1991 and were buried in mass graves. While
witness testimony provided strong indicators of where these
graves were located, our team watched for surface depressions,
exposed subsoil, and vegetational anomalies consistent with clandestine burial locations. Areas appearing suspicious were further
investigated using the probe. In all instances, we were able to document differences in compaction, consequently enabling us to not
only identify graves but their horizontal boundaries.

I found that vegetational clues were perhaps the most obvious, yet frequently overlooked sign of a possible burial site. Increased, decreased, absent, or foreign plant growth relative to that
in the surrounding area often suggests what is going on below the
ground surface. These changes are especially obvious from low-
altitude aerial surveys. In cases where interment is known to have
occurred fairly recently (a few days to a few weeks) the burial site
will be characterized by absent or very new plant growth. Vegetation surrounding the burial pit will be destroyed or crushed from

trampling, the use of tarps to keep the area free of excavated soil, and the mounding of back dirt during the digging process. There will probably also be loose soil on the ground surface and mixed in with any nearby vegetation.

It is also possible to use plants to locate older graves. In this case, investigators look for vegetational growth that differs from plants in the surrounding area. Assuming that a body is placed in a shallow grave or wrapped in something porous such as a sheet or blanket before it is buried, the fluids of decomposition have the Miracle-Gro effect and will frequently cause an increase in the height and density of the vegetation. By contrast, if a body is wrapped in something that is nonporous, such as a shower curtain or garbage bag, or is placed in a container such as a cooler, which is then buried, the nutrients from the decomposing body will be unable to escape and provide nourishment to the vegetation above. Consequently, the plants over the grave may actually be shorter than those in the immediate area, particularly if root growth is impeded by the nonpermeable and impenetrable surface enclosing the body. The point I am trying to make is that investigators don't necessarily look for increased or decreased plant growth—they look for growth that is different relative to that in the surrounding area.

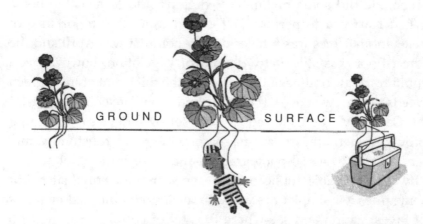

GROUND   SURFACE

Normal plant growth.   Increased plant growth   Stunted plant growth
                        caused by nutrients provided   caused by impeded root
                        by the decomposing body.   development.

Two specific incidents gave me a new appreciation for vegetational indices. Years ago, while working as an archaeological technician for a county-level Parks and Planning division, I accompanied my boss to a location in the woods where a survey crew had recovered possible human remains. As we traipsed through the briars and approached the location of the bones, he pointed to a cluster of yucca plants and commented how he bet there was a historic-period cemetery nearby. We were in the middle of the woods that happened to be in the middle of Timbuktu, so any ornamental plants were certainly out of place, but that was the first time I ever heard of the association between yucca and historic places of burial. After determining that the bones were not human, we decided to poke around a little. Within minutes we located two small, deteriorated headstones from a previously unrecorded historic-period family cemetery. These were about fifteen feet away from the yucca cluster. Even Ms. Cleo couldn't have made a prediction as good as that.

In the other instance, a young girl had been killed and the police had information that she was buried in a wooded area off the side of the road. Search teams and cadaver dogs had combed the area for weeks with no luck. Finally, a detective received additional information about the burial location and returned to the scene. He did some preliminary digging and located the body. When I arrived to perform the exhumation, the importance of vegetational clues was forever driven home. It was April and the forest floor was still pretty devoid of vegetation; however, you could trace the outline of the grave by the thick mat of lush, green weeds that grew above it. I became an immediate believer.

Certainly, sophisticated remote-sensing devices, including ground-penetrating radar, magnetometers, and resistivity meters, as well as aerial photography, and color infrared photography have valuable applications in the search for burial sites. But sometimes it is simpler to start with the less complicated methods of investigation and see where that takes you. It's a spinoff on Ockham's razor.

Bob and I worked on a lot of archaeological sites together, but only once did we get to bond excavating graves. One afternoon, Bob received a phone call regarding an unmarked, historic-period cemetery that had been inadvertently encountered when construction crews were digging a trench. After the police, the ME, and the state's attorney's office determined that the graves were not forensic in nature, the necessary permits were obtained and Bob got the contract to excavate the graves that were in the right-of-way of the proposed construction. I agreed to help him remove what remained of the coffins and do an analysis of the skeletons. Documentary historical research indicated that the managers of a nearby almshouse interred the remains in the field. The house was in operation from 1771 through 1965.

My friend April (the one with the Jersey mom) and I headed for the cemetery to help Bob when our Crime Lab shifts ended and, between the three of us, we excavated all the graves that were threatened by construction. The nearly complete bodies of sixteen people were then transported back to my house so I could conduct the skeletal analysis. At this point, I had been training in physical anthropology for a number of years and was excited about the prospect of examining the skeletons.

The trouble began almost immediately. All the bones were covered in sand and needed to be cleaned before the analysis could begin. They were also damp from the bad weather we encountered in the field and had to be air-dried to prevent molding. One slow, warm, and sunny day at the Crime Lab I slid by my house between calls and moved the beer boxes containing the human remains outside so they could dry out. My intention was only to allow them to get some air, but the road to hell is paved with good intentions and before long I had the paintbrushes out and was actively cleaning the bones. Considering that a person has 206 bones in his or her body and I had 16 people to clean, I had roughly 3,296 dirty bones and 512 dirty teeth to brush. I welcomed the opportunity to get a head start.

Time flew by, and before long piles of sand and bone surrounded me. That's when I heard the *whoosh*. At first, I didn't know what it was and wasn't too concerned by it. But then it got louder and was accompanied by a cracking sound. I stood up from a seated position on my deck, brushed the sand from my lap, and looked around. I was stunned when my eyes caught sight of what was happening in my neighbor's yard. The people behind us don't have a patio or deck, so they set up their barbecue grill in the driveway in a small alcove behind their house. I was horrified to see a ten-foot jet of flame shooting out of the grill's propane tank, igniting their house. Their rear porch was ablaze and the aluminum siding melted before me like candle wax. The roof was seconds away from becoming involved.

Needing to call 911, I started to key my radio mike—but stopped myself just before I pressed the button. *Shit, I can't call it in on the radio or they'll know I'm at home!* I ran inside the house and called 911 on the phone. After I gave the dispatcher the information, I darted back outside toward the skeletons. The fire was worse. I frantically started to pack the bones back in their boxes. I knew the fire department would be there in minutes and figured the police would come too. The last thing I wanted was for the police to see sixteen dead people laid out in beer boxes on my deck. I didn't want them to see me either. I rushed back and forth, from the yard to the garage, trying to put everyone away, but I could hear the sirens getting closer. I looked back toward the fire, which now threatened to ignite one of the big oak trees in my neighbor's yard. My eyes followed the branches. They were intertwined with those from a tree on my property, and my tree's branches hung over the roof of my house. *Shit!* Now I was afraid that the neighbor's tree would catch my tree on fire, and in turn ignite my house—and then the fire department would find the bodies of sixteen people and think they were all burned alive. I looked at my van, wondering if I could get all 3,296 bones and 512 teeth inside before the police came. But it was too late. Just as I opened the garage door, a police car flew down the street. It was Gorman—

the officer from the *Wheel of Fortune* scene. I saw his head turn toward the big white van that said FORENSIC SERVICES. He was probably wondering why Crime Lab was in the neighborhood. A few minutes later he walked up my driveway and into the garage. "Dana?"

I didn't know what to say. "Oh, hi!" I looked out the corner of my eye, trying to make sure a skull wasn't popping out of a box or no loose teeth were on the ground. "So, what brings you here?"

He looked at me like I had six heads. "Uh, the fire—you know, the one in your backyard." I looked over at the hoards of fire trucks and firefighters pulling big hoses down the street. "Oh, that. Yeah, I thought I heard sirens." They were ear piercing. I sounded stupid. He probably knew that I was the one that called it in because my name and phone number would have appeared on the KDT as the complainant.

He looked around the garage. "So, are you here on a call?"

I didn't want him to know I was at home while on duty. "Um, well, no. I live here." I hoped he wouldn't ask about all the pin flags in the bushes. There was one right behind him that said SQUIRREL. His eyes were fixed on my pants. I looked down wondering if my zipper was down and saw that I was still covered in sand. I nervously brushed it off. "I stopped by here to go to the bathroom."

Gorman looked amused. "In the garage?" He started to back out. "Well, I just wanted to say hi." I think he thought he was interrupting something. "So . . . I'll see you on the next one." He walked back over to the neighbor's house.

That should have been my first inkling that having sixteen dead people in my garage would create problems. In the days that followed, I completed the skeletal analysis and soon received a call from the director of the project who wanted to arrange the return of the remains for reburial. John informed me that the local community was aware of the discovery of the cemetery and was planning a formal graveside ceremony. The media would probably be present.

I was concerned. "Do you know that the bones are in beer boxes? How's it gonna look when I am all over the evening news stacking Saint Pauli Girl and Bud boxes in a grave?"

John was laughing. "Oh yeah. I forgot about that." The people were in beer boxes because I ran out of the archival-quality Hollinger boxes when we were in the field. In a moment of desperation, I walked to the liquor store across from the site and begged for some boxes. "Well, can you put them in something better looking?"

I hadn't budgeted for anything fancy. "I can get some more Hollingers."

"Let me make some calls and I'll get back to you." John was going to try to scrape up a few extra bucks.

While I waited, I browsed the Internet looking at coffins. There were stainless steel coffins, military coffins, wooden coffins, bronze coffins, and copper coffins that ranged between $600 and $7,000 in price. Monks made some of them, others were made in China, and some were made right in my own town. Options included pink crepe liners, gaskets, nameplates, waterproofing, and themes imprinted on the coffin's exterior surface. My favorite coffin was decorated to look like it was wrapped in brown paper. Big red-block letters across the lid read RETURN TO SENDER—EXPRESS DELIVERY. I bookmarked that page. I want to be cremated, but I still want that coffin.

John called me back about an hour later. "Okay, I got you twelve hundred dollars for some coffins."

"Well, I have some bad news for you." I cleared my throat and took a deep breath before I broke it to him. "It looks like twelve hundred dollars will get us two of the really cheap coffins and that's if we're lucky."

He didn't sound too surprised. I could hear his wheels turning. "Any chance we can squeeze everybody in two of 'em?"

I thought about it for a minute. "I suppose." I didn't know if he was joking or not. "Do you think the community group will frown upon it? And what about the dead people—they might not be too happy about sharing a crate with a bunch of strangers."

John sighed. "Well, either they play nice and share, or they go back in the ground inside beer boxes. Can you make some calls and try to see what twelve hundred dollars will buy us?"

I opened the yellow pages to the funeral section and started my calls. I had planned to get a bunch of prices, but that wouldn't be necessary. My first call would be my last. The woman who answered sounded young and her voice was a little too chipper for the business she was in. "Mohrland's Funeral Home, how may I help you?" She sounded like she was ready to take a pizza order.

I mocked her cheerful valley-girl tone. "Hello! I'd like to buy a coffin pleaaase!"

I caught her off guard. She was silent for a minute. "Um, okay, ma'am." I could hear her rustling around for a pen. "Would you like to come in and visit our showroom?"

"No."

"No?" She sounded surprised.

"No. I just want to buy a coffin. I don't care what it looks like."

She hesitated. "Okay, then. How 'bout I take like, your name and number and I'll have one of our directors give you a call back?" Her voice was sickening sweet and she sounded like a complete airhead. "You can discuss arrangements with him." The intonation of the last word in each of her sentences was higher than the rest. She probably had fake blond hair and pretend boobs, and I bet she was filing her acrylic fingernails and admiring her fake-and-bake tan as we spoke.

She made it sound like I was pricing a new car. "I don't want any arrangements. I just want to buy a coffin. Maybe two."

I was confusing her. It was fun. "You need *more* than one coffin?"

I didn't miss a beat. *"Fer sure!* Actually I need sixteen, but it will probably be expensive. So one or two should do the trick. What are the cheapest ones you have?"

"Ma'am, um, it would be best if you came in and met with one of our directors and, like at that time you can like, discuss your needs." I could tell she was chewing gum.

I was trying not to crack up. "Well, I really don't need to visit the showroom and I don't really have any specific needs. I don't care what the thing looks like. All I care about is the fact that I only have twelve hundred dollars and just want to know if that is enough to buy one or two coffins." I covered the receiver with my hand so she wouldn't hear me laughing.

She was trying to be sweet but clearly hadn't learned how to deal with a customer such as myself in telephone answering school. She just wanted to pass me off to someone else. "Well, ma'am, that's why you need to come in. Our director will explain the services we offer and you can go over your budget."

"Services?" I was relentless. "I don't need services! I just need a coffin!"

She tried to change the subject. "Ma'am, is your loved one already like, here? At our establishment?"

"Stop calling me ma'am. And no, they're not at your *establishment*." The tone in my voice made it sound like that was the stupidest question I had ever heard. "And it isn't a loved one. It's a complete stranger. Sixteen complete strangers if you want me to be perfectly honest."

She was at a loss for words. It took a minute for her to compose herself. "Well, like"—I knew she was gearing up for the question that I was waiting for—"where are these sixteen *strangers* right now?"

I spoke loud and proud. "They are in beer boxes in my garage."

Now she thought I was prank caller. "Ma'am, I'm sorry but we can't help you."

I jumped in before the dingaling hung up on me. "Listen, I am serious. I need to purchase as many coffins as I can for twelve hundred dollars."

Now she was mocking me. "For the sixteen people in beer boxes in your garage, right?"

"Yes!"

"And these are like, real people?"

What kind of question was that? "Of course they are real. Real live dead people." My cheeks were starting to ache from smiling.

"And why are they in your garage?"

"Because that's where I put them after I dug them up out of the cemetery and now I have to put them back."

That must have knocked the polish off her toes because I was immediately put on hold. I wiped the tears from my eyes and wished I had been tape recording this conversation. A few seconds later a gentleman picked up the phone. "Hello ma'am. I understand that you are interested in purchasing a number of coffins?"

"Yes," I tried to sound serious. "I need to purchase as many coffins as I can, but am on a tight budget."

He sounded suspicious. "Well, my receptionist tells me that you're requesting no other services?" He was trying to get me to tell him what I told his little valley girl. She probably also had a pierced belly button and a Hollywood name like Suri or Shiloh.

"No, all I need are a few coffins."

I could tell he wasn't sure if I was joking or if I was serious. "Well, you can visit our showroom and we can discuss caskets and prices"—he hesitated—"but before we schedule an appointment, I need to ask you what these caskets will be used for?"

I didn't want a *casket* I wanted a *coffin*. Caskets are rectangular, decorative burial receptacles, while coffins serve more functional needs. In other words, they are cheaper. "I'm sorry, sir. Did you just ask me what the coffins would be used for?" He didn't answer. "I'll use them to bury dead people."

The man put me on hold again. He picked up a few seconds later. "My receptionist says that you told her that you have sixteen bodies in your garage and that you dug them up out of a cemetery. Is this true?"

"Yes, sir. It's the God's honest truth. And now all I want to do is put the people in a big coffin and rebury them. I'm trying to do the right thing."

He sounded startled by my honesty. "*Ma'am!* You have *committed a crime* by digging bodies out of a cemetery!" He was upset. "I am not able to help you and am going to have to make a call to the authorities. Will you at least tell me which cemetery these people came from?"

It was time to come clean before he called the police. I wondered if funeral homes had caller ID? "Sir, let me explain."

"Please do!" I envisioned him rocking back in his chair and propping his feet up on the desk.

After about twenty minutes of explaining and a call to the county archaeologist as well as the state's attorney to verify I was on the up and up, he was ready to talk business. He talked me into a single large coffin. It made me wonder what they did with supersized people, like Front Butt. I guess they had special coffins for people like that. That was what I needed—a Front Butt coffin.

"Listen," his entire demeanor had changed now that he was convinced I wasn't a serial killer or a freak. "One of my guys doesn't live far from you. How 'bout he stops by your place after work tonight with one that I think will work."

"A coffin?" I was surprised. "You wanna bring a coffin to my house?"

"I thought I'd save you a trip all the way out here." The funeral home was about thirty minutes away. "Unless you have a problem with it."

"A problem?" I laughed. "Anyone who has sixteen dead people in her garage shouldn't have a problem with a coffin in the driveway." Not to mention dead animals in the bushes.

Later that night a pickup truck pulled up outside. There was a silver coffin in the bed. The neighbors watched as I climbed in the back of the truck and inspected the coffin's dimensions. It was too small.

The next night a white coffin arrived. Again, it was too small.

The following night, a big brown coffin visited. It was too small as well. The whole situation reminded me of the joke about Larry LaPrise, the guy who wrote "The Hokey Pokey." He died in 1996 and the trouble started when they tried to get his left foot in the coffin. . . .

"The problem are the heads," I explained over the phone. "There's no way sixteen heads will fit in there with the rest of the bones. I don't want to crush them or I'll have sixteen ghosts haunting me for the rest of my life." I didn't want to put the heads in a separate coffin because dead people should have their heads within reach.

He must have anticipated my call. "I didn't think that one would work. I've been talking to the other guys here. We're gonna build you one at no cost. We'll donate it. It's for a good cause."

A few days later, the neighbors and I admired the great big baby blue coffin in my driveway. It even had pallbearer handles on the side and a hinged lid. It was the most beautiful coffin—ever. The only thing it was missing was the RETURN TO SENDER stamp on the side. I unpacked the beer boxes and reminded everyone to get along as I laid the bones to rest for what would hopefully be an eternity.

The people arrived at the cemetery and the ceremony took place without incident.

One coffin: Free.

Sixteen coffins: Thousands of dollars.

Driving down I-95 with sixteen people packed into a huge baby blue coffin bungeed to your roof rack: Priceless.

I have learned a lot of things from traveling around with dead people. Number one, if you take three boxes of dead people onto the D.C. Metro, make sure you have three boxes when you get off. Poor Mrs. Davidson's legs hadn't been exercised in years, so she decided to escape my custody and took a little jaunt around the nation's capital. She turned up at Union Station later that day. I have also learned that if you dig dead people out of a swamp, then hop on a plane before you've had a chance to shower, you'll probably end up with a row to yourself. It was kind of like the time Bob and I got into the hot springs in Iceland just before we flew home, not realizing that we reeked of sulfur. We wondered why nobody was sitting near us on an otherwise full flight home to the States. I didn't eat hard-boiled eggs for months. It also isn't a good idea to tell curious onlookers what you have in the box tucked under your arm—that is, unless you are being questioned by airport security.

I had been doing some research in Utah with a team of physical anthropologists, but family obligations required me to fly home a few days earlier than my coworkers. My boss asked if I'd take two boxes, each containing three skulls, back to Washington, D.C., with me. Some were fragmented and needed reconstruction, while others had to be measured and X-rayed. Since I didn't want the skulls to get lost or manhandled, I decided the boxes would serve as my carry-on.

Running late as usual, I quickly checked my bags and ran to the security terminal, clutching the boxes the way a quarterback clutches a football. I glanced at my watch. My plane was probably boarding. I tossed my purse and the two long brown boxes, which were bound together with strapping tape, onto the X-ray conveyor belt and watched them disappear into the machine as I walked through the metal detector. A few seconds later my purse reappeared, but not the boxes. In fact, the entire conveyor had stopped.

I looked up at the security guy examining the X-ray monitor. He was making a weird face. His mouth was open, and each time he squinted his eyes, his top lip curled back, exposing his tobacco-stained teeth. He cocked his head from side to side and then played with some of the controls, moving the conveyor back and forth. Every few seconds, he craned his neck forward like an ostrich as he tried to get a closer look. I was getting nervous, and the people behind me huffed and sighed, showing their impatience.

The security guy must have pushed a secret button because a few minutes later his supervisor approached. I looked at my watch again and wondered how long before departure they'd stop boarding the plane. The security guy with brown teeth whispered something to his boss, and then they both looked at the monitor, then at me, and then back at the monitor. They whispered again and called over the guy who had been manning the metal detector. I could feel their gazes burning holes in my skin.

I stepped to the end of the conveyor so that I could catch a glimpse of whatever it was that they found so interesting. Then I saw them—all six of them. Six big-eyed skulls staring right back at them. *Shit!* My mind raced as I tried to decide if I should just play it off or try to offer an explanation. How could I explain six heads in my carry-on?

"Miss," the supervisor called to me as she sent the boxes through the machine. "Are these your boxes?"

I wanted to deny it and just jump on the plane. "Uh," I just stared at them for a minute. "Those—uh . . ." They really weren't mine if you wanted to get technical, but I had to be honest. "Yeah. They're mine." I tried to play dumb. "Why, is there a problem?"

The woman took my boxes to a table at the far end of the conveyor. "I'm gonna need to open them." She wasn't very friendly and her pants were too tight.

"Open them?" I looked at the strapping tape that I had so carefully applied. "Do you have to? The contents are fragile—that's why it's taped up like that." She ignored me. "I'll tell you what's in there if you don't open it."

A State Police officer joined her at the table. Someone must have called for him too. He watched as she worked on the tape. I got up the nerve to say it. "There are skulls in there. Do you have to open it?" I was pleading. The woman pulled a roll of tape from her pocket and placed it on the table. It was her way of telling me she would retape the boxes once she was done.

Without moving his head, the officer's eyes moved from the box toward me. He raised his eyebrows. "Human skulls?"

"Yes, they're human." They acted like this was the first time someone put a body in their carry-on. I tried to make a joke of it. "I thought it was okay to carry them on because they don't have bodies, so they can't sit and won't need a seat." They gave me a what-the-hell look. "They don't need tickets or boarding passes, right?"

They ignored me. Some people just don't appreciate my humor.

"I promise they won't eat any peanuts or drink anything from the cart."

The security woman in tight pants finally got the lids off. She slowly peeled back the Ethafoam and reached through the Styrofoam packing, pulled out a skull. "Okay, then! I have seen it all now." She slid it back into the box and looked at the officer. Both were shaking their heads in disbelief.

A businessman in a blue suit was walking by as she pulled out a second head and a mandible. Men in blue suits with PDAs don't take well to human heads on a table in the airport. He stopped dead in his tracks and watched. I looked away, feeling embarrassed as if the woman in tight pants was waving around my dirty knickers for all to see.

The officer had seen enough. The supervisor put the heads away and began to tape the roof back over their heads. "Okay. I'm gonna need to see some sort of paperwork stating you're allowed to have these things . . . these people, I mean these skulls."

I thought for a second. I didn't have any paperwork, and like a fool, my identification was in my checked bags. "I don't have anything."

The officer gave me a disapproving look and chided me. "Well, you better come up with something!"

I threw my arms up in the air. "If I had something, I'd give it to you." He stared at me. "I'm gonna miss my plane!" Now I was angry. "There's nothing in those boxes that's a risk to anyone on my flight. Can't I just give you some phone numbers and you can check it all out while I'm on my way back home?" I was pleading. "If you find something wrong, they can deal with it at the gate on the other end."

He pulled me off to the side. "How do I know you didn't just kill these people, or rob a grave?" He felt it necessary to restate what had become quite obvious. "You can't put a bunch of human heads in an X-ray machine in an airport and not expect someone to ask questions." He was right.

"Look, I was out here working and we are borrowing the skulls for research purposes. They are archaeological skulls, not modern ones." I interrupted the woman with the tape and opened the box again. "See!" I pointed to the lot numbers written on the skulls. "I swear to you, they are from museum collections. If I killed these people, I'd wrap them in carpeting, put them in my trunk, and drive them across country—I wouldn't pack them in a carry-on and fly!"

About ten minutes later I won my case, but missed my flight. I learned that there was a later departure, and when the plane finally took off, my little friends had their heads in the clouds.

CHAPTER 9

All Good Things Must Come to an End . . .

Working for the Crime Lab was kind of like working at a strip club. If you were at all bashful, it wasn't the job for you. On one of my first days in field training, I learned that inhibitions had to become a thing of the past or I'd wind up spending years in therapy. I was at the morgue with one of the detectives whose job I would soon steal, witnessing the autopsy of a presumed suicide victim, but I couldn't help but notice the woody on the man lying on the gurney next to me. I felt guilty about looking between the legs of a dead man and wondered if Jesus considered it a sin and gave me a black mark. I didn't want to have to sit in the confessional and say, "Bless me, Father, for I have sinned. In the week since my last confession I stared at the penis of a dead man." I'd be saying Hail Marys and Our Fathers until Armageddon.

The pathology resident caught me sneaking a peek and proceeded to show me how the man's penile implant worked. He let me feel the pump that was implanted in the guy's scrotum and showed me how depressing it several times moved a store of saline from the reservoir below into a cylinder that was surgically implanted in the penis, making it erect. To make it flaccid, you depressed a deflation site on the pump, which transferred the saline from the cylinder back into the reservoir in the scrotum. Now I'd have to tell the priest that I also fondled the scrotum of a dead man. I was doomed, especially if the priest peeked through the screen in the confessional and could attach a face to my sins.

So, that being said . . . you just can't be shy if you're going to survive as a CSI. That brings me to another frequently undiscussed bodily function whose remnants I frequently encountered. I don't know why people's cheeks turn red when its mentioned— after all, we all do it! Angelina Jolie, Cameron Diaz, George W. Bush, and even William Hung do it. Dr. Phil could be doing it as you read this, and I bet that Condoleezza Rice did it at least once already today. You know what I'm talking about: taking a dump.

Once I caught my old boss on the crapper. He was a man I completely respected, and part of me thought he had risen above the ranks of the rest of us who need to use the bathroom. I still recall seeing him sitting there, in a blue plaid shirt and a pair of jeans that were around his ankles. In both hands he held a wad of toilet paper and that surprised me because I thought most men folded the paper and most women crumpled. Regardless, when I opened the door, he was staring straight ahead. He looked at peace. I was in such shock that I couldn't even close the door—I just stood there, staring. He had to reach up and close it. We avoided each other for days after that.

I don't know why we're all so quirky about bathroom business. I worked at the Crime Lab with a girl who would spend each weekend at her boyfriend's place and squeeze her cheeks together the entire time. She would never consider pooping at his house, and they had been together for years. I felt bad for her when they went to Nags Head, North Carolina, for an entire week. Either she came back with buns of steel or was really hungry. Bob's friend once rented a hotel room just to take a crap while they were on a road trip because he couldn't "concentrate" at the rest stop. My current boss likes to fill the bowl with toilet paper first to prevent the splash effect, my best friend does the middump flush to prevent unnecessary clogging and odor, and my dad used to wrap his hand up in toilet paper before wiping and he called it his "little mitt." I even have a friend who won't sit on the toilet—not even her own—and another who cleans up with baby wipes to prevent unnecessary chaffing.

Women are especially peculiar when it comes to the secrets of the stall and there is an entire bathroom etiquette that I suggest all men thinking of becoming women in the near future should start learning. Ladies seem to have an inherent knowledge of the unwritten rules that govern what is and what is not appropriate bathroom behavior and these rules seem to be the most defined in the workplace. All women know that if you walk into a restroom and someone is in the last stall, farthest from the door, she is giving birth to something foul, but if she is in the first stall, closest to the door, she is just shaking the dew off the lily and will be on her way soon. It is never appropriate to enter a stall next to one that is occupied if others are free; doing so will cause the occupant who was there first to look at your shoes and then spend the rest of the day trying to figure out who you are. From that point on, you'll be known as "the Intruder." The woman in the unfortunate position of using the last stall also gets her shoes inspected and once her identity is known, you struggle to put that innocent face with the sounds and smells you experienced.

I used to work at a place where everyone took a paper toilet seat cover from the dispenser on the wall before they entered the stall. I did it too because I didn't want to be known as "Dana, the girl who doesn't use paper toilet seat covers." I faced the toilet (just in case anyone was watching my feet) and rustled the thing around for about five seconds and then just threw it in the bowl and hovered. I knew that a thin little piece of tissue paper wasn't going to protect my parts from whatever creatures lurked below.

You can tell sitters from hoverers from the distance between their feet. Sitters keep their feet close together in front of the bowl while the hoverers have them widely spaced on either side. If a bathroom doesn't have protective toilet seat covers, then those with their feet in front of the bowl get their shoes examined and everyone talks about them at lunch.

I always feel sorry for the people who sit and a little fart slips out. You know it's an accident because they don't even try to cover it with a cough or a fake sneeze. They definitely get their shoes looked at. This is really awkward if you're the only other person in the bathroom with them. It is hard to just sit there, or hover, silently listening to your neighbor let one rip. Sometimes I feel compelled to say something like, "Oh my, they're slippery little devils, aren't they!" or "Is everything okay over there?"

Then, of course, comes the hand washing. You always peek through the crack in the stall door to see who is coming and going and it is imperative that you see your stall mates make a stop at the sink and wash their hands. There was one woman in the Crime Lab who never washed her hands after watering the flowers and everyone steered clear of her contributions to the Christmas potluck luncheon. Hand washing or the pretend eyelash in the eye also serves as a ploy to see if anyone is in the bathroom if you have the urge to use the last stall. If someone is already in there and you're not quite crowning yet, you just pretend to wash your hands or get the eyelash from your eye, and then make a few fake photocopies until that particular pair of shoes walks past you in the hallway.

But for the person who is so mindful of bathroom etiquette, there is nothing worse than being accused of a toilet crime that you did not commit. It makes you know how the dog must feel each time you let him or her take the blame for your gassy transgressions. This kind of thing is even worse when you are in uniform though, because everyone knows that people in uniforms don't take dumps or have to fart and I sure as hell wasn't taking the blame for a turd that was located in the bathroom of a 7-11.

The store had been stuck up and I had just finished processing the scene and was getting ready to go. I decided to take advantage of the bathroom before I headed to my next call, so I slipped into the back while the officer and store clerk were busy talking. They didn't even see me head for the bathroom because their backs were toward me as they calculated exactly how much money was missing from the register. This store was one of my regular places to stop and get coffee and I knew the clerk would let me use the bathroom as he had done so many times before.

Answering Mother Nature's call with a boatload of equipment around my waist was always an uncomfortable task. Since my radio was secured in a holder on my belt, the first thing I had to do was unclip my lapel mike; otherwise the cord that connected the mike with the radio prevented me from pulling my pants down. Once the mike dangled in front of me, I was free to unbuckle my belt. But I learned from experience that this was a critical step; I absolutely, positively could not let the belt ends go. The few times I had done this, all my equipment slipped off and fell into the toilet. I had already ruined two pagers and a cell phone thanks to unbuckled pants. Once I had a belt end in each hand, then I had to unhook, unbutton, and unzip my pants and wiggle them as well as my underwear down low enough to engage in a hover. Over the years, I managed to get pretty quick at it. I got my pants into position, held onto the belt, and backed up over the can to begin watering the flowers. That's when I looked down and saw a mound of toilet paper in the crapper beneath me.

Ewww! I jumped forward and turned around to get a better look. I wondered how I hadn't noticed it earlier. I used my foot to flush and stood there holding my pants around my knees by the belt as I watched the toilet decide if it wanted to flush or not.

At first I heard a gurgle, then another one, and another. I gave it the look. *Don't even think about it!* The toilet tried to swallow everything in its bowl but it just didn't seem to have the room in its stomach. *C'mon! I think I can, I think I can!* It didn't have the confidence that I had in it. *C'mon!* I hoped the officer and clerk couldn't hear me having a conversation with the throne. It gurgled again and I could hear the water in the tank running. I stood there staring into the bowl, trying to *will* the paper down the hatch. But instead, I watched as the water started to rise and noticed that the turbulence was stirring up all sorts of oddly shaped turds that had apparently sunk to the bottom. *No! No!* I begged it to stop as I tried to get my pants up. *Please!* The water rose higher. *No!* It was starting to overflow and I stood there not knowing if I should drop my pants into the mess on the floor and turn off the water feeding the tank, or get my pants up and buckled and then turn it off. I backed up as I watched paper and turds crest the top of the tank and spill over onto the floor. I jumped for cover onto a milk crate. *Oh God! Oh God! Oh no!* I hoisted my pants up and fumbled with my belt and zipper, but things were happening quickly and I watched water and turds and paper start to wash under the wide gap beneath the bathroom door and into the back storage room.

Once I was buckled, I did the jump-and-scoot maneuver on the milk crate and shimmied it over to the toilet, where I could reach the water knob. I managed to get it turned off, but not before the bathroom was destroyed. There was water, millions of shreds of toilet paper, and little smeary brown turdlets everywhere. I knew that a few Little Debbie's had washed beneath the door and were probably resting comfortably next to the Slurpee machine. I prayed that the officer and clerk were still engaged in conversation because I didn't want them to think this was *my* mess!

I adjusted my shirt, reattached my lapel mike, and listened at the door to make sure the coast was clear before I ran for cover. I found the officer and clerk exactly where I had left them, with their backs still toward me. I grabbed my print kit, waved good-bye, and bailed out the door. I felt like I had just committed a hit and run.

Later in the night I handled another call with the same officer. It took everything I had not to laugh when he told me how he went to use the bathroom in the 7-11 before he left and found shit all over the place. He said he could tell that the clerk thought that *he* was the one who clogged the toilet and made the mess. The officer was mortified about something he didn't even do and told me he could never show his face in there again! I was very sympathetic.

It's a shame that they don't make toilets the way they used to. If people are eating more now than they did thirty years ago, I don't understand the rationale for making the water-holding capacity and outtake holes smaller. When I was ten, Dad installed a new toilet and proudly explained that it was as powerful as those on cruise ships. Chris and I knew better than to sit and flush—unless we were in the mood for disembowelment.

It is a fact that most people overeat, and this is particularly true on Thanksgiving. The unfortunate thing is that all of the delicious food that comes with the holiday eventually has to go. But sometimes getting rid of the blessed meal can be deadly. One poor soul was unable to resist the turkey gravy knocking at the back-door any longer. He pulled his car over on the shoulder of the road, dropped a load in the gravel, had a heart attack, and died. I don't want to be found like that—dead on the side of the road with my pants around my ankles being photographed by Crime Lab as I lie next to my supersized holiday leftovers.

Other people's last meals weren't always quite so elaborate— they didn't eat off of the fine china, use the silverware that their mothers got as wedding presents, or wipe their mouths on linen napkins folded like swans. Some people enjoy the simpler things in life. I once handled a suicide where the victim left a receipt on the kitchen counter that showed that he went to the grocery store about an hour before 911 received the call for shots fired. The receipt had four items listed on it: peanut butter, grape jelly, Wonder Bread, and a gallon of milk. On the table in front of the body were a partially eaten peanut butter and jelly sandwich and a glass of milk.

In 1994, Georgia-Pacific conducted a survey of people's bathroom habits and quirks and issued the *Quilted Northern Bathroom Confidential Report*. According to this survey, 74 percent of the respondents admitted to reading while riding the porcelain bus, while 47 percent talked on the phone, 23 percent watched television (who the hell has a television in the bathroom?), and 11 percent had a snack. One person confessed to playing the guitar and another meditated, but no one admitted to committing a crime while he or she was on the pot.

Georgia-Pacific needed to send a questionnaire to the guy in my neck of the woods who committed burglaries while he was pinching one off. In three weeks, this guy hit at least five houses. I knew it was the same person, not only from the fact that the burglaries were all in the same neighborhood but also because of the personal signature he left at each of his scenes. It was his calling card, so to speak.

Modus operandi (MO) is a Latin term meaning "method of operation" and it refers to the actions that are necessary for a perpetrator to commit a crime. Attributes of a burglary, for example, that come together to form the MO include the nature of the offense, location, time, means by which entry was gained, tools used, disguises worn, property taken, and so on. But sometimes perpetrators do something that is above and beyond what is necessary to execute a crime. They engage in behavior that has nothing to do with achieving their goal of burglary, robbery, or whatever the offense might be. This is called a signature and it is the means by which a criminal expresses him- or herself.

I had handled five burglaries in a two-block radius over the course of three weeks, and while I suspected the crimes were related, the unique calling card the suspect left behind confirmed it. This weirdo targeted single-family homes in an older neighborhood not that far from where I lived. All the houses in the development looked the same, right down to the screened-in front porches; the only thing that distinguished them was the color of the exterior paint and the style of lawn ornament. Since it was July, everyone had American flags waving in the front yard breeze. This was the first thing the burglar went for.

With flag in hand, the suspect climbed up the porch steps and entered through the unlocked storm door. The flag was then put in its new location: usually draped across the porch window or over a few chairs. That's when he (and I say *he* because women just don't do stuff like this) would get out his screwdriver and pry open the front door to the house. Once inside, he headed straight for the master bedroom and opened closets in his frantic search for a shoebox. Once he found one, he tossed the shoes on the floor and bee-lined back to the porch, stopping in the kitchen only long enough to grab a dishtowel or a sponge.

Feeling patriotic, he squatted down next to the flag and did what any other good American burglars would do: he shit in the shoebox. The dingle berries were wiped off with the dishtowel or sponge, which was then placed inside the box before the lid went back on. This nice package was left on the porch next to the front door for the homeowner to discover. Nothing was ever reported missing.

The shoebox shitter seemed to plan his crimes around the time he had to go, but for others, nature called when it was most inconvenient. I handled a lot of shitty burglaries and was directed to numerous bathrooms to see the floaters and sinkers of all shapes and sizes that the perpetrators left behind. For many criminals, the urge to go was probably a physiological response caused by the adrenaline rush that accompanied their crimes. On one scene, we could actually follow the path of the burglar because he left a trail of little nuggets and toilet paper in the victim's backyard, as well as in the yards of four of their neighbors. I envisioned him trying to hold a television in one hand and the waistband on his pants in the other as he scooted through the neighborhood making his escape, dropping turds the entire way. To think, I used to believe only dogs poop and walk at the same time.

Sometimes the burglars let some drop not because they had to, but because they wanted to. Being broken into was bad enough, but it was like rubbing salt in the wound when the burglar left a pile right in the middle of the living room floor. Usually, this happened when the suspect knew the victim, but didn't particularly care for them.

I saw this for the first time a few weeks after I was released from field training. The crime scene was located on the second floor of an apartment building in one of the county's shadier neighborhoods. I ascended the concrete stairs and could smell marijuana coming from one of the nearby apartments. I didn't care; it masked the stench of urine in the stairwell. I tried to over-look the garbage littering the floor and the roaches that met their demise from the Timberland and Air Jordan foot traffic. I took a minute to admire the artistic talents of those who spray painted their works of art on the walls and wondered who Akiria was. She seemed to be pretty popular with the boys.

When I got to the second floor of the building, it was pretty obvious which unit had been burglarized. Apartment 2C was missing the door; in fact, it was lying flat on the living room floor. A middle-aged man with a jiggley beer belly hanging out beneath a faded black Lynard Skynard concert T-shirt must have heard me come up the steps. He greeted me with a metal pipe in his hand. He didn't look like he was in a good mood.

I stood in the doorway and pretended to rap my knuckles on the missing door as I said, "Knock, knock." The man with the belly and old shirt didn't look amused.

"Took you Goddamn long enough to get here." He pointed to the door with the pipe. "Would you look at this shit?"

I looked at the door lying on the ground. It was dented around the lock and the doorframe contained toolmark impressions. Whoever knocked it down used something big, like a crowbar. The suspect would have made a lot of noise. I knew the neighbors had to have heard something—but in these parts of town, people never seemed to see, hear, or know anything when the police asked questions. I had to step on the door to get inside. "So, do you know where they got in?"

My humor wasn't appreciated. The man lit an unfiltered Camel using a lighter that resembled a pair of breasts. The flame came out of the left nipple. He threw the breasts on the coffee table when he was done and then took a long puff. "What, is this a big joke to you?" He let the cigarette dangle from his lips as he spoke, "I didn't wait no two hours to listen to your wisecracks." I pissed him off. "I'll tell you one thing, there won't be any laughing goin' on when I find out who the hell did this." He smacked the pipe in his palm. "Just you wait till you see what I do to 'em." He puffed again. "See who's joking then."

I changed the subject. "What did they do once they were inside?"

The man motioned for me to follow him to the bedroom. "I'll show you what they did." I followed him, trying not to think of the other women who made the same walk for some headbanger lovin'. He yanked the Camel from his mouth and pointed to the floor. "That's what them assholes did." He threw the pipe on the bed. "And when I find out who them little mother fuckers are, I'm gonna take care of it myself. I won't be callin' for the law. That's for damn sure."

"Well, whatever you do, make sure you do it before four in the morning so I don't get stuck on overtime." He liked that joke, because he smiled.

I wanted to laugh when I saw what the suspect did, but I didn't want to make him angry again. Perched in the middle of the carpeted floor were two extraordinarily long orangey-brown, solid turds. One of them was intact and its girth appeared painfully large. The other turd was the one that troubled me. For reasons known only to the suspect, he took it upon himself to use his bare hands to smash and smear it into the carpeting. I could make out the streaks in the light gray carpeting caused by his dirty little fingers.

"Okay then!" I really didn't know what to say. Usually, if a suspect left personal evidence behind, it was something like a jacket or set of keys. We then asked the homeowner if he or she recognized it. I didn't think that was appropriate in this case. That isn't to say that shit isn't recognizable. There is a product out there called Turd Twister, which is basically a template that you crap into. It enables users to shape their shits into amazing designs such as Christmas trees, moons, shamrocks, and gingerbread men. It's even dishwasher safe. But the shits lying on the bedroom floor in front of me were just the run of the mill variety. "Can you show me what else they did?"

"Yeah, I'll show you." The man went to the bathroom and pointed to a bottle of Pert shampoo on the vanity next to the sink. There was shit all over the bottle. "They took my shampoo from the tub and washed their damn hands with it." He stood there staring at me. I felt obliged to pretend to examine the bottle for fingerprints.

"Did they take anything?"

He motioned for me to follow him into the kitchen. "Look at that." He pointed to the coffee pot. "Them jackasses made a pot of coffee and then took the can. It was a brand new can too."

We walked back to the bedroom and stood side by side, staring at the turds. "So"—I tried to keep a straight face—"they broke down the door, made some coffee, shit on the rug, smashed it in with their hands, and cleaned up with Pert?"

The man just nodded.

"Must have been some pretty strong coffee!"

I had to run before he killed me.

It wasn't just bad people who found themselves having to face nature's call at the most inopportune times. I was right there with them. One time, I got caught watering the daisies in front of a bunch of CSIs, archaeologists, and federal agents who were trying to enjoy a quick break. We were surveying a wooded area for some unmarked graves, and I had become separated from the rest of the group as I worked on something several hundred feet away from them. I walked up to join everyone for lunch, but decided to take advantage of my last minute of privacy and get rid of the Gatorade that was making my bladder feel like it was a water balloon on the verge of bursting. I unbuckled, squatted, and started to go when I heard the giggles. Still squatting, I looked behind me only to discover the people I was working with lying on the ground taking a siesta. Since the bushes had no foliage on the bottom, I became known as a Moonie. My mother would be very upset to hear that I converted.

Then there was the time I was on a bus in Croatia and my bladder couldn't hold it a second longer; we weren't scheduled to stop for two more hours. I shoved a peanut bag that I found on the floor down my overalls and tried to be discrete about what I was doing—but that just made everyone else on the bus think this crazy American was busy with her hands down her pants petting her own poodle. I filled the cellophane bag to the top, only to discover that it was now stuck down my pants and I couldn't get it out without getting sloshed. It wasn't a problem for long because I soon further discovered that the bag had a hole. I'll spare you the rest of the details.

The Crime Lab vans didn't have windows in the back, so if we were tied up on a major call, particularly one in the middle of nowhere, most of the girls peed in the paint cans that were supposed to be used for arson evidence. I know of at least two guys who did that too. We all played dumb when our supervisors wondered why we went through the paint cans so fast.

Probably the hardest thing about my job was dealing with the most disgusting and awkward situations involving total strangers and doing it with a straight face. Take farting for example. It is like religion in a lot of ways. Just as it is inappropriate to force others to share in your religious convictions, it is entirely wrong to force them to endure the smell coming from your back alley. When I was in high school, my friend's boyfriend stopped by her house to pick her up for a football game. While he fiddled with something on the bumper, she slid into the car and let one rip. That was when she noticed the other couple sitting in the backseat. But at least she was embarrassed. Some people could care less!

You tell me, how is it possible to stand in some guy's living room and ask him to provide details of the crime that has just occurred, while he is letting wet-sounding bubbles, toots, and squeaks tear out of his ass? It smelled like someone crawled up this guy's butt and died! I excused myself from the house about three times so that I could get a breath of fresh air before I went back in for another round. I tried so hard to keep a straight face, but when he bent down to get something out of a file cabinet, the loudest of all of them registered as a tremor on the Richter scale. That was it! I asked him if he needed me to call an ambulance. He looked at me and asked, "For what?" That's when I lost it and told him that we had to talk outside or I'd come back later. I thought for sure I was on *Candid Camera* or the *Jamie Kennedy Experiment*.

If all good things must come to an end, it isn't always necessarily the rear end. I saw my share of vomit, too. I had a guy who bought two cabbages from the supermarket, then vomited and died in the parking lot, and a guy who was so upset that the police locked up his son that he vomited corn on my boots. People yakked in the tub and in the toilet and the department issued us special ventilators to keep them from hurling in our mouth while we were performing CPR. I hate vomit. I really don't like it at all.

Only on two occasions did I see people from my own department lose their cookies. On one scene, a man had been killed and bled out into the street. The fire department, for whatever reason, decided to pour hydrogen peroxide onto the blood just as my co-worker was getting ready to reach into it and feel for a projectile or casing. The blood was already starting to clot and it foamed because of the peroxide. I couldn't watch as she felt through the frothy soup of clots. She made a few trips to the bushes. I almost joined her.

Another time, a man shot himself in the head with a rifle. In high-velocity gunshot wounds to the head, it isn't uncommon for the massive discharge of gas to force the brain out of the skull. Oftentimes, it is relatively intact. In this case the brain landed on the suicide note. An officer who was still in field training was ordered to help me. I gave her the task of getting the note out from underneath the brain. It didn't go over well, and she looked like a mother bird feeding her babies as she hung over the back deck and hurled into the bushes.

I handed the officer a stick of gum and the rest of my Diet Coke. She took them both and then sat in the police car for a while. Those who got sick on the job were often humiliated, but in the Crime Lab, we never made fun of those who did it. In a way, it was a somber reminder that we were all human and what we were forced to see, think about, and touch was real and wrong. It was wrong for people to die in such states, and it was wrong not to be affected by it. The young officer finally came back about fifteen minutes later and apologized to me for getting sick. I will always remember how her apology made me feel; much like I'll always remember how watching the autopsy of the girl in the red gingham suit and white shoes made me feel. Why should anyone feel the need to apologize for having the emotional responses that were normal—the rest of us were the ones with the problem.

But as long as I had a problem, I might as well make the best of it. I headed off to check out the guy who died watching Animal Planet while masturbating and breathing nitrous oxide.

CHAPTER 10

As Much Fun as a Barrel Full of Monkeys . . .

On <u>CSI</u> they don't talk about farting victims. There are no hobbits that carry on conversations with an imaginary spouse, and people don't die with cabbages. But the truth is stranger than fiction and as one of my friends say, "You just can't make this shit up!"

When our Crime Lab shifts ended, we all congregated around the lunch table and compared stories—and were there ever stories! April told us about hanging over the face of a dead guy as she looked for injuries when she was startled by his voice. He said, "Hi. This is Jim. I can't come to the phone right now." She freaked out and spun around to discover the answering machine on a nearby table. Then there was the time that she found herself alone in a basement with a dead guy. As she walked around, she accidentally stepped on a board that happened to be under his arm. She almost died too because his arm suddenly flew up as if he was trying to grab her ankle. Something similar happened to me when I was photographing the face of a dead woman. My camera was only a few inches away from her nose as I tried to take a picture of a scratch when she suddenly started to hiss at me. I just about soiled my knickers and tore out of that room like a bat out of hell.

The ME assured me that it was just gasses settling, but I wasn't convinced and made an officer stand next to me while I finished processing the scene. The officers got a spook from time to time, too, and I cannot imagine anything more startling than the detective who found a body covered in maggots. As it turned out, the person was still alive.

Debbie talked about the woman who asked her if she saw sparks while she turned the lights on and off, and described a scene involving a dead guy on the grill at a local restaurant. Apparently, he was trying to break in from the roof and got stuck inside a grease vent, where he asphyxiated. After his body relaxed, he shot through like a hot knife through butter. Dave handled the veterinarian who performed self-euthanasia in the bank's safety-deposit box room, and Denise caused a car accident when she leaned into the van on a busy street to get her camera. I wonder what that driver was looking at! I spilled black fingerprint powder into the batter at Dunkin' Donuts, Jason met a woman who asked him to look inside her ass because it was burning, and Kathi handled a call where the guy had no qualms about admitting to having sex with the dog. On midnight shift, we all knew the woman who had a tanning bed in her living room and answered the door naked after her boyfriend beat her up each week.

There was the shooting that occurred when something went wrong while a bunch of guys were trying to act out a scene in a gay porn flick called *Double Handful*, the guy who overdosed and whose friends filled his pants with ice before leaving him to die, and the burglary victim who wouldn't let me into his place at two in the morning because the hour was inappropriate for a decent woman to be out and about, much less inside his apartment.

We all got a kick when officers asked us to check panties for seamen (as opposed to semen)—I felt the need to salute and start singing the Village People's "In the Navy." Jocelyn got shit dripped on her head, Cathy got chemicals in her mouth, Carrie went to the ER because of pepper spray, Bob had a lice exposure, and someone must have gotten worms because they were found floating in the men's room toilet. We all got into car accidents.

All the civilian investigators in the Crime Lab came from different backgrounds. Some had been security guards, one was a train crash examiner for the National Transportation and Safety Board, one had been a police officer in Kansas, a few were former ten-print examiners, and one even managed the Taco Bell around the corner. But the one thing that we all had in common was a sense of humor. You had to have one in this line of work.

One story that we all got a kick out of was the man who was strung out on crystal meth. It all started when the police responded to a domestic disturbance and found the wacko bouncing off the ceiling. He had pushed his girlfriend through the plasterboard wall and then fell back through the glass coffee table in the living room. His girlfriend was okay, but he was shredded like mozzarella cheese.

The guy wasn't too happy to see the police and decided to start swinging punches, so the officers didn't hesitate to wet him down with pepper spray. When he was finally in custody, I had to go to the hospital to photograph his injuries; primarily to cover the department's ass since force was used against him.

I parked in a spot outside the emergency room that was reserved for the police. As soon as I exited my vehicle, I could hear blood-curdling screams emanating from inside the treatment wing. The closer I got, the louder they got and I felt terrible for the kids in the waiting room who needed stitches and had to listen to the unreassuring wailing of an adult behind the blue double doors.

I was directed to a part of the emergency room that I had never seen before and was greeted by several police officers and nurses. I initially thought I was witnessing a new interrogation technique as I watched the nurses hose down the naked, shackled suspect with cold water. They were cleaning the pepper spray off his body so that they could treat him. I soon realized that he wailed not when the cold water touched his skin or washed through his open cuts. He screamed when pepper-laden cold water washed over his manliness. He played with fire and he got burned.

But screaming and wailing wasn't as ominous as moaning. I

was in the Lab late one night putting evidence inside one of the lockers when I heard something start to moan, like it was in horrific pain. *Uhhhhhhhhhhhh*. It scared me shitless! I spun around catching a glimpse of a large trash bag inside one of the lockers. That was where it was coming from, but I certainly wasn't going to be the one to investigate it. I made a mad dash for the door, but my rubber-soled boot caught on the carpeting and I fell flat on my face.

One of the detectives was just rounding the corner. He stopped and looked at me.

"Mike!" I scrambled back to my feet. "There is someone in that bag." I beckoned for him to come inside the room. "Listen." We both stood there silently craning our necks to hear, but there was no moaning. Mike combed his moustache as he listened. He looked like Sam Elliott and had a twisted, but funny sense of humor. Mike had been in Vietnam and I loved hearing his stories about how the women would pee standing up. He extended his thumb and index finger; and went on to explain how they'd press the thumb against their urethra and the urine would stream down their thumb and across their index finger and they could direct the flow with what I understood was pretty amazing precision. I wondered why they didn't just keep their hands dry and squat. If anything, I thought something like that would be a neat party trick.

Mike gave up. "You're crazy. I don't hear anything." He walked over to check his mailbox, which was really a repository for all the stuff that didn't fit into his desk any longer. I stared back at the trash bag and it acknowledged me with another moan. *Uhhhhhhhhhhhh*.

"Mike! It's doin' it! Come here—fast!" I was hysterical. He tossed his mail back in his pigeonhole and walked back over to me shaking his head and twisting the end of his moustache.

"It's not funny, hurry!" I pointed to the locker. "There is someone or something alive inside that bag!" I knew it sounded crazy, but I didn't care. "It sounds like someone is dying in there."

The moaning stopped just as Mike approached. "*What* are you talking about?" He listened to the sound of silence for another second. "I don't hear a damn thing."

We both stood there staring into the doorway of the room. "Go check the tag on the bag. See what kind of case it's from." I certainly wasn't going to do it. Mike went in and I waited at the door.

I pointed to the bag. "That one."

Mike used his master key to open the locker. "It's from Rob's suspicious death earlier today." I was vaguely familiar with the call. I heard him talking about it at the lunch table. He was complaining because the guy died in a motel room and since his identity was unknown, Rob had to collect all his property for safekeeping. "I think Rob knows better than to package a body." Mike slammed the locker's door, walked toward me, and turned off the light.

I stood in the doorway so Mike couldn't leave. "Just wait here a second! It will moan again!" It was silent. "Moan, damn it, moan!"

Mike waited for a few seconds and then pushed me aside so that he could close the door. "Let's go—you need some sleep."

Before the door could close all the way, I grabbed it. "Listen, listen!"

Uhhhhhhhhhhhhh! He raised one eyebrow and flipped the light back on and jokingly put his hand on his weapon.

"See, I told you!"

He opened the locker again and handed me the bag. He was smiling. "If you think there is a body in there, you need to check it out."

I carried the bag into the Processing Lab to search for a body and that's when I discovered what it was. I could feel the pager vibrating through the bag. It had apparently been lying against the metal shelf and each time it alerted, the vibrations made the moaning sound. We all laughed about that one for weeks—but it just goes to show how something so familiar to you can become foreign when your frame of reference is eliminated.

We played a lot of jokes on one another in the Lab, and one of the biggest pranksters was a guy named Steve. He would make fake spiders out of balls of paper and attach a thread, which he would tape to the tops of doors. The best was when he hid a paper spider in the hatch of a car in the Crime Lab garage. When Cathy opened it, the spider fell down and dangled from the thread only inches away from her face. She broke all her fake fingernails trying to get away from the thing.

When the detectives were still assigned to Crime Lab, the joking was out of control. It was fun, but crazy. One guy filled the vents of one of the vans with pepper spray and turned the blower to high so that when the next person started the ignition, he or she would get blasted. The peppered detective retaliated and filled the vents with black fingerprint powder; a deed reciprocated by stuffing the vents with a million paper circles removed from the hole puncher. When one of the detectives was on an extensive crime scene on a scorching hot summer day, one of the others slid by his location not to offer assistance, but to hide an open can of anchovies under the liner in his trash can. It was there for days before someone discovered the source of the smell. That started the "let's hide gross food " string of attacks and I even got pulled into it when I discovered a moldy tuna fish sandwich shoved in the back of my desk.

Annie lived at the Crime Lab and could usually be found hiding beneath desks, peeking over file cabinets, snoozing in the hallway closet, or hanging from a noose somewhere. She was a full-sized mannequin that had been murdered a bunch of times and only wore a raincoat and boots. Annie looked like a flasher with matted hair and a bloody face, and had undergone numerous plastic surgeries to have silicone scars added to her body and a hatchet imbedded in her head. Annie was popular and a regular guest at the Lab's Christmas luncheons and baby showers. When some of the new people were in training, they were processing a mock murder scene in the woods. Once again, poor Annie was the victim. But even the general public was sympathetic to her plight, and a few people called 911 to report a bunch of men dragging a naked, bloody woman with a hatchet in her head through the woods by her hair.

Annie's arms came off and got lost. As a matter of fact, I can't remember if Annie ever had arms. She reminded me of the county's police helicopter, which always seemed to be without its doors. The doors were probably with Annie's arms, but I knew better than to complain about the missing doors ever since I cursed like a sailor about them the time I went up in the chopper to take aerial photographs. I thought I was mumbling to myself; nobody told me that the helmets had voice-activated microphones in them.

I still laugh when I think about sneaking Annie into one of the other investigators' van. I was hysterical as I followed the van down the highway watching other motorists point to the naked, bloody, armless woman wearing a raincoat with a hatchet in her head looking out of the back window. That was only to be topped by the looks we got when we drove around the highway in hairnets, goggles, and full respirator masks. We did it just for the hell of it. Childish, I know, but fun.

Having a full-sized mannequin in the Lab was almost as fun as having Ray Charles dressed in a tuxedo and holding a Pepsi hang out with us. One of the detectives also named Ray, picked up this life-sized cardboard cutout at his part-time job and drove around with him everywhere. We would run into Ray Charles and his Pepsi in the hallway, in the parking lot, and once I even found him sneaking a peek in the ladies' room. Ray took Ray Charles to crime scenes with him too, but Ray Charles was banned from the Lab when a defense attorney noticed him in the background of some homicide photographs, still wearing a tuxedo and holding the same bottle of Pepsi.

But the fun didn't end there. Keith, one of the dayshift people, had been temporarily assigned to midnights and wasn't too happy about it. Trying to make the best of a bad situation, I decided to go out of my way to welcome him to the shift. It was a Friday night and the time seemed perfect to hang a big sign from the back of his Crime Lab van. We had rolls and rolls of brown paper in the Lab that we used to wrap evidence and keep work surfaces clean. I taped a huge sheet of paper to the back of his vehicle and wrote only two innocent words on it: I'M COOL!

The following morning, once Keith finished threatening to kill me, he sat at the lunch table telling us how he drove around most of the night not knowing about the sign. He went from call to call, through the strip of bars on the main drag, across the interstate, over the river, and through the woods wondering why people in adjacent cars were slowing their speed to get a good look at the man in the police uniform driving the Crime Lab van with a big sign that said I'M COOL. Keith said some people beeped at him, others gave a thumbs up, and some pointed and laughed. It wasn't until his shift was halfway over that an officer reluctantly told him about the sign.

Paybacks were hell and for the next several months I found all sorts of similarly embarrassing signs on my personal vehicle. A full-fledged war was launched. The next opportunity arose when Keith was back on dayshift. He wore his departmentally issued coat that said CRIME LAB in great big letters across the back. I taped a note below CRIME LAB that read, BUT YOU CAN CALL ME MR. CSI. I was delighted when Keith returned to the lunch table that afternoon and told us how he walked around all day wondering why people were calling him Mr. CSI. He'd probably still have the note taped to his back if it weren't for the kind-hearted man at the credit union who tapped him on the shoulder and said, "Mister CSI, eh?" He pulled the note off Keith's back and handed it to him.

When new people started, we didn't hesitate to set them up either. After all, the detectives did it to us. I answered the telephone when I was in field training to hear "dispatch" on the other end tell me I had to go process a recovered stolen dog. So, doing unto others as had been done to me, I put on an accent and called the Lab from a phone around the corner. I pretended to be a victim wondering when the Crime Lab was going to show up to process the tusks of my wombats for latent prints since they had been handled by a potential burglar (wombats don't even live in the USA, nor do they have tusks).

Another time, in a thick English accent, I begged the technician to come to my home to have my girl processed for latents so I could figure out the name of the guy I just had great sex with, and other times I called the Lab claiming to have been recently abducted by aliens and needing my body scanned for foreign objects. The best were the calls where I requested detailed information on how to properly destroy blood evidence and reduce a body to ash, leaving the impression I had just killed someone.

I shouldn't be so quick to make fun of the other people because there were plenty of times that the joke was on me. The drying locker was perhaps the grossest room in the Crime Lab. It was where we air-dried wet evidence and stored things with bugs. The room smelled like a combination of blood, garbage, and cheese and I hated going in there for fear something would drip on my head or land on my cheek. When I first started working for the department, we hung our wet evidence on new hangers attached to clotheslines that were strung from one end of the room to the other. The problem was that the room was small and you always found yourself walking like a hunchback under the goopy things hanging above, and who the hell wanted to get blood clots in their hair? The other issue was that, although we were careful, there was the possibility for cross-contamination between cases. Eventually, the clotheslines gave way to separate drying cabinets so that evidence could be kept apart.

One day I opened the door to the drying locker and scanned the room for anything with wings that threatened to fly into my hair. I hated bugs as much as I hated vomit and even had my first car accident when a locust got tangled in my hair and I jumped out of the car while it was still in drive. When I was sure the coast was clear, I garnered the nerve to run inside and hang my evidence. That's when I saw it: it was the biggest Goddamn bug I ever saw in my life and it reminded me of the beetles on pins in Claudine Plisko's basement. Her father was an entomologist and as kids we loved going over to her place to look at the impaled beetles in the cabinets and her miscarried sibling that her parents kept in a glass canning jar surrounded by flowers. Remember—you can't make this shit up!

The bug was about two and a half inches long and it had a three-inch wingspan. It was green and black with big yellow eyes that probably had X-ray vision. I shrieked when I saw it and ran out of the room before it laid eggs on me. I grabbed some embalming spray that had been on the shelf in the room for years and sprayed the hell out of the thing, hoping to pickle it—but it didn't even flinch. I sprayed it again and again—letting it soak in a cloud of poison, but when the cloud dissipated it was still hanging there, glaring at me with its beady eyes. Finally, I got the broom and gave it a whack. The bug fell from the vent and slammed onto the floor. I beat it and beat it and beat it and then tried to smash it under a metal trash can, but it was a tough guy and I couldn't crush it. Finally, exhausted, I surrendered my attack and assessed my damage to the thing. That's when I saw MADE IN TAIWAN on its abdomen.

I have a tendency to put my foot in my mouth a lot, but the latest things that rolled off my tongue seemed to make for good lunch table stories. My problem is that I say what's on my mind, even if it isn't always appropriate. I try to think before I speak, but my brain seems to be hardwired to my mouth and before I know it, something has slipped out. Once I had a student named Mandy. I called her name on the first day of class as I was taking attendance, and before I knew it, the fact that I have a dog named Mandy blew through my lips with the force of hurricane winds. I couldn't stop it, then spent the rest of the class apologizing to her in front of her thirty-four classmates. It really wasn't meant to be offensive though.

Then there was the guy who had the horrible bruises on his face, and I didn't hesitate to tell him how bad they looked, only to discover it was a birthmark, and then he showed me the small contusion on his forearm. There was also the victim with the worst handwriting on Earth. I told him that penmanship wasn't obviously his strong point and that's when he showed me the one and a half fingers on his right hand. He lost the other ones in Vietnam. *Nice.* And I can't forget about the guy who was shot in the ass and the bullet lodged in the shaft of his penis. He was unconscious and was waiting to go into surgery. As the trauma resident pulled aside the bandages revealing the obvious hump beneath his skin, I scolded him and said it was a crime against his lady friends to take something like that out. Someone whopped me upside the head with a metal clipboard for that one.

And along came Tom Matte. I never heard of him because I hate football. As a matter of fact, there aren't many sports I do like; synchronized swimming and ice skating, do those count? I don't even know how you play football and I don't want to learn. I have better things to do with my time, like bury dead animals in the yard. Bob would later tell me that Matte was a famous halfback/running back for the Baltimore Colts and between 1961 and 1972 he made fifty-seven touchdowns and tied for sixty-third with Natrone Means, Wilbert Montgomery, Jim Nance, and Ken Willard on the NFL All-Time Rushing Touchdowns List. Whatever, good for him. Maybe I'd be more enthused if I knew what the hell a running back was and what it meant to rush. I thought rushing was when girls tried to get into sororities.

I found myself in a football predicament when an officer raised me on the radio and asked if I would respond to a burglary of a garage. He stated that he knew this was not something Crime Lab would ordinarily respond to, but hoped I would help him as a favor. I agreed and shortly thereafter arrived at a large house and was met by the officer and the homeowners. I learned that after the suspect entered the garage, the victim's SUV was broken into and searched. As I rummaged through the truck's interior looking for items to fingerprint, I uncovered a Baltimore Ravens seasonal parking permit that was on the floor buried beneath the contents of the glove compartment. The couple was overjoyed to see that the permit had not been stolen. That's when a bout of diarrhea of the mouth kicked in. Before I knew it, things were slipping out. "I wouldn't have stolen it either."

The man, who was big, hovered over me as I kneeled on the floor of his garage and dusted for prints. He wanted an explanation. "What do you mean you wouldn't have taken it?" He was smiling, so I knew he was pulling my leg. "Do you know how much that thing is worth?" I tried to blow it off, but he was persistent. "What, aren't you a football fan?" He tapped my shoulder. "Don't you support your team?"

I ignored the officer's gestures to shut up. He knew I told it the way it was. I turned to the big man and my lips just started moving before my brain was even involved. "I don't get why people enjoy watching a bunch of big, fat, dumb guys jump on each other." The officer buried his face in his hands. It was over. I had called Tom Matte a big, fat, dumb guy who liked to jump on other men. That weekend, Bob turned on the television and guess who was announcing the football game? None other than my new friend Tom.

I got to poke through a lot of sports stars' underwear drawers when their homes were broken into. If I knew who the hell half of these people were, then maybe I'd be prouder about having peeked at their skivvies. As far as I know, I was in the homes of at least five football players, two baseball players, a jockey, and a jouster. I also visited the abodes of two actors and the weatherman from one of the local news channels. I didn't see the weatherman's underwear. I would have liked to, though.

When I had to do a search warrant in the middle of winter on another football player's house, my mother left a message on my answering machine after she saw my cameo on the news. "Dane, you didn't look too happy. Is everything okay?"

When I saw the close up of my face on the six o'clock news, I saw what she was talking about. It was clear I was ranting about something.

I called my mother back and explained, "I was walking down the sidewalk, through two and a half feet of ice-capped snow, hollering to the homicide detectives that in two weeks this dude makes more than I make in a damn year and he can't even pay to get his flippin' sidewalk shoveled!"

I might have been poor next to this guy, and my sidewalk might have been chewed up because I threw the wrong kind of salt on it, and I might not have had a salt water aquarium built into the middle of my living room table—but at least my walk was shoveled.

CHAPTER 11

Out of the Mouths
of Babes . . .

Crime Lab isn't normally dispatched to calls that are heart warming. As a matter of fact, I didn't respond to a whole lot that was warm. Within a few weeks of taking the job with the department, it became quite clear that rescuing kittens from trees and returning lost kids to their overjoyed parents were pleasantries only the cops got to enjoy. We didn't help old ladies change flat tires. Instead, we were called on when the old lady didn't park far enough over on the shoulder and got intimate with the grille of a passing eighteen wheeler. The walls of the Crime Lab would never look like those in the police precincts, thickly wallpapered with thank-you notes and letters written by victims of crime and citizens in need. We were nobody's heroes. We were the crew with stomachs of steel that showed up when a nasty job needed to be done. We were the grim reapers of the department that appeared only when something was dead, almost dead, bloody, gross, or contained juice that leaked from someone's eyes, ears, nose, mouth, ass, or crotch. I wanted to put a slogan just below the CRIME LAB stamped on the backs of our coats that said: IF YOU KILL THEM, WE WILL COME. We did the stuff that nobody else wanted to do: we were the condom collectors, the vomit samplers, pubic pluckers, the semen swabbers, and the dumpster divers of the department. Life's unpleasantnesses were our business, and we would perform unthinkable tasks without hesitation and with smiles on our faces—and you didn't even have to say thank you!

It is kind of ironic that the Crime Lab is so visible on television, when in reality it is anything but. I always thought it was funny when people found out where I worked. They'd tell me they didn't even know that the county had a Crime Lab. I'd go on to explain that they have existed in places other than Nevada for a number of years now. The truth is that, unlike the activities of the police, all that happened in the Crime Lab did so behind closed doors. Maybe that is part of the draw of shows like *CSI*—it lets some people act on their voyeuristic tendencies and peek through the keyhole in the Crime Lab door just like I peek through the bathroom stall door to see if people are washing their hands. Since we are really like the secret society of Masons, the public doesn't know about the backlog of cases in the Latents and Serology Units. It doesn't realize that Gary has to process evidence from over 1,000 cases a year as well as maintain the SICAR (Shoewear Identification Comparison and Recovery) database, perform shoe and tire examinations, keep up supplies in the processing laboratory, and squeeze in trips to photograph the outsoles of new shoes at Target and Footlocker. The public is unaware that the wanted posters and enhanced surveillance tapes they see on the eleven o'clock news were done by Carrie and Graham and that the prints that caught the axe murderer down the street were recovered by Kim, who did it on seven hours of overtime. They don't have a clue that Debbie, who should have picked up her kids at the sitter's house an hour ago, was forced to stay late to digitally enhance Kim's prints and that Joyce, the latent fingerprint examiner who normally doesn't work on Saturdays, got called in to enter them into the system. The public isn't aware that its taxes paid to send several of us all over the country to conferences and footwear identification, tire examination, computer forensics, and trace examination schools—to name only a few. There is a lot that goes on behind that big black door that says CRIME LAB.

For me, one of the worst parts about my job was the complete lack of recognition for a job well done. None of us in the Lab begged for acknowledgment, but a pat on the back from time to time was nice; whether it was from a victim, a supervisor, an officer, or a detective. It made the overtime, the finger in my mouth, and the mung stuck to my shoes all seem worth it. Occasionally, one of the assistant state's attorneys would write a letter thanking me for my hard work, but that and a few other miscellaneous "attagirls" were about it. If we recovered critical evidence from a crime scene or managed to get fingerprints, hairs, or blood that provided a lead in a case, the CSI as well as the Crime Lab were the best thing since sliced bread. But for those murders, rapes, and robberies where the evidence just wasn't there, the Crime Lab suddenly sucked and so did the CSI who handled the case. One day we were great, and the next we were all a bunch of lazy losers.

When Thanksgiving and Christmas rolled around, we didn't hold out much hope that the local businesses would send *us* deli trays and pastries. It was yet another reminder that we were anything but cops. As the night drew on and the hunger pangs stabbed in our stomachs, we found ourselves grazing through the leftovers in the precinct roll call rooms. Our job was thankless and our unit was invisible.

I tried to imagine some of the letters that would adorn our walls if people *were* to realize we existed and send us thank-you notes. They might go something like this:

Dear Madam,
    Last week I was taken into custody as a possible suspect in a sex offense. You responded to the scene to collect some of my pubic hair. I am writing to commend you on the fine pluck job that you did. The pain was minimal and your words were comforting. You turned what would have been an otherwise awkward situation into a joyous occasion.

And no wall would be complete without one like:

Dear Ms. Kollmann,

Last week I was the victim of a crime. I left the mall and approached my car only to find the driver's side door covered in what appeared to be semen. You jokingly referred to the case as a drive-by shooting. Nevertheless, you confidently swabbed up a nice-sized glob and transported it back to the Crime Lab. You must make your parents very proud.

A decade in the field had forever changed me. When I started working for the Crime Lab, I was goofy but shy, not very assertive, and lacking self-confidence because I didn't have much experience. But dealing with the dark side of life, day in and day out, made me into a completely different person—a person I wasn't quite sure what to think of. I liked the self-confidence I had come to acquire and I was a good investigator—and I am not embarrassed to say that. But what I didn't like were the preconceived ideas I had begun to formulate about people I had never even met. I didn't hesitate to think that the woman walking down the street in the middle of the night was a pavement princess peddling her booty and the kids on the corner were trying to hustle a few nickel and dime bags of crack. I wondered what the real story was regarding the victim who had been beaten with a pipe, and what the homicide victim did to get himself into such a hopeless predicament. I assumed that all skinny women with Jurassic-era facial features were heroin junkies and only criminals and archaeologists wore Timberland boots. I had become more distant from my friends outside of work and even my family to a certain degree. But the thing that bothered me the most was that I had really started to lose touch with feelings of sympathy and even empathy. I don't think it is healthy to live in a world where you are forced to dull the sensations of the most basic human emotions.

The fact that there really were truly innocent, good people out there was driven home the night I met a little boy named Alex. It was the night before Christmas and Alex came home from picking up his grandparents only to discover that the grinch had paid a little visit while he and his family were gone. As Coolio would say, these grinches were "taught by the scholars who don't read books," and they took their business seriously. Hell-bent on ruining Christmas for everyone, they didn't waste time squeezing down the chimney (or in this case breaking through the sliding glass door) and taking all the goodies from under the tree.

It was about midnight, and despite the damper that must have been cast on this family's holiday spirit, the place still looked cheerful and festive from the outside. Santa and his reindeer were on the roof and a big inflatable snowman swayed in the wind. The house was outlined in red and green lights and Christmas balls hung from the cherry tree next to the sidewalk. There were two big toy soldiers on either side of the front door. A face peered out of the upstairs picture window as soon as I pulled into the driveway. A few seconds later the front door flew open and a man in his mid-thirties rushed out and met me at my van. "Can I help you carry something?" He was breathy and sounded desperate to get me inside.

People were under the false impression that I'd collect fingerprints, rush back to the Lab and examine them, notify the officer of a print hit, and would be made an arrest within the hour. The reality was that I'd collect prints (assuming there were any) and at the end of my shift I'd drop them in a lock box. On Monday morning the latent examiners would get them from the box, but violent crimes took precedence over property crimes and there was always a case backlog. Hopefully, prints from a burglary would make it into the system in a week or two. If there was a hit, the burglary detectives would be notified. They would then do their investigation and if necessary issue an arrest warrant. None of this happened overnight, and the chances of victims getting their property back were slim. I handed the man my clipboard and pretended to hurry.

I walked into the living room to find Mom, Granny, Gramps, and Alex sitting side by side on the sofa and staring silently at the pile of torn paper, ribbons, and empty boxes that were left scattered beneath the Christmas tree. Alex was the first to greet me. He darted off the sofa and ran toward me in his dinosaur pajamas. He was about four or five. "Daddy says you gonna catch the person that stoled the presents."

He was a cute little boy with blond hair and big blue eyes. I patted his head. "I'm sure gonna try." Alex inspected the gadgets on my belt and asked for a description of each and every one of them. I didn't tell him how many times each of them had fallen in the crapper. I pulled my flashlight out of the holder on my hip and handed it to him. "Can you help me out by holding this?" Alex's jaw dropped and he looked at his mother in disbelief. She smiled and gave him a subtle nod. "It's heavy, so hold it with two hands." I felt sorry for this kid. Christmas is supposed to be a magical time, not one ruined by a junkie who forgot to do his shopping.

"So, Alex," I talked to him but glanced at Dad to make sure he was listening to my questions. "Do you think you can show me where the bad person got in?" Alex was full of energy, even at midnight, and danced toward the sliding glass door, shining the flashlight on the broken shards that lay on the floor. The glass explained why Alex was wearing tennis shoes with his pajamas. "Right here and he throwed a rock." Dad listened but let Alex do the talking. He was the man of the house.

I gave Dad a little smile as I listened to Alex hypothesize about the angle and speed with which the rock was thrown. When he was finished, I asked him to show me the other rooms the bad guy went in. I was happy to learn that the crime scene was confined to the living room—or so Alex thought. Dad would later inform me that Alex's presents from Santa had been stored on the top shelf of the master bedroom closet. They were also missing.

I rummaged through my fingerprint kit as Alex held the flashlight over my shoulder trying to light everything up for me. "Why don't you help me carry a few things over there." I nodded toward the tree as I handed Alex fingerprint cards, envelopes, scissors, and tape. He scurried away and stacked the items beneath the tree while I grabbed my powders and brushes.

I looked at the mess before me and wondered where I should even start. The bulk of the processing would involve finger-printing wrapping paper and department store clothing boxes. I decided I would use three different techniques to try to get prints. The lids to the clothing boxes and much of the wrapping paper were shiny, preventing the oils from being absorbed into the sur-face. I would process these using standard black powders. The bases of the boxes had a normal, matte finish and would have likely absorbed the oils from the fingertips. Porous surfaces such as these called for magnetic powder. Finally, I would collect a few pieces of torn gift wrap as evidence and transport them back to the Lab, where they would be processed with a chemical called Ninhydrin, which reacts with the amino acids in fingerprints and turns the latents a bright purple color. They are then photo-graphed.

I started with the lid to one of the clothing boxes. Alex's eyes bugged out of his head as he watched me slide on my cafeteria lady–style plastic gloves. I just needed a white jacket, a hairnet, and a chicken patty to complete the part. Unless a scene was bio-hazardous, we didn't normally wear latex gloves while finger-printing because of the expense and because it was possible to leave latents through the latex (shhh, don't tell the bad guys). However, the last thing we want is to have *our* prints show up on a crime scene.

I shook my powder before opening it and heard the pennies in the jar clink against the metal lid. These kept the powder from clumping. My brush was old and greasy from processing too many fast-food joints and I had been meaning to trade it in for a new one. I swirled it in the lid to my powder to lightly coat the bristles and instructed Alex to stand closer to me and hold the light. I twirled my brush so it danced over the box surface and within seconds, prints begin to emerge. I was told my ability to twirl a fingerprint brush is what got me the background part of a CSI on the television program *Homicide: Life on the Street*.

Alex was ecstatic as he watched the prints come into view and literally danced for joy as he looked on. "Mommy, Daddy, Granny!"

He ran over to the sofa where they were all sitting. "See!" He pointed to me! "Did you see—she's gonna catch the man!" Alex came back over to me and watched for a second. "It's a black man, right?" I just looked at him. "A black man was in our house today, right?"

I was taken aback. "I don't know who was in your house today, Alex, but I'm gonna try to help figure it out." I moved the box back and forth trying to get a better look at the prints that developed.

"It was a black person. I know it was!" I ignored him, waiting to see how his parents would address it. I was appalled and didn't like this family anymore. Why on Earth would a five-year-old boy associate skin color with a crime? I wondered what his parents were teaching him or what conversations he overheard. Alex, as cute as he was, would wind up being another one of the county's lost causes.

Alex didn't drop the issue either. He made sure everyone was aware of his discovery. He clutched his grandmother's knee, "Granny, a black man came here and stoled all our presents." He ran to his mother and squatted in front of her yelling, "Mommy, the bad man is a black man."

Finally, his dad piped in. His voice was stern. "Alex, enough! Just calm down and be quiet."

Dad's scolding registered in Alex's voice. "But, but, Daddy, it was."

"Alex!" His dad pointed to the sofa. "Go sit next to your mother and don't say another word!"

Alex's lip quivered and his mother stroked his hair as she explained it could have been black people, white people, or purple people that broke in. She was overwhelmed by everything and started to cry.

I lifted the prints from the cardboard box and transferred them to the white card before I started on another one. Alex watched my every move and tried to help me by shining the flashlight in my direction from his time-out position on the sofa. "Daddy,"

Alex's voice was soft and pleading. "Can I go over and help the lady, please?"

Dad relented. "Okay, but I don't want to hear a word come out of your mouth."

Alex flew off the sofa and was back at my side. He shined the light on the box that I was dusting and took in my every move. More prints developed and Alex saw them too.

"Daddy, Daddy," he squealed, "I told you so! There were black people in our house today! Black people that stoled our things!" Alex was waving my flashlight around like it was the light saber in *Star Wars*, but I snatched it from his hand before he smacked himself or Gramps with it. I wasn't even sure Gramps was even still alive because he hadn't moved since I got there.

I waited for Dad to cut in. It took only seconds. "Alex, enough!" Alex stopped running in place and hung his head low. He knew he was in trouble. He went back to the sofa and started to cry.

"Alex, look at me," his mother wiped his tears and pulled his face toward hers. "I don't want to hear any more talk about who you think did this, okay?" He nodded. "Do you understand me?" Alex rubbed his eyes and wiped his nose on his pajama sleeve and nodded again.

He sat in his mother's lap and both of them watched me as I hit the jackpot with prints. The prints looked fresh, too, and I was confident they belonged to the suspect. After a few minutes had passed, Alex called his mother in a soft voice. "Mommy," he started sobbing again. "Bu, bu, but I know the bad people were black."

Mom took Alex off of her lap and pulled his hands away from his face. "Alex!" Alex resisted and tried to bury his face in her lap. He was hysterical now. "Alex! Look at me!" She was yelling. "Alex, that's it. Go to bed! I have had enough of this. How many times did we tell you not to say that? If I hear it one more time, you are going to be punished all day tomorrow too. Do you understand me?" I had a feeling Alex was going to feel punished anyway when he woke up the next day to no presents.

Alex had squirmed away from her and stood in the middle of the room, watching me. "But—but." Now Dad was involved again and had grabbed Alex by the arm and was proceeding to drag him to his room. "Alex," he warned. "Do *not* even say it. Do *not* say it."

Finally, Granny, who hadn't said a word up to this point, but at least she had moved, piped in. "Alex," she had a shaky old lady voice. "Why do you think the people were black?" Nobody had even bothered to ask Alex this question before, just assuming he was being derogatory.

Alex ran to his grandmother and grabbed her hand and then pointed to the box I was dusting. He started sobbing again, "See, see, Granny." His voice trembled and he looked at his father and his mother before he went on. "See, the fingerprints on the boxes are black."

Epilogue . . .

I don't regret a day of being there, and I don't regret a day of being gone. When I started in the Crime Lab, the detectives gave me the nickname "Short Timer." I got that name because I was back in graduate school, working on my doctorate in anthropology, and what person with a Ph.D., who was sent all over the place to assist in forensic and archaeological investigations would want to be charged with the task of sprinkling fairy dust on a shed burglary in the pouring rain in a bad neighborhood at 3:00 A.M. in the middle of the winter? They ate their words because, almost ten years later, I was the most experienced civilian fairy-duster in the Lab and fell only under Mike, the detective with the handlebar moustache, in terms of seniority. I loved it there, I met some of my closest friends there, had some of my best times there, and I certainly found myself in the most bizarre situations there.

My decision to leave was bittersweet and was about a year in coming. I didn't pick the time to resign, the time picked me. I had nearly completed my dissertation coursework requirements and was beginning to see opportunities outside the Lab that were more lucrative, more flexible, more accommodating, and more challenging—both academically and professionally. I probably would have stayed in the Crime Lab if there had been a realistic expectation of promotion, but for civilians these opportunities were limited. I was beginning to feel like I had outgrown the position and felt my skills were being underutilized on the majority of the calls that I handled. I sometimes felt like a glorified garbage collector. I needed more responsibility and was somewhat appeased in that I was completing my training as a shoe and tire examiner, and conducting the training for the new hires, but it was more than just that. I was sick of the bullshit calls that I was forced to handle because the department was afraid to say no to their taxpaying citizens. I was also growing tired of the midnight shift and my experience was biting me in the ass. The Lab's managers didn't want the most "unsupervised" shift to be staffed by primarily new people and they were reluctant to approve my transfer to day shift anytime in the foreseeable future. I didn't blame them for their decision; I didn't like it but understood. There was also the problem of retention. Because so many of the new people were quitting, rumblings came of rotating shifts and rotating days off. This completely undermined the "good" days off that I had finally come to claim through seniority. Besides, an ever-changing schedule would keep me from taking and teaching my university courses. I just wasn't happy anymore and the possibilities outside the Lab were driven home when my best friend, April, went into the Federal Bureau of Investigation Academy and another close friend, Caitlyn, secured a position as a document examiner with the Department of Homeland Security. And there I sat, on a stranger's washing machine, staring at the pearly whites of the dingo that thought I was the next best thing to rawhide. It was time to move on. I just needed a little push.

That's where Elias came in. Fifteen months after we began the adoption process, we received word to travel to Guatemala to get our baby. I went on maternity leave, but knew I wouldn't be coming back. I even packed my things before I left. Two weeks before my leave ended, I resigned.

When people find out what I did for a living, they always ask me why I quit, how I coped with what I saw, and what my most interesting calls were. The "quit" question is easy—I just tell them that if the job was anything like *CSI*, I'd still be there. The "coping" question is harder to answer. I really want to tell them that crime scenes are like enemas: if you have enough of them, you get used to them. But I refrain and usually just say that I tried to focus on the good and think of the importance of what I was doing and how my work could help put the person responsible away for a long time. I leave out the part about all the shed burglaries. I explain that the dead are gone, so I tried to think of the living, of that mother who will never have her son back, and the hard work that I did was as much for her as it was for her child. I wanted all crime victims to have their day in court. As far as the "most interesting calls" question—now I can just hand them a copy of *Never Suck a Dead Man's Hand* and go on my merry way.

While I don't miss the Lab's endless list of rules du jour, overtime, shift work, and the uniform pants that made my butt look big, I do miss my friends, and the crazy calls, and the shoe and tire examinations.

In the short time that I have been away from the Crime Lab, I have been busy. I finally finished my doctorate, which was a huge accomplishment and something that I probably could not or would not have done had I not quit the Lab—the time just wasn't there. While I wrote my dissertation, I also wrote this book. Though writing was an enjoyable experience, I do *not* recommend writing a book and a dissertation at the same time. I survived—somehow. I have also been doing archaeological and physical anthropological work, both locally and abroad. Most recently, I was part of a small research team working on Mayan remains in the Petén region of Guatemala. I have also done some archaeological compliance review at the county level and GIS work for the state. I continue to teach undergraduate and graduate-level forensic science classes at a local university and hope to be a part of their expanding curriculum.

The big news is that Bob and I recently went back to Guatemala and brought home a second baby boy, and for now, I am just taking a break and enjoying my time at home, trying to make certain that my boys grow up as normal as possible. Consequently, my Mom has promised not to introduce them to the "Ways of the Family," although some of her quirks have already rubbed off on them. They are plucking "good luck" hairs at the beginning of each month, stepping on dropped combs, and they know they're supposed to do something with spilled salt—they're just not quite sure *what* it is. Their inquisitive nature is keeping Bob and me on our toes, and I listen as he tenderly fabricates stories about why our bushes stink so badly and why Mommy is always stopping her truck on the side of the road and putting "things" inside of garbage bags. Despite our best efforts, it appears my cover is blown. Earlier this week, I eavesdropped on a conversation that my three-year-old son was having with the puppy after discovering the pooch chewing on a bone I had just bought at the pet store.

"Frodo!" Elias was yelling. "Frodo, drop it!"

Frodo cowered and dropped the bone.

"Frodo, bad doggie. Mama's gonna be mad." Frodo had a dumb look on his face.

Elias grabbed the bone and tiptoed to the front door. "That's Mama's bone, Frodo."

I peeked around the corner as Elias went out on the front porch and threw the bone in the hedges. Frodo followed behind, looking confused. Elias then walked over to the stash of pin flags hidden beneath the boxwoods and removed one with a hot pink flag. He threw that into the bushes in the vicinity of the dog's bone. Once he had readjusted the flag and the bone, he tiptoed back inside.

"Time out, Frodo. You no touch Mama's bones."

Acknowledgments . . .

I know it sounds clichéd, but this book would not have been possible without the assistance, support, and guidance of so many individuals. For fear of leaving people out, I offer a general thank-you to the many, many individuals who offered their assistance in one way or another. This of course includes all of my friends at the "Crystal Palace." It was at there, where I spent about one third of my life, that I met my co-workers—many of whom have turned out to be my closest friends and bring a smile to my face whenever I think of them. Bonnie, Cathy, Padula, Gary, Haddock, Kathi Michael, Bob Huncher, Graham, Keith, Denise, Deb, and Pat Kamberger—thank you for making the past decade and then some so much fun.

I also have to thank the many new friends that I have met along my book-writing journey. Corinne Botz inspired me to write after I reviewed early versions of chapters in her book *Nutshell Studies of Unexplained Death*. Corinne, thanks for lighting the fire of opportunity under me! Then comes Bob Mecoy. I was a no-name wannabe writer with nothing but a big idea, but Bob took a chance on me. Bob is the only literary agent I have ever known—and I don't want to meet any others! I must also thank my friends at Kensington Publishing Corporation. Michaela Hamilton, whom I have never met in person, but feel like I know well enough to read her mind, is deserving of much praise, especially for her patience as I freaked out over photo requests, had meltdowns over typos, and cried because of five-day deadlines. Michaela was enthusiastic every step of the way and kept my chin up when I was ready to throw in the towel. There are also many other editors and artists at Kensington who contributed to my book in one way or the other. I never even got to learn the names of these people, but their work does not go unnoticed.

I must also thank my friends and family here at home, who have suffered through the two years it has taken me to write both a book and a dissertation. Mom, Chris, Vicki, Kassidy, Christina, and Lindsey—thanks for hanging in there with me. Bob, thanks for your support, and I promise that I won't make you eat spaghetti and canned sauce ever again, just as I promise my boys, Elias and Miguel, that they will never, ever have to watch *Dora* or *The Polar Express* again. Mama is back! And poor Alicia—your search for typos has now reached an end.

I sincerely thank all of you.